Advanced Praise for *The Global Heart Awakens*

"Anodea Judith addresses the very issue that is now coming into focus as the key to a sustainable and humane future. All the strategies in existence cannot take us to the shores of a better world if they lack the element of love. But love, when informed by practical and realistic strategies, can. This is what *The Global Heart Awakens* shows us, and what we must all take to mind—and to heart!"
—**Ervin Laszlo**, philosopher, systems theorist, and author of over 75 books

"Few have articulated with such original insight the underlying themes behind our planetary crisis and how, if we all pull together with bright vision and profound love for our world, we can make it through the initiation to our planetary adulthood."
—**Lynne Twist**, author of *The Soul of Money*

"Anodea Judith is one of the great sacred storytellers of this generation. She is engaged in the most urgent work of our time: to re-narrate the great story of our being and becoming in a way that allows us to see the patterns that connect and to chart a course for a better tomorrow. She is at once sage, shaman and seer. Read this book now."
—**Dr. Marc Gafni**, author, Your Unique Self

"Anodea Judith's big-picture thinking is full of original insights and wise guidance for our time. With a gift for weaving science and mythology, she shows how both are necessary to shepherd us into a thriving future. Here is a much needed feminine voice in the evolutionary story. "
—**Michael Dowd**, author of *Thank God for Evolution*

Science has revealed that the planet is deep into its sixth mass extinction—this time, the direct result of human behavior. This book provides illuminating insight as to how we arrived at this crossroad and how, if we change our perceptions of life, we can heal the environment and ourselves. Read this book and help save our world."
—**Bruce Lipton**, author of *The Biology of Belief*

"Anodea's work helps us reimagine the Big Dream for ourselves and the world. She is an exceptionally wise woman whom I turn to for guidance, insight, and answers. Now, with this book, she makes her deepest wisdom available to us all."
—**Marcia Wieder**, CEO/Founder, Dream University

"*The Global Heart Awakens* explains why and how we can meet the urgent challenges of our time with our hearts as well as our minds, and thus provides us with a marvelous example of spirituality-in-action. Judith's clear and refreshingly feminine voice demonstrates advanced erudition as well as a lifetime of spiritual experience."
—**Steve McIntosh**, author of *Evolution's Purpose*

"*The Global Heart Awakens* offers us a powerful template for personal and collective transformation. With her signature insight and her capacity for bringing together ancient wisdom with cutting-edge social, scientific, and psychological research, Anodea has created a vision that can inspire and empower your evolutionary journey for years to come. Highly recommended."
—**Sally Kempton**, author of *Meditation for the Love of It* and *Awakening Shakti*

"Anodea Judith is a wise woman for our times for our times who calls us to our evolutionary destiny. At a time when our civilization is overwhelmed by the content in our heads, she offers us the context of the heart."
—**Steve Bhaerman** (aka Swami Beyondananda), coauthor of *Spontaneous Evolution*

"Demonstrates convincingly that our collective transformational challenge mirrors the one facing individuals: to use all our capacities—physical, emotional, intellectual, and spiritual—manifesting as the awakening of the global heart."
—**John Stewart**, author of *The Evolutionary Manifesto*

"Anodea Judith offers deep wisdom and a feminine perspective on the full sweep of our human history. She brilliantly shows us how we've now arrived at a time when we can create a new world based on love."
—**Marci Shimoff**, #1 *NY Times* best-selling author of *Happy for No Reason*

"*The Global Heart Awakens* provides an intelligent and insightful perspective of human history and of consciousness evolving into heart-connected living. I especially appreciated Anodea's understanding that 'the most fundamental aspect of love is *caring*.'"
—**Deborah Rozman**, President and CEO, HeartMath, LLC

"A powerful guide through the violence and brilliance of the past up to the present and beyond—a beautiful piece of work."
—**Barbara Marx Hubbard**, author of *Conscious Evolution* and *Birth 2012 and Beyond*

"Masterfully exposes the mythic underpinnings of the human crises and awakens our imagination to the possibilities now at hand."
—**David Korten**, author of *The Great Turning*

The
Global Heart
AWAKENS

Other Works by Anodea Judith

Wheels of Life: A User's Guide to the Chakra System

The Sevenfold Journey: Reclaiming Mind,
Body, and Spirit through the Chakras
(with Selene Vega)

Eastern Body, Western Mind: Psychology and
the Chakra System as a Path to the Self

Contact: The Yoga of Relationship (with Tara Guber)

Creating on Purpose: The Spiritual Technology
of Manifesting through the Chakras
(with Lion Goodman)

Chakra Balancing: A Guide to Healing and
Awakening Your Energy Body
(multimedia)

The Chakra System: A Complete Course
in Self-Diagnosis and Healing
(audio set)

Beginner's Guide to the Chakras (audio)

The Illuminated Chakras: A Visionary
Voyage into Your Inner World
(DVD video)

The
Global Heart
AWAKENS

Humanity's Rite of Passage from the
Love of Power to the Power of Love

Anodea Judith

Shift Books

P.O. Box 151117 • San Rafael, CA 94915
www.shiftmovement.com

Cover design by Thomas Wolfe

ISBN-13: 978-0-9848407-6-2
LCCN: 2013904963

Publisher's Cataloging-in-Publication

Judith, Anodea, 1952-
    The global heart awakens : humanity's rite of passage from the love of power to the power of love / Anodea Judith. -- Rev. ed.
    p. cm.
    Includes bibliographical references and index.
    Rev. ed. of: Waking the global heart.
    LCCN 2013904963
    ISBN 978-0-9848407-6-2

    1. Civilization, Modern--21st century. 2. Love--Social aspects. 3. Civilization--Philosophy. 4. Social evolution--Psychological aspects.   I. Judith, Anodea, 1952- Waking the global heart. II. Title.

CB430.J83 2013   909.83
                          QBI13-600048

First printing May 2013

Printed in the United States of America on Forest Stewardship Council certified paper

10 9 8 7 6 5 4 3 2 1

Contents

ACKNOWLEDGMENTS

The global heart awakens as a result of many minds and hearts working together, while gratitude opens the individual heart. So I would like to express my heartfelt appreciation to the many people who have helped shape this work over its many years of development.

It began with my former husband, Richard Ely, whose scholarship and love of history, philosophy, and science made for endless fascinating discussions over the early years of formulating these ideas. Richard also created the history charts in the first edition of this book, which will be made available on the book's website, GlobalHeartAwakens.com. I am grateful to Dawson Church of Elite Books for recognizing my vision early on, as he published the first edition, Waking the Global Heart, in 2006.

Little did I know when I first met Stephen Dinan and his wife, Devaa Haley Mitchell, creators of the Shift Network, that 10 years later they would be leading a world-changing organization and publishing this book. I continually admire Stephen's broad vision and hardworking dedication toward the bettering of our world. Devaa is a quintessential embodiment of the divine feminine, and she continually reminds me of what is missing in our world. I would also like to thank Lion Goodman, coauthor of my previous book *Creating on Purpose*, for it is Lion who first introduced me to Stephen and Devaa.

I can't express enough appreciation for Byron Belitsos, who has shepherded this book from inception to publication as editor in chief and publisher. Byron continued to envision possibilities while fastidiously handling the many details of bringing this book to fruition, from editing to marketing and putting together the team that made it all possible. In addition, many thanks to Elizabeth Rose Raphael, whose wise developmental editing brought out key points from a feminine eye; to Elissa Rabellino for copyediting; to Theresa Duran for proofreading; to Deb Tremper for typesetting; and to Thomas Christian Wolfe for the cover design.

I'm grateful to James O'Dea for writing the foreword, but even more for his life's work in the areas of peace and compassion, not to mention his Irish eloquence. Molly Rowan Leach helped to shape the book's launch—and thanks in advance to all the people who will spread the word about this book, and who help spread these important ideas through your contacts and conversations.

On the home front, I'm eternally grateful to my office manager, Shanon Dean-Milon, who handles everything else while I write; to Gianna Perada for formatting the manuscript; and to Ramone Yaciuk, who gives me wonderful support and keeps me laughing and loving.

But most of all, I want to thank all those evolutionaries who are helping to shift consciousness on this planet in all the many ways that this occurs. May we live to see our visions come true.

Anodea Judith
Novato, California
March 2013

FOREWORD
By James O'Dea

Mystics have long understood that the heart is mysteriously powerful. Yet, it is in the special nature of its power that the heart is never susceptible to any form of coercion or manipulation. So it is that you will find in these pages a call to a mature understanding of the role of the heart in human destiny—and of the hour that is now upon us on planet Earth.

The heart is our gateway to all things higher, but to access its prodigious vitality and reach, we must move beyond the very developmental strategies that bring us to its threshold. The heart will not open unless it is released of ego fixations and crude power plays.

The Sufis say the heart is like a great mirror that must be polished. As we deepen in compassion, service, and selfless love, we begin to experience the most generous universe of the heart; we see reflected in it the true nature of our higher intelligence with all of its strength, creativity, and beauty.

It is this journey to the heart and its qualities that Anodea Judith impeccably maps for us as individuals and as a collective. The scale and inclusiveness of her vision calls us to witness the awakening of humanity's heart in this epochal period of our evolution.

The global heart is awakening not in response to an inventive new philosophy but as a reality emerging from scientific, evolutionary, cultural, spiritual, and mythic perspectives. The heart is a representative of wholeness and cannot be reduced to being a partisan of selective ideologies or the privileged worldviews of those few deemed to be in the know. That is why you will find the resonance of holism throughout this book and the moral and intellectual coherence to back up its narrative of planetary whole-system transformation.

Open this book and you will find a great heart guiding you—one that calls you to recognize that we, as a species, are finally ready to end our adolescent rebellion and demonstrate that we are capable of embracing wisdom, nurturing peace, and evolving to love.

AUTHOR'S PREFACE

When I was a young child, my parents had an impossibly messy drawer in the kitchen that held string, wire, and various kinds of fasteners. Whenever someone reached into the drawer to use one of these things, the contents came out in a great tangled blob, only to get thrown back again with frustration. One of my favorite things to do—and one that kept me happily occupied for hours—was to empty the drawer and untangle the strings. I would patiently follow all the threads through their maze, untying the knots, until the tangle was neatly separated into usable little piles. It gave me a great deal of satisfaction and, of course, pleased my mother to no end. I have been following threads in one way or another ever since. In this book, I attempt to untangle the collective threads of our human story and reweave them into a vision that can guide us to the future.

If it weren't for the certain knowing that everyone who is aware of today's global challenges feels small in the face of them, I would never have had the courage to write this book. In fact, over the many years I've worked on the manuscript, I tried to give it up many times, but somehow it wouldn't leave me alone. I told myself that it was out of my reach or over my head—that other people wrote books like these, but not I, a woman who is wildly in love with this world. It is this love that wouldn't release me from my task, that kept me awake at night over the years, that compelled me to pore through texts and sit at my keyboard to bring you these words.

So much for using this preface to convince you of my qualifications.

What is more important, however, and the method to my madness in this humble beginning, is that most people stay out of the kitchen, not because they can't take the heat but because they think they don't know how to cook. Most people are stopped by beliefs in their own inadequacy—thinking they don't have the tools, the experience, or the education to make a suitable offering.

I challenge that belief. I instead insist that the new world we are creating needs *everyone*. Passion and dedication are as important as skills. Help can be found and skills can be obtained if the passion and dedication exist. But there are innumerable skills going to waste for lack of passion and purpose. Amateurs built the Ark, while professionals built the *Titanic*.

I didn't have all the skills I needed when I began this book. I am a psychotherapist by training, a writer and workshop presenter by profession, and a visionary philosopher by heart. My talent is recognizing patterns in both the individual and collective psyches, and my claim to fame is my articulation of the Eastern system of the chakras as an archetype for wholeness and a template for transformation. Having spent nearly 40 years looking at life through the lens of the chakra system, which has long been regarded as a path to personal evolution, I became aware of how this system offers us a potent map for our collective evolution. This path makes sense of our past, guides us through the present, and illuminates a positive future. It is this vision I wish to share.

In my role as a psychotherapist, I spent over 20 years watching individuals struggle with the wounds lodged in each of their souls from the collective gestalt of our human follies. Wrongs that never should have been committed, beliefs that served no positive purpose, and suffering that could have been avoided—these were the constant realities tugging at my heart. As I handed over the tissues hour after hour, year after year, I came to the conclusion that it is not enough to bandage the wounds—*we have to stand up and address the slaughter*. For it is clear to me that unless we unravel the threads of the archetypal patterns that govern our collective lives, we will not be able to fathom the many crises that are brewing on the global horizon.

I confess that I am a historian not by training but only by interest. Historians typically focus their expertise on a particular area of history and are expected to refrain from speculation. As a result, one does not get the overview that puts these facts into a broad—and admittedly conjectural—evolutionary perspective. I instead regard myself as a storyteller and weaver. From my perspective as a therapist, I am interested in the formative experiences of our collective childhood that led to the beliefs and complexes that feed our present social imbalances and environmental crises. This storytelling begins with the prehistory of our common beginnings and continues through the present into a visionary framework for the future.

As the past makes up only half of this book in order to leave room for the future, I had to be very selective in what I chose to write about. For that reason, it is primarily the story of *Western* history that I tell in this book, in sweeping broad strokes that illustrate the archetypal dynamics and inner psychology of our common ancestral childhood. This is partly to keep the storytelling down to a manageable size but also because it is the *values* of Western culture that pose both the greatest threat and the greatest promise to our collective world. And while this is changing rapidly as Third World countries enter the global playing field, it is primarily the Western world that has the technological capacity to change the trajectory that has been moving toward a mass extinction of everything we hold dear.

We can take the reins of the future into our own hands only by understanding how those reins got hitched onto the animal that is now leading us astray. For this reason, we need to understand the past, from our earliest social beginnings in the wilds of the Earth—far predating the beginning of masculine rationality—so as to fully comprehend where we are now. In addition, we need to gather threads of what is missing so that we can weave a new tapestry of wholeness. In particular, the common telling of history is literally a masculine story that mostly ignores the feminine. Here I offer my feminine voice to speak up for what has been tragically lost and for what needs to be reintegrated if we are to become whole.

I ask you, beloved reader, to review with me these stories in the unfolding human mystery play for the sole reason that I believe that each of you has a part to play in the current act. Looking at the programs we were given for this drama, we see that our current time is usually referred to as the postmodern era. If that is so, then what's next? The post-postmodern era? And then the post-post-postmodern era? What if we instead were to regard our time as the *predawn era*, that liminal realm between the wee hours of the night and the new day? It is always darkest before the dawn, yet that does not mean that I believe we are yet at the darkest point. Instead I wish to light some lamps in preparation for that darkest point—so that we don't get lost in the dark when and if it does arrive, and that we don't *lose heart* in the depths of the trials that I believe lie ahead of us.

To say that things will likely get darker before the new dawn may sound alarmist to some, and I have no objection to that term. If the cancer is spreading, if the ship is sinking, if the building is burning, then sounding an alarm is one of the sanest things we can do. But even more important when sounding an alarm is to propose an alternative. To yell "Fire!" in a crowded theater with no exit signs or to watch the *Titanic* go down without enough lifeboats only leads to despair.

Many people today are sounding alarms about our environment, our economy, our governments, and our social injustices. And many people are getting lost in despair. What I believe is needed at this time is not only a realistic evaluation of our collective situation but a story of hope. Not the kind of hope that says to a child, "Don't worry, it will all be OK, just go back to sleep," but the kind of hope that employs all of our efforts in creating a mature vision of what's possible. For in my many years of attending to the wounds of the human heart, only the presence of hope could lighten and heal the heart. When hope arises, there is a deeper opening to new possibilities—and to love.

A viable vision of the future can be created only by all of us. I offer here both the dark and light sides of our collective story, which I hope will ignite your own love for this glorious world and the incredible beings that live in it, and will illuminate your part in the astounding future that awaits us all.

From the heart,
Anodea Judith

Evolution is the Gods' way
of making more gods.

INTRODUCTION

Setting the Stage

 The only myth that is going to be worth talking about in the immediate future is one that . . . will be exactly what all myths have dealt with—the maturation of the individual, from dependency through adulthood, through maturity, and then to the exit; and then how to relate this society to the world of nature and the cosmos. . . . And until that gets going, you don't have anything.[1]
—*Joseph Campbell*

The human drama is nearing its denouement. The great unveiling is approaching, a time when the power structures of the world begin to crumble and people of the heart sing out a new truth. Many voices are joining the chorus, many feet are walking the path, many minds are dreaming possibilities. For beneath the crises that are looming at every level of civilization, the global heart is awakening, beating out the rhythm of a new and glorious dance.

As we meet for coffee, for dinner, for business meetings, or for romantic dates, the conversation buzzes like an audience murmuring between acts. What's going on? What will happen next? What's wrong? Who's right? What should we do? What *can* we do? And most frightening of all are those of us who wonder if we'll even survive into the next age. For the emerging generation is watching in despair as those in charge recklessly spend their inheritance with little regard for the future. Yet the question of "What's going to happen?" could more appropriately be shifted to "What can we create together?" For we are becoming cocreators of our future destiny.

In the theater of our world, we are simultaneously audience and cast, playing to an instantaneous-feedback system that continually shows us our reflection. Here we see how the combined actions of seven billion humans are slowly weaving the global tapestry into a new picture. The threads of this tapestry were spun from archaic forces long ago, and then woven over time by the myths, legends, and heroic deeds of our ancestors. To weave a new picture, we must engage with these archetypal forces and take them into our own hands—with maturity, with consciousness, and most of all with heart.

As the curtain rises on the next act of our drama, we find that center stage is now everywhere, broadcast from televisions, radios, newspapers, magazines, and the Internet into living rooms, cars, airports, and our cell phones. As news of both discoveries and tragedies ripples through the global brain, the gaze of collective attention is focused like never before. Some viewers are just waking up, rubbing their eyes in confusion. Others have been watching for quite some time, with growing concern. Still others prefer to remain asleep, doing their best to ignore the signs that point to an impending and massive shift at every level of civilization. Change is in the air, and we all have ringside seats. Yet we are far from mere spectators.

You who are dreamers and poets, executives and laborers, healers and teachers, entrepreneurs and factory workers, artists and visionaries, parents and lovers—each of you plays a part in bringing forth the new dawn. You are the ones who will be leading humanity's rite of passage into the next age. For the global heart's awakening occurs as each of us opens to the power of love and joins together in the creation of our future. Physically, the heart is an organ that keeps us alive through a network of cells beating together. Spiritually, the heart is the center of love, the primordial force that unites us and makes our lives worth living. Globally, the heart symbolizes a new organizing principle for humanity—as I endeavor to show in this book.

Immersed in technology yet hungry for the sacred, we have a deep longing for a story that fosters progress but honors sustainability, creates order but allows freedom, utlilizes power yet increases cooperation, and brings a long-needed balance to the archetypal masculine and feminine. The stories we tell ourselves shape our world. They guide our relationships to each other, to the environment, and to the future. The 21st century is calling for a new myth to guide us to the next age of humanity.

Our collective initiation from the *love of power* to the *power of love* is the drama of our time. Ours is an era that future historians will call a time of Great Awakening, a time when humanity's monumental challenges stimulated the birth of a new era, a time when the best and the worst of humanity played their parts in the fate of human evolution. But if future generations are alive to tell this story, it will be because the best of humanity prevailed and pulled together with a love so profound that the seemingly impossible was achieved.

You are part of this story, as your note joins with countless other voices singing a new song. You begin wherever you are, as you face that difficult rite of passage between what has been and what is becoming. On the personal level, this liminal zone occurs between your old ways of being and the new ways that call to your heart. On the collective level, it is the shift between past and future organizing principles.

This drama is a love story on the grandest scale—not an adolescent tale of romantic projection and happily-ever-after fantasy, but a tale of how to live from our hearts, cocreating a world run by what we love more than what we fear, connection more than separation, collaboration more than competition, embracing mystery as much as certainty. It is a story that looks at love, not as a mere sentiment but as a profound *social organizing principle*, indeed the self-organizing principle that mirrors the myriad relationships within nature's web of life. When this principle of love is truly understood and applied, miracles are possible.

Creation and destruction have always happened simultaneously, longtime partners in the evolutionary dance. Like characters in a mystery novel, whose separate stories come together as the plot is revealed, both crises *and* opportunities are converging upon each other in this grand denouement. Which will prevail remains a mystery, but if the outcome were certain, it wouldn't capture enough of our attention. Even more, a certain outcome would allow us to remain passively asleep rather than rolling up our sleeves and becoming an active part of the process.

On the side of destruction, the convergence of crises is becoming ever more apparent. As rising temperatures cause food and water shortages; as economic disparities, racism, and sexism fuel social unrest; as failed states amass guns or, worse, nuclear weapons; as rising sea levels engulf coastlines and displace hundreds of millions; as population expands into a world where the air becomes foul and land turns to desert—as all these crises and many more unfold, we face the biggest challenge that humanity has confronted since our ancestors stood on their hind legs millions of years ago.

While this perfect storm of crises gathers on the horizon, human creativity is simultaneously racing to the scene. Technologies connect vast numbers of people with instantaneous communication, offering ever-increasing opportunities for mass collaboration and higher collective intelligence. Socially responsible investing is shifting money toward innovation and sustainability, funding improvements in green technologies. The best of the world's spiritual traditions are widely available, allowing the pursuit of higher consciousness to become mainstream. Science is piercing the very nature of matter while producing abundant data about human effects on nature. Our methods of healing are becoming more holistic, with faster means of diagnosis and treatment. Our systems of travel, food production, and education are all shifting toward the capacity to do more with less effort. Technology is innovating so rapidly that any statement I make about it could be out of date within months. Social innovation is sprouting everywhere: through neighborhood coalitions seeking to become locally sustainable; alternative communities learning to share resources; nongovernmental organizations addressing issues of social justice, environmental sustainability, democracy, peace, and the study of consciousness; conferences, think tanks, and research groups; social media, online courses, and collectively created encyclopedias of knowledge.

Individuals have more personal power than at any time in history. In most countries, we can go where we want, say what we want, and create our own books, websites, YouTube videos, podcasts, and tools of all sorts for enhancing every aspect of life. Developed countries across the globe have stores full with most any item we could want, and we can even order it from the Internet with the click of a mouse and have it delivered a few days later.

But the question remains: What is all this *for*? What is its purpose? Why has this freedom been important, and what is our *collective purpose* at this amazing confluence of events?

In order to develop the wisdom necessary to deal with these immense issues, and to find a new myth that will guide us to a thriving future, I believe we must inquire into the essential questions asked by myths and legends of all ages: *Who are we? Where do we come from? Where are we going?* The answers to these questions will give meaning to the drama, reveal our purpose, and define the parts that each of us plays. It is to these questions, embedded in the human mystery play, that this book is addressed. Three major sections will explore these questions in depth. Here I offer guidance for our journey ahead, not only as individuals but as creators of the emerging story of what we are becoming together.

Part One, "The Drama of Our Time," examines each of these three questions in brief. It begins by looking at who we are as a species in the context of our time. I show that our current crises not only are initiatory ordeals but are what Barbara Marx Hubbard has called "evolutionary drivers," which are demanding a shift to a new social organizing principle. I suggest that we will emerge into the next age of humanity in part because we have successfully endured the "Underworld" journey of these initiatory ordeals. I describe the stages of initiation as a metaphor for how we transform ourselves and our culture. These stages, though difficult, have an evolutionary purpose.

Part Two, "Our Long Journey Home," deals with the question "Where did we come from?" or, less eloquently, "How did we get into this mess?" Here we look at the long sweep of human history, examining how the beliefs and values of the past have contributed— both for better and for worse—to our current planetary situation. In this historical journey through cultural evolution, we explore the dynamics of masculine and feminine influences in each era of history, as well as correlating each era to developmental stages of childhood. I also map these stages onto the yogic system of the seven chakras, a field I have studied and written about extensively.

Rather than a history of dates and battles, this section tells the human *story* of our long journey to where we are now, from the Paleolithic Stone Age to the present. In particular, it looks at the often-untold feminine side of the story, featuring the Great Mother and her subordinated daughter, who is now maturing into adulthood and reemerging into equality and fullness.

Through understanding our past, we can better see how we evolved into our current love of power through our middle childhood and have been moving steadily toward an organizing principle of the heart, now ripening as we mature through our cultural adolescence into early adulthood. This history is by no means exhaustive, making up less than half of the book, and is largely focused on Western culture, yet it digs into the ancestral memories that predate all civilization. These pages also look at the mythologies, key initiations, and developmental tasks that brought us to where we are now. I suggest that while the first seeds of heart-based principles were cast thousands of years ago, we have not yet realized the full flowering of a heart-based paradigm. You might say we've suffered from arrested development in our love of power, a topic explored more fully in the pages ahead. I believe that we are only now ready to actualize this principle on a global scale. The history in Part Two sets the pattern for understanding what is coming next.

Part Three, "Where Are We Going?" looks at the dynamics of Sacred Partnership and also delves into the Divine Child archetype as richly described in Jungian literature and elsewhere. Building on these constructs, I look at the elements of an emerging myth that could guide us in cocreating a thriving future of heaven on earth. Chapters 14 and 15 examine the theoretical guidelines of the next organizing principle, based on the power of love and the integration of archetypal polarities. The final chapters in this section first examine the personal practices that help us to open our hearts and then describe the global trends, already under way, in such areas as peace, economics, and democracy, that indicate we are moving toward the global awakening of a heart-based paradigm.

My hope is that my telling of our collective story—as we travel both the light and dark terrains of our past—will give the reader hope during a time of crisis and change: hope for a thriving future, for a world sustained by love, and for the eventual unification of heaven and earth.

Part One

THE DRAMA OF OUR TIME

WHO ARE WE?

Adolescent Initiates

As a species, we are no longer the subject of the evolutionary process. We have become the authors of it.
—*Lynne Twist*

As the curtain rises on the unfolding evolutionary story, we see that we are the most recent guests to arrive at the party. In fact, our arrival dominates the scene, as our species spreads wide across the earth in an indescribable array of diversity and adaptability. Though we stand on the genetic building blocks of all that has come before, our capacity is unsurpassed. With calculating brains and opposable thumbs, self-healing bodies, and relatively long life spans, it appears there is little we can't do—and herein lies the simultaneous promise and peril of our species. It isn't just about what we can *do*, however, for we also have immense capacities for consciousness, and for discovery, learning, innovation, and creation.

We may not be the pinnacle of evolution, but we are the first to become aware of it. It took 3.8 billion years since the first living cells appeared for evolution to produce creatures with enough consciousness that they could become conscious of evolution. And now we are the first to realize that we can consciously evolve. This gives us a significant distinction in the evolutionary matrix.

We are also the first species capable of harming the planet's ecosystem, perhaps irrevocably. While many species have damaged their own local habitats, no complex creature has had the ability to cause damage planetwide. However, we are also the first species capable of realizing the terrible consequences of what we are doing. That means we're the first species capable of doing something about it, though our capability doesn't guarantee that we will.

Just in case you think global warming and our excess of carbon dioxide is impossible to change, consider the great oxygen crisis that threatened the future of life 2.4 billion years ago. It all started with the appearance of photosynthetic bacteria around 3.5 billion years ago— an evolutionary necessity, since photosynthesis produces oxygen as a waste product. Prior to these cyanobacteria, complex life would have been impossible, since there wasn't much free oxygen in the atmosphere. But after a billion years or so, oxygen accumulation became toxic. The result was the most significant extinction event in Earth's history, annihilating bacteria everywhere. Greenhouse gases were *lost*, which caused a global cooling that triggered one of the greatest ice ages in geohistory, sometimes called Snowball Earth. Most of the planet was covered in ice and slush.

How did it get solved? Michael Dowd, author of *Thank God for Evolution*, explains this process of catastrophe leading to creativity:

> Because it was precisely this bad news that forced different kinds of bacteria to cooperate in ways they had never done before, which eventuated in cells with a nucleus that could breathe oxygen, then communities of multicellular organisms. So! No oxygen pollution crisis equals no cooperation, no community—nothing more exciting than anaerobic bacteria.[2]

If a planetary crisis like that can turn around with only the simplest of organisms, then what is possible with advanced intelligence, scientific instruments, communication devices, and the Internet? One thing I love about who we are as humans is that we're the only species that can discover things like this.

Homo sapiens sapiens—the scientific term for our current iteration—implies we are an organism that not only has consciousness (*sapiens*: to know) but *knows* that it knows—is self-aware and self-reflective. And we can know that our consciousness is just beginning to learn how to cooperate—to join with others like the single-celled organisms of our archaic past. The path of evolution moves toward increasing the scale of cooperation, making ever-larger wholes from increasingly complex groups of parts. From the 2.6 billion years it took single-celled organisms to become multicelled creatures, from small nomadic tribes to the settled villages that grew into walled cities, from powerful city-states to individual nations to our emerging global civilization, *evolution coordinates the emergence of ever-larger collectives.*

As humans, we are the ones capable of recognizing who we are, what we can do (and not do), and even more: what we are a part of. For we are the only species to realize that those sparkling diamonds of light that grace the night sky are actually billions of galaxies of distant stars, infinitely expanding. That makes us the first to see our planet as a jewel in a vast universe that we have barely begun to explore or even understand. How can we possibly end it all before we embrace that quintessential mystery?

Cultural Adolescence

Stop, be still and listen, because you're drunk,
and we're at the edge of the roof.
—*Rumi*

Amazing as we are as a species, we are only in our adolescence. Birthed from the primal womb of nature after billions of years in gestation, we have risen out of Stone Age infancy, crawled across the land in our toddlerhood, and labored through thousands of years of sibling rivalry to arrive at the present time—in the throes of our adolescent initiation. Our next task is to become adults—parents of the future—cocreating a world that can sustain the evolutionary experiment.

Many agree with my belief that we are in our adolescence. Author and researcher Duane Elgin, after questioning people across cultures—from India to Japan, England to Brazil—reported that over two-thirds of those he surveyed agreed that humanity is in its adolescence.[3] It's easy to see why. We need only turn on the television to see adolescent behavior raging through all ages, races, creeds, and genders. Creative but disrespectful, powerful but reckless, narcissistically obsessed with our looks, and bursting with repressed libido, we are sorely lacking in social and environmental conscience. We are fascinated by flashy gadgets and fast movement. We are driven by the whimsy of our desires, expectant of quick fixes for our problems. Like teenagers thoughtlessly cleaning out the refrigerator while entertaining their friends, human populations are insatiably consuming the once-vast oceans and forests in the attempt to satisfy their voracious appetites.

And why not? Hasn't Mother Nature always kept her cupboards well stocked in the past, free to her children, just for the asking? Hasn't our sole responsibility been to consume the resources provided for us and use them to feed a growing humanity? Did we ever think it was possible that Mother Nature's cupboards could run out? As children, we are provided for, and at adolescence we often abuse that privilege. As adults, we become self-supporting and eventually able to support and care for others. Adults typically know how to keep their homes clean, and we can extrapolate this toward a planetary adulthood that maintains a clean and healthy environment. However, it is clear that we have not yet matured into this stage.

Adolescence is a time when physical growth comes to a halt. It's the time when we take that prodigious life force and learn how to grow in a new dimension. At best, this dimension is spiritual, growing toward deeper understanding of ourselves and our world. But if this passage is blocked, adolescents act out recklessly, often harming themselves and their environment before they understand what they are losing.

To become adults, adolescents who have previously been nurtured, cared for, and educated by elders must learn how to provide for themselves, and others in turn. They must learn about the meaning of life, the structure and order of the world, and their purpose within it. Yet they are also compelled—by the unique life force within them—to question and change that structure as they grow into it. It is a tumultuous time, as any parent knows, and there are days when we may look at our teenagers with exasperation and wonder if they will ever grow up, much as I feel when I listen to the evening news today. Yet we have no choice but to move forward as best we can.

Just as adolescence marks the end of physical growth, *our human population has grown to its adult size and can no longer continue to expand in a physical dimension.* We have reached (if not surpassed) the carrying capacity of our biosphere. The world's population has more than doubled in the last half-century, climbing from 2.5 billion in 1950 to over seven billion at the time of this writing.[4] Just for perspective, this means there has been more population growth in the last *half-century* than in the previous two to three million years since humans first appeared! If not checked, this number could double again in the next 50 years, with disastrous consequences. From the depletion of topsoil and underground aquifers to the diminishing oil reserves that bring our groceries to the table; from the disappearing forests and the creatures that live there to the greenhouse gases that are raising global temperatures; from urban smog to waste disposal; from the billions who live in poverty to the epidemic diseases that threaten entire populations—every facet of human and nonhuman society is affected by our unchecked population growth. What Malthus predicted back in 1798 is now a reality:

> The power of population is indefinitely greater than the power in the earth to produce subsistence for man. Population, when unchecked, increases in a geometrical ratio. Subsistence increases only in an arithmetical ratio. A slight acquaintance with numbers will show the immensity of the first power in comparison of the second.[5]

Not only must population growth be curbed, but we need to change our view of progress and our narrow definition of success. Ever since the Industrial Revolution, progress has been measured by incessant growth. Growth is measured in terms of more products, bigger markets, larger infrastructure, and ultimately greater profits. The success of a company is almost always defined by its expansion rather than by its social contribution—whether that means building more housing developments, expanding roads and highways, infiltrating indigenous cultures with Western products and lifestyles, or simply crafting a way to make more with less. But if we are to survive, our "industrial growth society" must place its value on something other than growth before we exhaust our life-support systems. The entry of the word *downsizing* into our vernacular shows that much of this expansion is already reaching its limit and turning around. Learning how to live sustainably is part of the maturation of our species.

As with adolescents who have grown incessantly since their birth, unchecked growth has been the driving force of humanity's history since its beginning. Prehistoric nomads focused on images pertaining to birth. The Bible tells us to go forth and multiply. Conservatives today try to thwart abortion and even birth control. In earlier eras, when the world population was smaller and survival meant propagating the species, this might have been appropriate. With the vast expanse of Earth still unexplored, we didn't think we'd ever run out of resources. Yet the ceaseless growth of our long childhood created its own momentum, now hard to stop, and we're in the growth spurt that is typical of late adolescence. Like the infamous ship *Titanic,* such a colossal system is difficult to turn around—even when we see the iceberg up ahead. Yet in order to survive, we must harness that creative urge to multiply and point the evolutionary arrow in a new direction.

We are now facing a collective adolescent identity crisis. Our challenge is to foster a new identity, as evolutionary agents of a larger matrix and as parents of a new millennium. But we are not yet adults. As Jean Houston has said, we are "people of the parentheses,"[6] living in a nebulous space between the old era and the new, neither child nor grown-up, undergoing the tremendous changes of adolescent transformation. In one way or another, this transformation will eventually come to us all. We may resist the call and remain stubbornly attached to the old ways, or we can surrender to the transformation and advance to the other side. We cannot remain the same and still survive. If we do survive, we will emerge transformed.

In this initiation, there are no authority figures who will solve the big problems for us. For the task of initiation is to awaken our own inner authority. Where most previous religions have posited either a Mother Goddess or a Father God as an external source, the current trend in spirituality is to awaken the divinity within as an internal resource, through practices that open a direct connection to higher and deeper states of consciousness. Not only are we "on our own" in terms of parental guidance, but we are simultaneously the first generations saddled with the responsibility of saving the entire world. Our ancestors' challenge was to save their tribe, expand their empire, or defend their country. Now the protection of the planet and its entire population is at stake. That alone demands an unprecedented level of species maturity.

CHILDREN	ADOLESCENTS	ADULTS
Dependent	Independent	Interdependent
Continuous growth	Growth spurt	Growth stabilized
Lives in present	Rebels against past	Plans for future
Parents are gods	Parents fall from grace	Become parents
Obedient	Rebellious	Cooperative
No power	Reckless power	Shared power
Needs help	Resists help	Gives help

Figure 1. Stages of maturity.

WHERE DO WE COME FROM?

Culture on the Couch

If this link up [between past and future] does not take place, a kind of rootless consciousness comes into being, no longer oriented to the past, a consciousness which succumbs helplessly to all manner of suggestions and is susceptible to psychic epidemics. . . . In as much as man has cut himself off from his roots he may be swept to catastrophe by his dangerous one-sidedness.
—C. G. Jung

In tribal cultures, an essential part of a rite of passage was to teach *the history of the tribe from the beginning of time.* Only initiates who understood the forces that shaped their history were allowed to become elders in the tribe. This was not to inhibit innovation by binding initiates to an inflexible tradition, but to *ground* their actions in an understanding of the larger matrix.

As a former psychotherapist, I know the value of excavating the past. Clients in crisis need immediate solutions, but their deeper healing comes from identifying the events, beliefs, and assumptions that created their crisis in the first place. I have repeatedly seen how healing the wounds from the past frees people to create their future and how avoiding this work holds them back. But after spending a few decades bandaging the wounds of my clients, I decided instead to stand up and address the slaughter. I knew I needed to address the social causes of these wounds and to find their sources.

With a world in crisis, we can't create a thriving future unless we look at the wounds we carry from our collective history. The traumas, challenges, and even solutions to former problems have all led to our current situation. Rapidly expanding populations created the need for order and control, leading to political domination and subordination of individuals. Wars to settle disputes left entire populations traumatized, and this deep wounding created a tendency to perpetuate violence in subsequent generations. Industrialization raised the standard of living but created pollution and mechanized lives. Motorized transport increased our freedom to travel but contributes to global warming. Computers solve innumerable problems but may be driving us away from more personal connections.

Most of the crises we face as a planet have their source in the West. Therefore, the collective healing we now need requires a deep examination of Western history. As a former psychotherapist, I'd like to engage you in a thought exercise to help us understand why the past is important: Imagine Western Civilization as represented by a client in psychotherapy (we'll call this person "W.C." for short), and let's put this wayward culture on the couch in a therapist's office.

It wouldn't take long to recognize many of the traits of a client in crisis: a rapidly deteriorating home environment, mounting debt, health issues, increasing drug use, violence, instability, and alienation. We would see a masculine psyche largely in denial of its feminine, an inflated ego in denial of its shadow, and an addiction to power in denial of its costs. Worst of all, we would see a client with suicidal tendencies and the means to carry them out. A dire situation indeed.

If we imagined the contents of the media—the television, novels, and movies—that represent W.C.'s dream life, we would see adolescent love stories, with characters in perpetual youth following the lure of their libido but seldom forming mature partnerships. We would observe persistent violence, which, when it occurs in dreams, represents intense conflicts within the psyche. We would see frequent explosions blowing up the institutional buildings that have been

W.C.'s central community experiences. We would observe repeated examples of parental order cracking down on rebellious shadow figures, but seldom do the criminals seek redemption, nor do the parental figures offer rehabilitation. We would see insatiable consumption to fill the growing emptiness, and a huge pretense that everything is fine the way it is, a state that therapists call *denial*.

With these observations in hand, we might well ask: What are the assumptions that have led to W.C.'s unhealed situation? What are the archetypal influences that have led to the West's prevailing destructive beliefs? What are the wounds from our collective childhood that we must heal in order to overcome our addiction to consumption, media-fed narcissism, political gridlock, deep denial, and destructive suicidal tendencies? And how do we heal these wounds so that we can quickly steer ourselves away from self-destruction and toward a planetary adulthood of wholeness and vitality?

In order to work with this client, we would explore W.C.'s history. We would quickly discover that he has no memory of his mother, having lost her long ago. He would speak of growing up with a distant father, spending most of his time in institutions, fulfilling prescibed roles and duties. To survive, W.C. would have had to armor himself against the constant squabbling with his brothers and the separation from his sisters. Such a background would create a rather psychopathic personality. No wonder our civilization is insane enough to be destroying itself on the very threshold of its potential rebirth into magnificence!

For this reason, Part Two of this book delves into our collective story—not just *history*, but *our* story—the story of humanity's development from primal birth through childhood to adolescence. In it, we examine the events that led to our nightmares, while mining the gifts that can lead to our dreams.

To support my argument that we are, indeed, adolescents "coming of age in the heart," I map the eras of human history onto the stages of childhood development. Again, the history in this telling is largely

Western, because it is Western culture that seems the most adolescent at this time (with other cultures either more or less mature), and it is Western culture that has the greatest influence on the shaping of the global tapestry right now—for better or worse. But this story also goes back to prehistoric roots that are common to us all.

So much of our history tells us about the deeds of men—*his-story*—that we scarcely notice how much the feminine part of the story is missing. For this reason, my narration goes all the way back to our ancient mother and examines various ages in light of the feminine or masculine valences or memes, as seen through four different aspects: the original *Static Feminine*, its overthrow by the *Dynamic Masculine*, the era of the stabilizing *Static Masculine*, and finally the recent emergence of the *Dynamic Feminine*. We will come to understand how *all four* valences are needed in our roles as mature parents, coming together in sacred partnership to birth what I call the Divine Child of the future.

The Chakra System as an Evolutionary Map

For in the chakra system, the heart is the very center
of being, with three chakras above and three chakras
below, integrated within the crucible of the heart.
—*Anodea Judith*

An equally important thread that runs through my telling of this tale comes from the Eastern tradition of yoga, as described by the map of the ancient system of energy centers known as the *chakras*. As a comprehensive system, the chakras form a profound formula for wholeness, not only for individual awakening but also for the evolution of society as a whole. As a result of my life's work in this area, my deep understanding of the chakra system has illuminated a pattern that leads me to believe that we are moving from a culture largely organized around the third chakra, which is associated with power and ego-based consciousness, to a new organizing principle more reflective of the heart chakra. The new era, now emerging, is characterized by integration of polarities, balance of gender, hyperconnectedness among its parts, and the qualities of empathy, compassion, relatedness, and peace.

In my previous book, *Eastern Body, Western Mind: Psychology and the Chakra System as a Path to the Self*, I chart the correlation between the chakras and individual childhood development, showing how the chakras awaken sequentially, from bottom to top, starting with our emergence from the womb and continuing as we move through adulthood and beyond. In the book you now hold, I map this pattern onto our collective development, showing how it also parallels childhood development. A simple chart showing how these stages map onto the chakras appears in *Figure 2*. (Please bear in mind that because these are huge eras of human history, their dates are not exact, nor do they start or stop at any single event or time.)

When mapped onto collective development, the progression through the chakras begins at the survival-oriented root chakra of our ancestral beginnings. It moves gradually upward, through the establishment of farming and shipbuilding (second chakra) and later evolves into the building of city-states, empires, and our modern nation-states (third chakra).

We're now at the threshold of the global heart, the era of planetary adulthood. We have been slowly emerging into the fourth chakra, with the advent of rational philosophy, human rights, women's rights, democracy, and a spiritual revolution that is moving beyond dogma toward compassion, higher wisdom, and personal connection with the divine. I argue, however, that we're now suffering from a syndrome of arrested development in our journey to the heart. Parts of our collective psyche are moving forward, while other aspects remain trapped in the egoic third chakra's love of power. We are trapped in a fragmented society divided against itself with the separation of archetypal dualities, such as heaven and earth, mind and body, masculine and feminine, civilization and nature, spirituality and science, and rational versus mythic. A divided world cannot fully enter the heart. Nor can it find peace.

So, what's the solution to these divisions? In chakra theory, *it is only by embracing the full spectrum of human consciousness that we can bring about a true awakening of the heart.* This involves developing the upper chakra realms of communication, vision, and spirituality (chakras five, six, and seven, respectively) and *integrating* them with the lower chakra attributes of the body, the emotions, and personal power (chakras one, two, and three, respectively). In spite of our arrested development, modern technology has enabled upper chakra capacities on a planetary scale, through the communication of words, images, and information via mass media and the Internet. Now that this has occurred, we have arrived at an unprecedented threshold: we may, for the first time ever, be able to integrate our collective upper chakra capabilities with our lower chakra practicality and finally be ready to create a heart chakra paradigm of wholeness and integration.

A valuable aspect of the chakra system is that it can address both personal and collective awakening in the same map. The twofold map I provide in this book allows us to see how our personal evolution along the chakra system contributes to our collective evolution and vice versa. In this way, we can address both inner development and outer action, each one informing and enhancing the other.

Students of integral theory may wonder how this schema maps onto the system put forth by Clare Graves and Don Beck and adopted by Ken Wilber, known as Spiral Dynamics. In this system, various colors and labels are given to the prevailing set of attitudes, values, beliefs, and behaviors (called *memes*) for stages of cultural development. It is beyond the scope of this work to reiterate the entire Spiral Dynamic model (which can be found in numerous sources, especially in Wilber's writings). But I will occasionally make reference to it, as this depiction of the evolution of culture and consciousness also addresses the need for integration of all stages in a comprehensive evolutionary model. *Figures 2* and *3* show how these elements correspond to each other.

For the first time in our long history, we have the means to see the big picture, both in space and across time, thanks to electronic media that bring us news from around the world, as well as a massive accumulation of scientific data about everything from subatomic particles to the environment to the composition of distant stars. Now we can look back and see where we've been and make conscious decisions about where we're going. We'll discover that the question is not just about creation—how it all started—or about destruction— how it will end—but about *evolution*: how an entire planet of infinite complexity evolves to a higher, more conscious and sophisticated system of organization.

Chakra	One	Two	Three	Four	Five	Six	Seven
Sanskrit name	Muladhara	Swadhisthana	Manipura	Anahata	Vissudha	Ajna	Sahasrara
Meaning	Root support	One's own place	Lustrous gem, jeweled citadel	Unstruck, unhurt	Purification	Command center	Thousandfold lotus
Location	Base of spine	Sacral area	Solar plexus	Heart	Throat	Brow	Top of head
Element	Earth	Water	Fire	Air	Sound	Light	Consciousness
Psychological association	Grounding, security	Pleasure, sexuality	Power, autonomy	Love relationship	Communication, creativity	Intuition, imagination	Consciousness, intelligence
Individual developmental phase	Womb to 1 year	6 months to 2 years	18 months to 3–4 years	4–7 years	7–12 years	Adolescence*	Adulthood
Historical time period	Paleolithic	Neolithic	Bronze and Iron Ages	Began c. 600 BCE	Began in Renaissance	Began in 20th century	Now dawning?

Figure 2. Chakra correspondences.

* I have described in my earlier works how the heart phase begins in the socialization of early childhood, while adolescence is equated with the opening of the sixth chakra. The reason we are now at our adolescence culturally, yet still not consolidated in the heart, is that we are suffering from arrested development, a topic dealt with fully in these pages.

In both individual and cultural development, the opening of a particular chakra does not mean that its development is completed in that phase. Often, higher levels of realization are necessary in order to consolidate a previous chakra phase.

In the collective tasks, as seen in *Figure 3*, we have achieved, at least partly, the tasks of the upper chakras, yet we have not yet arrived at peace and freedom for all. I argue that global communications in the fifth, sixth, and seventh chakra realms are necessary to achieve a global awakening in the heart.

Chakra	One	Two	Three	Four	Five	Six	Seven
Element	Earth	Water	Fire	Air	Sound	Light	Consciousness
Task	Survival	Procreation	Power	Love	Communication	Vision	Realization
Age	Infancy	Toddlerhood	Early childhood	Middle childhood	Pre-adolescence	Adolescence	Maturity
Approximate beginning	Earliest humans	10,000–8,000 BCE	3000 BCE	550 BCE	Renaissance	1900	1960s
Gender valence	**Static Feminine** Mother only	**Static Feminine** Mother/son	**Dynamic Masculine** Brother/sister	**Static Masculine** Father/daughter	**Static Masculine** Father/daughter	**Dynamic Feminine** Erotic partnership	**Sacred Marriage** Mature partnership
Initiatory experience	Hunting	Procreation	War	Asceticism	Scholarship	Mystical awakening	Union of masculine and feminine
Central belief	Nature is all	Magic influences Nature	Conquest is power	The word is law	Knowledge is power	God/dess dwells within	Heaven on earth
Organizing principle	Nature	Seasonal cycles	Imperial authority	Written word	Industry	Visionaries	Evolutionaries
Challenges	Survival	Population expansion	Coordination of labor	Cohesion of diversity	Mechanization, complexity	Meaning, purpose	Implementation of vision
Technology	Hunting and gathering	Farming, animal husbandry	Irrigation, metalwork	Weaponry, architecture	Machines, movable type	Computers	Consciousness
Collective living units	Nomadic clans	Villages	City-states	Kingdoms	Metropolis	Urban sprawl	Eco-villages? Space colonies?
Population of units	Tens to hundreds	Thousands	Tens of thousands	Hundreds of thousands	Millions	Tens of millions	Billions
Accomplishments	Primitive art	First temples, megaliths	Writing, mathematics, irrigation	Law and order	Literacy, science, free enterprise	digital networks human rights	World peace
Spiral Dynamic color	Beige	Purple	Red	Blue	Orange	Green	Yellow/Turquoise

Figure 3. Chakras and elements of cultural evolution.

WHERE ARE WE GOING?

Coming of Age in the Heart

We are coming to a place where the road ends. From here on out, we will be making the road as we walk it, in ways we've never had to do before. We now have the job of forging our own evolutionary destiny, and being prime agents of the process of evolution here on Earth.

—*Tom Atlee*

Evolution is the Gods' way of making more gods. This is a basic premise of this book. You can replace the concept of God with whatever term, gender, or pantheon you like, but the point is that evolution proceeds, not only toward greater complexity and freedom but also toward ever more potent powers of creation and destruction. We are approaching a divine awakening of our potential on a scale never before possible. When we can influence the course of life on our planet through global warming, species extinction, or gene splicing—to say nothing of nuclear warfare— we are approaching the power of gods. But have we evolved the wisdom and grace equal to that power? If not, what does it take for us to get there?

Some say it will take a global disaster for humanity to wake up. They may well be right, for we know that rites of passage include *some* kind of death. Certain destructive values and behaviors are so deeply embedded in Western culture, and are so pointedly unsustainable, that clearly *something* needs to die. Do we need to do some kind of global detox in order to remain healthy? Natural and man-made disasters have always occurred; the difference today is one of scale. Because of population density and the global scale of the many related problems we have created, disasters now affect millions. On some level, they affect us all.

Disasters do open our hearts. This was evident in the outpouring of public support following the attacks of September 11, 2001, the tsunami of 2004, and the flooding of New Orleans during Hurricane Katrina in 2005. Earthquakes and hurricanes, floods and droughts, all break down the isolation of individuals and awaken a sense of community. Disasters are one form of initiation that we will examine more closely in the next chapter.

However, a proper initiation can also *mitigate* disaster by awakening a guiding vision. Without that vision, we are stuck in outdated belief systems, with only guilt to guide our current behavior. We know we shouldn't drive so much, use so much, waste so much. But most people feel they have little alternative. We are immersed in power systems that lead individuals to believe they have little control. Others are not even aware of their impact. Nor is it easy to give up privileges we have come to rely upon.

By contrast, a guiding vision can give us something to move *toward* instead of something to move *away from*. No disaster was necessary for people to switch from an electric typewriter to a word-processing computer; it was simply a better idea. It didn't require a failure of the telephone system to make room for cell phones. When a better way becomes apparent, we choose it naturally. *A destructive lifestyle is simply ignorant of a better way.* What's needed is a vision of the future as an organizing principle, much as the blueprints for a house organize the laborers who build it. Without something positive to move toward, we are much like an adolescent who is acting out, suffering from a lack of guidance.

The culmination of billions of years of evolution now rests in our hands. It signals an extraordinary need for responsibility and a driving imperative to wake up. At the very least, it requires the maturity of adult wisdom and behavior. But even more, it calls for an awakening of the global heart. For love is the key to that which endures.

The Balance of Power and Love

It is not power that corrupts but fear. Fear of losing power
corrupts those who wield it, and fear of the scourge
of power corrupts those who are subject to it.
—*Thomas Jefferson*

One of the hallmarks of the heart chakra is balance. While our collective center of gravity may be shifting from power to love, or third chakra to fourth chakra, it doesn't mean we give up one for the other; instead, we find balance and integration between them. Both power and love are vitally necessary for social coordination. The shift we are going through is more like an upgrade in our collective operating system, one that builds upon the previous platform.

Many see power and love as a kind of either/or duality. Carl Jung spoke to this: "Where love reigns, there is no will to power; and where the will to power is paramount, love is lacking. The one is but the shadow of the other."[7] Politics that falls on the side of compassion is often criticized as weak. Dismantling nuclear weapons, "coddling terrorists" through negotiation, funding humanitarian efforts, working for peace, even taking care of the environment—or truly caring for much of anything—is seen by some as soft, effeminate, or ineffective. Whereas those who wield power and wealth are often seen as selfish, insensitive, oppressive, or manipulative.

Politics without love becomes tyranny. But love without power is childish idealism. We don't give up our power to move toward love. Instead, we stand firmly in our power, our feet planted together on commonly held sacred ground, our collective will aligned with purpose, guided by informed and educated minds reaching toward the infinity of the stars. What shifts is the primary organizing principle through which we see and organize our world. Martin Luther King expressed this beautifully in a 1967 speech:

> Power properly understood is nothing but the ability to achieve purpose. It is the strength required to bring about social, political, and economic change. . . . There is nothing wrong with power if power is used correctly. . . . And one of the great problems of history is that the concepts of love and power have usually been contrasted as opposites—polar opposites—so that love is identified with a resignation of power, and power with a denial of love. . . .
>
> What is needed is a realization that power without love is reckless and abusive, and love without power is sentimental and anemic. Power at its best is love implementing the demands of justice, and justice at its best is power correcting everything that stands against love.[8]

The shift I am describing moves our center of consciousness to a higher level, integrating power and love. It happens in our personal lives as we expand from lower to higher centers of consciousness and from narcissism to planetary awareness and service. It can happen in our economics as we seek to distribute resources for the optimal functioning of the planet and its human and nonhuman inhabitants, operating with both compassion and the wisdom that sometimes has to make hard decisions. It is a shift to an organizing principle in which decentralized power can create greater abundance, relevance, and efficiency.

The shift from power to love takes us from a chain of command to a web of connection, from hierarchy to holarchy, from competition to collaboration, from an ego system to an ecosystem, from greed to green, from markets to networks, from unlimited growth to sustainability, and from the love of power to the power of love.

Power-paradigm characteristics	Heart-paradigm characteristics
Hierarchy	Holarchy
Chain of command	Web of connection
Competition	Collaboration
Markets	Networks
Stockholders	Stakeholders
Either/or	Both/and
Mind over body	Mind-body-spirit integration
Exploitation of nature	Deep ecology
I–it	I–thou–we
Rational	Mythic-evolutionary
Male dominated	Partnership
Expedience	Aesthetics
Empire	Earth Community (David Korten)
Ego	Essence (Barbara Marx Hubbard)
Procreation	Cocreation (Barbara Marx Hubbard)
Ego system	Ecosystem
Individual	Relational
Unlimited growth	Sustainability
Greed	Green
Imperialism	Participatory democracy
Militarism	Peace and social justice
Adolescence	Adulthood
Belongings	Belonging (Jeremy Rifkin)
Web 1.0	Web 2.0, 3.0

Figure 4. Comparison of heart and power paradigms.

Love as an Organizing Principle

Love is the social equivalent of gravity.
—*Morris Berman*

From the first cries of a newborn to the last breath of a parent, from the excitement of our first romance to the beauty of nature, or as mundane as our favorite food or movie, we use the word *love* to describe them all. As teenagers we draw hearts on our notes, fantasizing about our latest attraction, and call it love. As bereaved, we wail over the loss of our loved ones, whether from death, betrayal, or rejection. We improve ourselves in order to be more lovable, and we hold love as an ideal across time and cultures.

While the most common association with love is the romantic love between two people, any mature definition includes far more than that. The Greeks, for example, had four basic words for love, and this is a good place to start.

Eros, or romantic love, tends to be the most compelling. Romantic love begins in attraction, has strong urgings in the body, seeks expression through the erotic, and desires union with the beloved. Romantic love can be strong or fickle, lasting or fleeting. As anyone knows, it is a powerful force to contend with, one that rules much of our lives.

Storge, or affection, is the feeling of care we develop for another, such as parents for children. It can also mean the need for consistency in love, the task of enduring tough situations, keeping commitments.

Philia describes a kind of brotherly love, the love between friends that grows over time. Aristotle described it as a kind of dispassion, while Plato distinguished it from physically expressed love, giving us the term *Platonic love.*

Agape is unconditional love and moves toward religious devotion, ecstatic states, and a larger connection with the world around us.

Agape is the kind of awe we feel in religious experience, an unmovable faith in the divine, a melding with the great realm of spirit that we sometimes call universal love.

In these pages, I will add yet another use of the term *love*: as an *organizing principle for human society*. This organizing principle is based on connection, collaboration, cooperation, empathy, caring, generosity, peace, appreciation, compassion, higher consciousness, integration, and wholeness. I use the word *love* to denote the kind of grace that holds things in relationship, as a force that arranges constituent parts into a whole. We find this grace in the body, when bones and joints are properly aligned and move freely. We find it in a family, when the internal relationships are appropriate and there is harmony in the home, benefitting all members. We can find it in the garden or wilderness, when the plants have formed a balance of color and shape that sings with beauty; or in an orchestra where the instruments play well together.

As an organizing force, I also use the word *love* as a principle of *exchange,* or perpetual reciprocity, that allows things to continue in relationship, such as the give and take of scratching each other's backs. When that reciprocity is maintained, so is the relationship. This can be seen in any mature ecosystem, where the exchanges between parts are optimized so that everything gives and receives in a kind of perpetual balance that maintains the whole. This kind of love is necessary for sustainability—for what has perpetual reciprocity can endure through time.

In terms of application, I refer to love as a principle of *caring,* or taking responsibility for the well-being of yourself, another person or group, or anything outside oneself, such as your neighborhood, the rain forest, or children in poverty. Service, charity, altruism, and generosity fall under this umbrella of love. Caring is rooted in a feeling in the heart. It is also the basis of vocational passion, the compelling desire to give something back to the world, to see something protected, healed, or improved.

In addition, I regard love as a kind of *entelechy*, meaning an invisible force that draws us toward future fulfillment through the longing in our hearts. Such longing is for a state that does not yet exist and is the underlying force for creativity. Entelechy is driven by our values, what we appreciate, and what gives us meaning. Examples of love as entelechy would be feeling drawn to become a healer because you see the potential of helping others, being drawn to work in a country because you love the culture, or being drawn to study something that would enhance your development. It even occurs as we feel drawn to a person who later turns out to influence our destiny. Barbara Marx Hubbard calls this *vocational arousal*, meaning the kind of excitement we get from our work when it is meaningful, beneficial, and evolutionary.

Finally, as a larger, more spiritual concept, there is a *universal love* that exists as a field in which we are all enveloped. This love is an evolutionary principle that seeks optimization of all the parts of a system from what could be called a divine source. You can see it in the exquisite way the intricate web of relationships gives us the perfection of life: the snow that reflects light in winter and stores water for streams in summer; the loss of leaves in the fall, with their incredible burst of color, to fertilize the soil; the fact that the moon is highest in the winter when nights are long and dark or that the cycle of the seasons gives us renewal of life. This profound force of organizational consciousness exists beyond any single entity and keeps our incredible world functioning beyond our understanding. To describe this perfection, I use the term *universal love*.

For humanity to evolve into our planetary adulthood and "come of age in the heart" is to *fall back in love with the world*—to stand in a place of power and use that power in service of love. In the realm of the heart, we reconstitute the archetype of sacred partnership: balanced, respectful, and mutually enhancing. Here we are inspired to act from passionate dedication, not spineless obedience; to be repossessed by the sacred, rather than dispossessed by its lack; to be pulled forward by an evolving vision from the future, rather than held back by the decaying patterns of the past.

The Path of Maturity

The future enters into us in order to transform
itself in us long before it happens.
—*Rainer Maria Rilke*

The path toward wholeness, which Jung called the archetype of *individuation*, is now being thrust upon the collective psyche. Individuation is the soul's process of maturing and awakening to its true nature. It often begins in a crisis that forces deeper self-examination. Here we find forgotten selves; reclaim disconnected parts, such as our shadow or wounded child; and bring our inner masculine and feminine into balance and relationship. This process calls us to break the confines of cultural conformity and begin to live authentic and embodied lives.

Just as it occurs for individuals, our task is to *collectively* face our hidden shadow of violence, greed, and domination and stop projecting it onto others. We must balance the powers of masculine and feminine not only in socioeconomic status but also in terms of our innate values, making emotional intelligence as necessary as cognitive genius, nurturance as important as accomplishment, receptive wisdom as valuable as creative expression.

Our current age of power has delivered vast knowledge, sophisticated technology, and personal freedom, greater than at any time in our history. Yet the shadow side of our power has created pollution and tyranny, as well as inflated military budgets across the globe that rob funds needed to combat environmental issues such as global warming that pose an even greater threat to our future security.

Power and domination, where one part rules over another—such as mind over body, male over female, white over black, one nation over another, or civilization over nature—has typified our world for the last several millennia.

The age of power also brought us the initial steps of individuation from an undifferentiated tribal unity, much as our personal autonomy emerges from an initial fusion with our mother. As we will see later, separating from the archetypal Mother and giving birth to the ego brought us what Joseph Campbell and others call the Heroic Age. The heroic journey has been a rightful quest for power, but this quest has now overshot its mark.

The Hero's journey mirrors the initiation process: heeding a call to serve something greater, separating from what is known, and even dissolving the structures of one's individual consciousness. The Hero enters the belly of the Underworld, faces trials and ordeals, meets and merges with archetypal forces, opens to new vision, and is ultimately reborn before he finally returns. We are all at different stages of this heroic journey. Some of us are experiencing dissolution; some of us are in the Underworld; others are battling in their ordeals; and many are discovering and opening to archetypal forces, returning with new vision. We are all a part of this initiation, each in our own way.

The final step in the Hero's quest is the *return home,* where the fruits of the quest—the elixir of healing or the enlightened vision—are brought back to a broken and ailing world. The Hero's quest begins with the striving of an individual but ends in the healing of community. The quest illuminates our power, but the return is an act of love. To turn the fruits of our power back toward the repair of our environment, the serving of people's needs, and the healing of our culture is to come back home again. But we return home different than we left—older, wiser, more expanded, and more capable.

From Caterpillar to Butterfly

We know what we are, not what we may become.
—*Shakespeare*

The evolutionary biologist Elisabet Sahtouris has suggested a metaphor for transformation based on the story of the butterfly.[9] This process of metamorphosis has so many parallels with our collective rite of passage that we will refer to it again and again throughout these pages, as a guiding image for our collective changes.

Caterpillars are spineless larval creatures that eat voraciously throughout their larval life. When a caterpillar nears its transformation time, it begins to eat even more ravenously, consuming everything in sight. The news media so often calls individuals "consumers." Is that unconsciously indicative of our larval state? As a result of this consumption, the caterpillar's body becomes heavy, bursting its skin many times, until it is too bloated to move. Attaching to a branch (upside down, we might add, where everything is turned on its head), it forms a chrysalis—an enclosing shell that limits the caterpillar's freedom for the duration of the transformation. Within the chrysalis a miracle occurs. Tiny cells that biologists actually call "imaginal cells"[10] begin to appear. These cells are wholly different from caterpillar cells, carrying different information and vibrating, so to speak, to a different frequency—the frequency of the emerging butterfly.

At first, the caterpillar's immune system perceives these new cells as enemies and attacks them, much as new ideas today are often viciously denounced by the powers that be. But despite this attack, the imaginal cells are not deterred. They continue to appear, increasing in numbers until the new cells are numerous enough to organize into clumps. When enough cells have created structures along the *new* organizational lines, the caterpillar's immune system is overwhelmed.

The cells of the original body dissolve into a nutritious soup for the growth of the butterfly.

When the butterfly is ready to hatch, the chrysalis becomes transparent (much as the Internet is making many hidden actions transparent). The need for restriction has been outgrown. Yet the struggle toward freedom is part of the process. If the chrysalis opened too soon, the butterfly would die. As the butterfly emerges, it fills its wings with the liquid "soup" and then flies away to dance among the flowers.

These two wings (a "right wing" and a "left wing," we might note), both necessary to fly, are coordinated from the central *core* of the butterfly. In a similar way, the core within each one of us can be seen as an *axis mundi* that runs from crown to base, connecting heaven and earth. As we come into our core through the gradual dissolution of our "caterpillar consciousness," we discover that the internal map of the chakras is part of our core identity, guiding us on the evolutionary journey. Once we recognize our core, we can balance the right and left wings of our consciousness, so to speak, and take flight toward a new way of being. Can you see how this analogy helps us to understand the awakening of the global heart? Humanity is transforming its collective body from the unconscious, overconsuming bloat of the caterpillar into a lighter creature of exquisite beauty, grace, and freedom.

This coming-of-age process takes us to a new mythic reality, a larger story that is ripe with meaning and direction. It is not a passage that ends in the gray grimness of adult responsibility, denying the colorful spirituality of childhood innocence. Rather, it is a reclaiming of wholeness that denies little and embraces all. From this abundance we can better love and cherish our world.

This book is the story of that passage. It takes us through the twists and turns of humanity's childhood, showing how previous organizing principles ordered society. It examines the masculine and feminine valences of each era preceding our own, along with the chakra-related challenges of each step of our development. And it shows us how to engage with the initiation and transformation that is now before us. From the love of power to the power of love, this rite of passage from separation to reunion is the emerging myth of our time.

INITIATION

Answering the Call

When you step further into the story you came to live, not only does the mythic territory open, but the deep self moves and the world of imagination and meaning comes towards you.
—*Michael Meade*

When fate arrives at your door, there is no lock strong enough to hold it back. It may find you asleep, unprepared, too busy, or defiant, but these states are no deterrent. Destiny does not wait for your mood to change. When the time is ripe, the rite of passage begins. Such rites eventually come to us all.

Sometimes initiation begins more gently, with a call tugging at our hearts. Rainer Maria Rilke said, "What goes on in your innermost being is worthy of your whole love; you must somehow keep working at it."[11] That inner being longs to dissolve petty distractions and open to something larger—whether it be a project, a community, or our collective future. This pull, emanating from the deep unconscious, invisibly guides our lives toward greater meaning and purpose. Known as *the call*, it comes in many forms. It may begin as a restless dissatisfaction with your daily life or a deep depression. It may arise from your gut churning over the daily news or an inspiring story you hear from a friend.

However the call finds its way into your private chambers—whether by inner longing or a sudden event—it changes the course of your life. Often such calls begin with a blunder: a simple lapse of attention that lets unconscious urges rise to the surface just long enough to take over the reins and steer us in a new direction. It might be an affair that ends your marriage or a sudden injury that makes a dead-end job impossible to perform. It may come from a tragic loss or even an unexpected boon. It may seem like a random quirk of fate, but looking back upon it later, you find that the hand of destiny was clearly marked by your own fingerprints. Joseph Campbell saw these blunders as the result of suppressed longings, "ripples on the surface of life, produced by unsuspected springs."[12]

If, by whatever means, you are called to the path of initiation, know that you are not alone. Many are now hearing the call. Many are waking up from the dream, only to discover that it was a nightmare. Awake to the call within their hearts, they begin to move toward a new destiny.

When you first hear the call, it may seem that nothing you know fits the new challenge—for its very purpose is to bring you to a new realm. Like the caterpillar wrapped in a chrysalis, you cannot know who you are becoming when the process begins. It's only in hindsight, looking back from the other side of the transformation, that you finally understand. You can resist the process and remain as a caterpillar, or you can relinquish control and emerge as a butterfly. But once you begin, you cannot remain the same.

When the old world is stripped away, it reveals another world hidden beneath. A reluctant mother, bent on pursuing an adult career, discovers the magical world of children. The homeowner ravaged by fire or flood discovers the freedom of living without possessions. The lover who engages in a secret affair discovers vital parts of herself coming back to life. Each loss, though difficult, brings a new awakening. Each cloud has a silver lining.

Traditionally, initiation was a way of bridging the past and the future through a meaningful exchange between elders and youth. Tribal societies believed that a failure to initiate their youth would create a generation that would destroy their culture. Since our culture doesn't provide the kind of "wisdom" initiations that occur in indigenous tribes or spiritual communities, we have far too many people, both in and out of power, who are incomplete adults with arrested development. Then the initiation process finds a back door into our lives—with nervous breakdowns, health issues, midlife crises, drug addiction, neighborhood gang wars, or military combat. While rare individuals may find their way to spiritual awakening through these paths, it's certainly not the best way to produce such wisdom. Perhaps, by acknowledging the need for consciously created spiritual initiations, we can better guide our youth to adulthood.

Collective Initiation

All life is a process of breaking down. But the blows that do the dramatic side of the work . . . don't show their effect all at once.
—F. Scott Fitzgerald

In the same vein, humanity's lack of wisdom and foresight are leading us to extreme forms of collective initiation. As modern culture continues its ecologically destructive path into the future, we can see that in many parts of the world, whole villages and cities, even countries, are facing these tragic wake-up calls. Earthquakes and tsunamis, hurricanes and floods, droughts, disease, economic collapse, wars, political oppression, and acts of terrorism are disturbing or destroying lives by the millions. We can regard these events as initiatory ordeals on a collective level. They will touch greater numbers of the world's population, eventually touching us all, either directly or indirectly. Like contractions in a birth process, they will increase in frequency and severity until we birth a new way of being. Fasten your seat belt and take a deep breath as you read through some of the initiatory challenges that are looming in our future.

Let's begin with climate change. The majority of scientists agree that our world is reaching a tipping point of escalating catastrophe. While the danger limit of atmospheric carbon has been estimated at 350 parts per million (ppm), the world reached 400 ppm in the summer of 2012.[13] The fact that carbon levels were only 280 ppm prior to the Industrial Revolution of the 19th century points to human activity as a primary cause. Because the measures to reduce carbon emissions have been too meager and too late, we face a runaway system in which greenhouse gases will increase and temperatures will continue to rise. Carbon dioxide levels are expected to rise at the rate of 2 ppm per year over the next several decades. While this may not sound like a serious increase, a mere 50 years brings us to 500 ppm, a level that will produce large-scale catastrophe.

Exactly how much warming will occur is unpredictable. Estimates range from 2 degrees Fahrenheit at the conservative end of things to 12 degrees as a more catastrophic prediction. This small rise in world average temperature may again seem like very little, yet for every two-degree increase there is a 10 to 15 percent decrease in crop production. Meanwhile, the United Nations says we need to *increase* food supply by 50 percent to feed the world's growing population. And this is just the tip of the iceberg.

Melting glaciers and polar ice caps will cause a significant rise in sea level, potentially displacing 350 million coastal inhabitants worldwide (greater than the entire population of the United States). Severe weather as a result of changing temperatures creates droughts in many areas and floods in others. Torrential storms, such as Hurricanes Katrina and Sandy, are likely to increase in severity, costing lives, homes, and billions of dollars. Disruption of ocean currents, such as the Gulf Stream, may cause extreme cold as well as heat, especially in northern Europe. Higher winds will dry out soil, requiring more water for cropland, while dying forests become tinder for fires. Microbes, frozen in the ice from the distant past, will enter the water system as glaciers melt, possibly spreading new diseases for which we have no antibodies. Reduced food supply, especially of the world's staples of rice, corn, and wheat, can bring wide-scale famine. Some crops, like corn, whose tassles dry out in extreme heat, cannot fertilize at temperatures over 104 degrees Fahrenheit.[14] Intense heat also takes its human toll, as it did in the European heat wave of 2003, which claimed the lives of 52,000 people.[15]

Climate change isn't our only issue, however. All of the above contributes to situations already occurring: economic disparities, racial tension, political corruption, disease, war, and terrorism. Underprivileged classes and Third World countries are always hit hardest by any disaster, be it economic, political, or "natural." Increased poverty conditions breed crime and social unrest. Lack of clean water for sanitation contributes to the spread of disease, while dense populations coupled with world travel can cause the spread of increasingly virulent flu viruses or more deadly plagues, such as AIDS or SARS-type diseases. Failed states—countries whose governments and economies are in collapse—can fragment into anarchy and violence, as the disenfranchised run rampant with guns or, worse, access to more powerful weapons.

Aside from climate change, many other problems plague our environment: Topsoil is turning to desert at alarming rates, with areas of soil degradation equal to the size of India and China in the last 50 years,[16] while Africa has a dust cloud large enough to cover the United States, coast to coast.[17] Meanwhile, air pollution takes the lives of 1.3 million each year, according to the World Health Organization.[18] Ocean fish stocks are collapsing along with a decrease in plankton, which not only comprise the base of the food chain for sea life but also produce half of the oxygen we breathe and draw down carbon dioxide. And while we're speaking of the smaller building blocks of nature, those tiny bees that pollinate our crops are disappearing at alarming rates, due to a phenomenon called Colony Collapse Disorder.

Meanwhile, the production of oil, upon which modern civilization now depends, will continue to decline, curtailing transportation while increasing the cost of everything, from heating our homes to manufacturing our products and packaging. Other critical sources of energy, such as nuclear power plants, are both expensive and vulnerable to meltdowns, as witnessed in the 2011 Fukushima disaster in Japan. And let's not forget that all this takes place in a world armed with enough nuclear weapons to render the extinction of all current life on earth.

It's hard to remain positive in the face of these statistics. Many see only doom and gloom, such as the full-scale collapse of civilization and the end of life as we know it. While the above predictions imply that a certain amount of disaster is coming, I choose to see these crises as a dire stimulus to human awakening, the initiatory drivers of evolution that force us to transform. The perfect storm of these crises converging upon each other creates a widespread planetary initiation whose impact will demand radical change in nearly every sector of society.

In fact, it is my hope that even the *warning* of the above facts will impel us into action, so that the worst of these crises can be avoided. Indeed, these realities should be front and center on the evening news, *before they happen* rather than after, yet denial is still rampant. Lester Brown, head of the environmental research firm Earth Policy Institute, describes all these factors and more in his *Plan B* series of books, which are widely available. The encouraging point that Brown makes, however, is that humanity has the means, both technological and financial, to address every one of these issues. What is missing is the collective and political will to make it happen.

And yet, even disasters have a silver lining. Rebecca Solnit, in her hopeful book *A Paradise Built in Hell: The Extraordinary Communities That Arise in Disaster*, describes how "natural disasters," while terrible, reveal that in fact everyday life is its own disaster of greed, corruption, isolation, or boredom. She states, "Horrible in itself, disaster is sometimes a door back into paradise, the paradise in which we are who we hope to be, do the work we desire, and are each our sister's and brother's keeper. . . . If paradise now arises in hell, it's because in the suspension of the usual order, we are free to live and act another way."[19]

Her book courageously explores major catastrophes, from the 1906 San Francisco earthquake to the one in Mexico City in 1985, from New York's 9/11 tragedy to the flooding of New Orleans, proving again and again that in the wake of these events, something joyful, beautiful, and lovingly powerful emerged. Despite the media's portrayal to the contrary, her research led her to conclude, "The prevalent human nature in disaster is resilient, resourceful, generous, empathic, and brave."[20]

Such tragedies are initiatory wounds. They shatter childhood innocence, humiliate adolescent arrogance, and replace complacency with a demand for action. But even more, they break through separation, open the heart to compassion, and awaken communities of cooperation and generosity. As physical walls tumble down, so do the walls between us. As bureaucracies crumble, new forms organize. As external power sources fail, we find internal resources. One survivor became so energized that he claimed, "It's as if the power grid went off and went right into me." Reverend James Martin, a Jesuit priest, said of his volunteer work in New York's 9/11 aftermath, "I have to say, for me, working down there has been the most profound experience of the Holy Spirit that I've ever had."[21]

Stages of Initiation

As you go the way of life, you will see a great chasm.
Jump. It is not as wide as you think.
—*Joseph Campbell*

Initiation may be instigated by a sudden event or occur incrementally through a series of events. The process of transformation, however, takes time, and the larger the system, the longer it takes to transform. Knowing the stages of initiation helps us to navigate our way through. Knowing there is a beginning, middle, and an end makes it easier to endure. We understand there is a purpose, and that gives it meaning. And we know that this initiation requires something of us, something wholly unexpected, transformational, even miraculous, that calls forth our greatest gifts. We know that we have to stretch and reach beyond our comfort zone, and that we will discover new gifts, powers, and capacities we didn't know were possible. And most important, we know that there is a rebirth on the other side.

Initiation begins with separation from what is known and familiar, entailing a loss of safety and predictability that arrests our attention. Elders in indigenous cultures might steal a youth from his home in the middle of the night to begin his initiation. The Divine Child in mythology is usually ripped away from his parents at birth and left to die, yet somehow he survives. Some contemporary examples could include the following: a young woman on the way to college discovers that she is pregnant; a fire destroys a home; a cancer diagnosis makes you change your lifestyle; a car accident kills your best friend. Victims who lose their homes, their villages, or their habitat are wrenched from familiar surroundings. Some lose their jobs, their family, or their community. Others lose loved ones: spouses, children, or parents. Neighborhoods and businesses disappear in a heartbeat, with no time to prepare. In a sudden wrench from normalcy, life is irrevocably interrupted. Such disruption rudely gets our attention: *all of it.*

The stage that follows this precipitating event is isolation and containment. Initiates are often bound and blindfolded in a dark room or cave. An unexpected fall might leave one stuck in a hospital for months at a time. One might serve time in prison. A power failure might leave us unable to communicate. Or this containment might result from oil shortages that make travel so expensive that we are confined to our communities. Often in this stage the effects last longer than the initial blow, and we are forced into a solitude or total abandonment that brings us to our knees. In that moment of surrender, we open to a kind of grace, if only out of desperation that nothing else will save us. The soul becomes open to the unknown.

Once we surrender, we can receive spiritual helpers, or what Joseph Campbell called "supernatural aid." Myths abound with the miraculous appearances of fairies that spin straw into gold, mentors who appear as if from nowhere, and magic animals that can transport a wounded child or warrior through desert, storm, or forest. During their period of isolation, initiates find their guidance in dreams, see visions of angels, or experience an auspicious synchronicity that gives them hope. Maybe we resort to prayer for the first time, now coming from a humility that didn't previously exist. Once there is this glimmering—however small—of sustaining power, vision, or purpose, one is ready to face the core of initiation: the *challenges.*

While spiritual aid may provide the needed support system, ordeals are what catalyze the transformation. Indeed, we cannot survive the challenges unless we transform. Ordeals are shockingly horrific, sometimes the initiate's greatest fear or worst enemy. They appear to be insurmountable, by definition bigger than the known powers of the initiate, for they exist precisely to awaken greater power than we thought possible. In the same way, the challenges and ordeals before us on this planet may seem insurmountable. Our powers as a people may seem lacking in the face of these deeply entrenched systems.

The most difficult stage of initiation is the one that involves some kind of death, either real or symbolic, before the transformation takes us through to the other side. In our coming collective ordeals, as in the disasters that have already occurred, there will be loss and death. Some will be the death of humans, some will be habitats, some will be whole species. Other losses will be customs, cultures, languages, businesses, bank accounts, relationships, hopes, and dreams. It isn't the death of everything, but it is enough to produce sobriety and instigate change. We all know about the people who die in floods or terrorist events (approximately 2,000 in Hurricane Katrina and nearly 3,000 at the World Trade Center), yet 3.4 million people are dying *each year* from a lack of clean water.[22]

It is not only the tragic loss of life that occurs, but also, and perhaps more important, the death of old structures. Political hegemonies, economic strangleholds, and beliefs in the sanctity of outdated systems die as well, allowing something new to arise in their place. Mexico City's 1985 earthquake cracked the political stranglehold of the PRI (the Institutional Revolutionary Party), which ruled Mexico with massive corruption at every level, eventually bringing it down by the turn of the century. Rebecca Solnit claims that the quake marked the rebirth of what Mexicans call civil society.[23] The Chernobyl nuclear disaster, horrible as it was, influenced politics in the Soviet Union, as Mikhail Gorbachev reflected in 2006:

> The nuclear meltdown at Cherobyl twenty years ago this month, even more than my launch of *perestroika*, was perhaps the real cause of the collapse of the Soviet Union five years later. . . . The Chernobyl disaster, more than anything else, opened the possibility of much greater freedom of expression, to the point that the system as we knew it could no longer continue. It made

absolutely clear how important it was to continue the policy of *glasnost*, and I must say I started to think in terms of pre-Chernobyl and post-Chernobyl.[24]

Similarly, it could be argued that Hurricane Sandy, which ravaged New York and New Jersey just prior to the presidential election of 2012, not only drove home the urgency of dealing with global warming but also tipped the scales in President Obama's favor and undermined the science-denying platform of the Republican Party.

As power grids fail, we find our own power. As walls tumble, we are forced outside to meet our neighbors and experience a new kind of community. As survivors are denied escape, they are forced to transform where they are. Political structures fail and fall; hierarchies prove inadequate, as they did in Katrina. Humans, eminently creative, give birth under duress.

One death we are certain to face in the coming years is that of our adolescent way of life, where we expect every whim to be indulged, every need to be granted, and where we continue to spin without purpose or understanding of our evolutionary destiny. This death will lead to the last stage of initiation: *rebirth in a new form*. Just what that will look like cannot be known when we are approaching initiation's gate. It is discovered through the process of initiation itself. Our only valid choice is to surrender to the process and use the best of our wits to see it through. We can make our values be our guide, integrity be our strength, and hope be our beacon of light. What we can hope for is that we emerge as a mature species—able to control our population and to live sustainably and peacefully with the help of amazing technologies to create an exhilarating future.

Initiation is a series of stress tests in which our character is challenged. Which will we choose? Vengeance or negotiation, war or peace, opposition or synthesis, the old ways that we know or the creation of something new? We face these choices daily, whether in large ways or small. They occur within our personal relationships, at work, and in our schools, hospitals, and government institutions. When we consistently choose a new way, we will move out of the testing phase of initiation and truly begin the next round of civilization. Longer-standing problems will still exist and new ones will arise, but our means of addressing them will be from a different perspective.

Initiatory ordeals are a way to hold the challenges we must face, giving them meaning in a larger perspective. Our future maturity as a species will result not from any single event but from a string of many such events. It is not a quick or easy process. It is a long, slow turning, an elegant confluence of creation and destruction in the eternal spiral of evolution, in which these events are instigators. A peaceful world may not occur in my lifetime, but a decline in violence is already happening, as we will explore further on. The balancing of genders, the integration of races, economic justice, and arriving at true sustainability is a huge shift with many moving parts, taking place over decades and centuries, yet it is already under way. Still, this change will occur more rapidly than changes have in the past: not only because it can but because it must.

The Underworld Journey

We're in a freefall into the future. We don't know where we're going. Things are changing so fast, and always when you're going through a long tunnel, anxiety comes along. And all you have to do to transform your hell into a paradise is to turn your fall into a voluntary act. It's a very interesting shift of perspective and that's all it is . . . joyful participation in the sorrows and everything changes.
—*Joseph Campbell*

Whether your call comes as a whisper or a command, a yearning or a sentence, how will you answer? How do you face this numinous passage? How do you prepare for entry into sacred realms?

Carl Jung said, "Only that which can destroy itself is truly alive."[25] In some cultures, the possibility of death was a very real element in their rites of passage. Failure to meet the challenges could end an initiate's life. Is it so different for us as a species? To naïvely continue in the same direction of mindless consumption, destruction, and distraction, and fail to initiate necessary changes, could bring life as we know it to a tragic end. The ultimatum is written on the walls that surround us: transform or die.

For us to emerge into this new form, the old form must be irrevocably altered—even destroyed. This is no easy process. Our lives are embedded in the old form. We are made from it, dependent upon it. We think with its images, judge ourselves with its values, unconsciously respond to its programming. It is this very death that we fight with such intensity, that we run from in our dreams, that we try to escape from through chemical obliteration. But it is this very death that brings us to rebirth.

Finding the entrance to the realm of the sacred is the first mystery that must be probed in preparation for initiation. This entrance is not a physical place but an attitude of openness within the psyche. The more you resist the unknown, the greater the breakdown must be. You must undo who you think you are and get down to your basic essence in order to build a new structure.

Both ascendant and descendant spiritual paths agree on this point, though their approaches are vastly different. Ascendant spirituality includes those paths that seek salvation through transcendence, by moving upward into etheric, intellectual, and/or meditative realms, leaving the heavier, earthly concerns behind in order to find ultimate truth. Such paths seek to dissolve attachment to the earthly, egoic self and its limitations in order to pierce through illusion and open to a more inclusive reality. Here ego death is voluntary, or hopes to be, but it may take many years or lifetimes of dedication before the last sticky vestiges of our attachments are extinguished. Transcendence is the central tenet of what is considered to be the world's perennial wisdom.

Buddhism, Zen, yoga, Christianity, Islam, and many New Age philosophies, as well as most people's interpretations of the chakras, all tend to focus primarily on ascending paths of consciousness.

The descendant path, though brutal, is faster and less equivocal. The death phase of initiation is one of separation, loss, and dissolution, mythically represented as a journey to the Underworld. This unpleasant downward journey strips a person of all false props and hopes, including those sought in the ascendant practices. In the Underworld, you don't relinquish your attachments—they are pried from your hands, destroyed before your very eyes, amputated without anaesthesia. Descendant paths strip you down—not only to your foundation, but to the core upon which such a foundation is built. Only then can you truly find roots that are solid, nourished by the deep, hidden layers of the collective unconscious. These roots are indestructible. They give strength for the journey ahead. By losing what we don't need, we find what is eternal. Such a path may not grace the top of our "fun list," but it is, nonetheless, tremendously effective.

Sudden losses are the most common form of ordeal. The wealthy executive who has to declare bankruptcy, the spiritual teacher who falls from grace, the athlete who gets permanently injured, the parent who loses a child—these are the kinds of personal ordeals that signal a spiritual initiation. To survive this journey, we must learn the rules of the Underworld as it has been described by mythologies throughout time.

The Underworld in Myth

It is by going down into the abyss that we recover the treasures of life.
Where you stumble, there lies your treasure.
—Joseph Campbell

The story of the goddess Inanna's descent to the Underworld is believed to be one of the oldest written myths, preserved on fragments of clay tablets from ancient Sumer that have been dated around 1750 BCE[26] The story tells how Inanna, tender of the great World Tree, travels to the Underworld to attend a funeral, something even a goddess cannot do without fundamental sacrifice. When she knocks on the Underworld gate, the gatekeeper, Neti, sends a message to Ereshkigal, the ruler of that dark realm, that the Queen of Heaven has arrived.

Seven gates open, one by one. At each gate something vital is demanded from Inanna: her royal crown, her necklace, the beads at her breast, her breastplate, her gold ring, her lapis measuring rod and line, and finally her royal robe.[27] With each loss, Inanna protests adamantly, "What is this?" Each time, the gatekeeper, Neti, scolds her: "Quiet, Inanna! The ways of the Underworld are perfect. They may not be questioned!"

Oh, how we protest when we tumble into darkness! How we shake our fists at whatever we believe in, how we whine to anyone who will listen, and, failing to find sympathy, how much we pay our therapists. Little good does it do. Better to surrender to the darkness and get on with it than to curse the sputtering candle. In that surrender, sweet and dark as it is, lies the humility that opens us to receive something new.

Herein lies the purpose of the Underworld journey. R. J. Stewart, in his book *The Underworld Initiation,* describes this explicitly:

> The breaking down of the personality, therefore, is regarded as inevitable and essential in magical growth.

The growth cannot occur without the clarifying break-down; hence the old term "twice born" for initiates. During dissolution, the constituent elements of the personality, both superficial and long-term, are reduced. What remains are the individual archetypes, resonating in harmonic pattern attuned to the Life Source.[28]

The Underworld journey, with its specter of death, awakens the urge to live. Our survival instinct is the indelible bottom line, a connecting link to all life, the fundamental trajectory of evolution. It is only when we face death and surmount it that the tremendous power of the survival instinct shows its true strength. All fears tumble in the face of this mighty one. It is this aspect of Underworld initiations that brings the initiate his or her strength for the trials ahead.

Faith in our future survival is the very core of the most enduring initiatory experiences known. The Eleusinian Mysteries, held annually in ancient Greece for about 2,000 years, were famous in the ancient world for granting initiates an unwavering optimism in the power of life. While the secret core of the ritual was never revealed, the story it enacted is one of the best-known myths today.

In this myth, Kore, the archetypal Maiden, is abducted into the Underworld of Hades, land of death. Here she must experience the mystery of Underworld initiation in order to grow from mere daughter and maiden to queen and goddess. Soil that is bleached dry by the burning sun has no fertility. Without a refuge of cool and quiet darkness in our soul, we "burn out." Kore must learn to embrace the darkness in the Land of the Dead in order to contain within herself the dark fecundity of the earth. Only through union with darkness can she later be penetrated by sunlight and contain the polarities that bring forth life. Thus we find that Kore's maturation from Maiden to Mother follows a period of darkness and loss.

The Underworld journey is about dissolution, the necessary break-down that precedes breakthrough. The purpose of this dissolution is surrender. Our current paradigm of power is based on achievement through force of will. Western culture operates under the myth that anything can be achieved if we just apply enough force. But few realize that the Hero's journey to power often includes an Underworld journey, where the Hero has been stripped of his power, the ego dissolved, so that later the power can be held in balance. When we deny the Underworld journey, we deny the humbling experience that enables us to hold that power with humility.

When all is dissolving, how do we keep from losing hope? How do we find an anchor to get us through? If the caterpillar dissolves into a nutritious soup for the butterfly, and we are to truly dissolve our egoic being down to our immortal essence at the core, what structure holds us while we fall apart? The caterpillar is held by the chrysalis, the broken bone by the cast. In the Hero's journey, that limit is referred to by Joseph Campbell as "the belly of the beast." This archetypal belly, after trapping its prisoner in his darkest hour, becomes the very womb of rebirth.

The belly of the beast represents a limit. The fetus in the womb grows prodigiously until the limit of the uterus is reached, and this stimulates birth. A fetus cannot continue to grow, or even survive beyond this point, unless it descends through the birth canal and enters the larger world.

Collectively, the parameters of our planet pose just such a limit on our cultural transformation, forcing society into a new birth. Butting up against our limits—of land, water, energy, and resources—we are forced to change our ways. Since it is obviously not our first birth, it has all the earmarks of being a rebirth, and hopefully one that will bring us great joy. But first we have to get through the Underworld.

Magnifying the Darkness

*Darkness cannot drive out darkness; only light can do that.
Hate cannot drive out hate; only love can do that.*
—*Martin Luther King*

Collectively, we are entering a kind of Underworld state, even as many signs of transformation are evident. The news media reports war and violence through the cultural nervous system on a daily basis, enlarging these issues to excess. Why this unbalanced broadcast of Underworld conditions at a time when we most need hope and inspiration? And why are innovations and positive trends buried in the back pages of the newspaper while crime and violence lead?

In my years of pondering the human condition, I have long wondered why we feature violence more than love—in stories, movies, television, news, and even children's video games. Why is it that sex, which at its best is an act of love and pleasure, is censored—while pain and violence are not only featured but glorified? We build monuments to military heroes. We create video games whose central goal is to kill as many as you can in the shortest time possible. Statistics tell us that crime rates, homicides, and violence have been in steady decline[29] over the last centuries, yet the reporting of crime dominates the media.

I offer two possible answers, and they both dance around the same pivotal point in the death–rebirth process. The first is that we *are* going through a massive dissolution process in our culture—and we cannot proceed through the initiation until we fully comprehend this. As economies or even entire nation-states fail, and as environmental threats increase, more and more people will be facing painful losses. Yet our culture's prevailing tendency is to avoid and deny. We distract ourselves with sensationalistic stories, sales at shopping malls, insipid "reality" TV shows that have little to do with reality, and the acquisition of more and more stuff. Things are dissolving all around us, but we simply change the channel and turn our attention elsewhere.

As long as we are distracting ourselves or denying the obvious, the darker issues must be magnified to get our attention.

Furthermore, the new structures arising, like the imaginal cells in the chrysalis, are outwardly attacked by the old system—the very pillars of tradition that are in the process of dissolving. New discoveries in science may be attacked by academics, alternative medicine is often attacked by allopathic practitioners, and spiritual diversity is attacked by religious fundamentalists. Are we approaching the state of an autoimmune disease, where our defenses will turn and attack the very structures of our collective body? It is encouraging to remember that the butterfly undergoes the same process and lives through it. Perhaps we will, too.

So what happens when we accept our dissolution and finally face our collective Underworld of violence and destruction?

We begin to turn things around.

Magnifying the darkness can awaken the light. When television broadcasted real-time scenes of carnage from the Vietnam War, a passionate peace movement was born. Rather than some intellectual concept of horror that was happening on the other side of the world, it came home to U.S. living rooms and spawned the largest antiwar movement of the 20th century. Now when scenes of natural disasters appear on the Internet, human compassion is awakened, and people band together to raise funds, volunteer, get the vote out, or create community.

The second reason why I believe violence holds such a spell is that we unconsciously hunger for that primal push of survival that makes us feel so incredibly alive. When we are removed from the natural environment by the many wonders of modern living, our innate survival instincts, wired as they are for extreme situations, go dormant. Our nervous systems, however, which haven't changed much in 150,000 years, are wired for more primal experiences.

As we have seen, awakening our core survival instinct is the vital turnaround from death into life. This floods the system with power and aliveness, a necessary ingredient for survival—both as individuals and as a species. In realizing that we can blow ourselves to bits with nuclear weapons, we give birth to a peace movement. The failures of allopathic medicine are generating an alternative healing movement. The threat of environmental destruction fuels the sustainability movement. Facing our shadow is the beginning of transforming our demons into our allies.

The mere instinct for survival isn't enough, however. The germinating seed that yearns for the future must be in the process of becoming something. For this we need intention, understanding, and information. The builder needs blueprints. The zygote needs the information encoded in the DNA.

To rise from the Underworld, we need a reason to live.

In the dark of the Underworld, removed from our normal way of seeing, we begin to create a vision. But for that vision to be sustaining, it must have deep roots. Those roots will now dig down into the earth, entwine with the threads of our past, and take us to an exploration of our collective history—the path that brought us to where we are now. It is from this sustenance that the stalk grows tall and strong, with roots deep enough to support our reach for the stars. Here we enter the womb of nature, the belly of the Great Mother. Her ancient threads are part of the tapestry we are weaving into our new story.

Part Two

OUR LONG JOURNEY HOME

IN THE BEGINNING

The Great Mother

Every threshold passage . . . is comparable to a birth and
has been ritually represented, practically everywhere,
through an imagery of re-entry into the womb.[1]
—*Joseph Campbell*

If a woman started going into labor but knew nothing about pregnancy or the birth process, she would surely think she was dying. If
you told her she was going to push out a fully formed baby from deep
within her belly, she would think you were insane. Yet we know it
happens all the time.

Birthing a new era may seem impossible in the face of our serious
problems, yet we are fully pregnant with possibility. We have already
experienced "contractions" in the form of oil, water, and food shortages; economic downturns; and natural disasters. They will come
faster and faster as the birthing proceeds, occurring around the
globe. Painful though they might be, each contraction forces a reorganization process, something new opening as a result of what is
closing. Rising oil prices steer us toward fuel-efficient vehicles, less
driving, and decentralization. A falling real estate market discour-
ages new home building, which in turn reduces urban sprawl and
deforestation. Rising food prices are spawning neighborhood gardens. Economic disparities "birthed" 2011's Occupy movement, call-

ing for a new distribution of wealth, the results of which remain to be seen. Creation and destruction are still partners in the dance, but now their pace is accelerating.

During a breath workshop at a retreat held by the Shift Network in 2011, I had a remarkable vision. The earthquake in Japan that triggered a tsunami and the meltdown of nuclear power rods in the Fukushima reactor had just happened, with whole towns destroyed, thousands dead, and many more lives, homes, and business threatened. The world was reeling with the implications, as was I. In my vision, I saw the decaying aspects of civilization—the floods, droughts, and earthquakes; the housing debacle, economic disparities, and political corruption; the oil shortages and food crises—as analogous to an eggshell breaking apart as new life emerges. Out of this fracturing shell radiated an almost blinding light, shining from a golden earth. By contrast, the shell was gray and brown, like a lifeless scab falling off a wound. The golden globe inside had unity while the outside was fragmented, with an infinite number of pieces falling away and crumbling into dust. In my vision, I saw how some people were trying to patch the eggshell back together, but they too were falling away as this remarkable process took place. What was emerging was so fundamentally new that it looked nothing like the shell. It was whole, radiant, alive, and astoundingly beautiful. It had a power that was awesome to behold. This is not to minimize the destruction, which caused incalculable suffering, but to find a silver lining of hope in such tragedies.

Barbara Marx Hubbard has written in her book *Birth 2012 and Beyond* how we are birthing a new kind of human, which she calls *Homo universalis*. "As universal humans, we are consciously integrating our social, spiritual, technological, and scientific capacities with our highest aspirations to create a world that works for everyone. We can now imagine living in a more synergistic, co-creative society with extended intelligence, life span, creativity, space development, green technologies, and much more."[2]

How do we birth ourselves as a new kind of human? How do we birth a new culture? How do we begin to build a new world while we are still embedded in the old world and still need many of the things the current system supplies? Can we imagine bringing forth something so large as a thriving planetary civilization through what seems like an impossibly small opening? Is there a mythological framework for this part of the story?

Even more important, what happens after the birth? We know that newborns require tremendous love or they fail to thrive or even survive. How then do we nurture the new state of being and continue to build a thriving culture in the midst of extreme challenges? What kind of love do we put into the foundation of our cocreated future? These are the questions we must ask as we face the daunting initiation before us. As with all initiations, the answers are found in the realm of mystery. Perhaps returning to our original birth in the womb of nature will give us some clues.

Out of the Underworld, into the World

The child is born out of the womb to the unconscious, begotten out of the depths of human nature, or rather out of living Nature herself . . . a wholeness which embraces the depth of Nature.
—C. G. Jung

The Underworld, like the chrysalis, is an archetypal womb of transformation. Dark and difficult as the Underworld journey might be, it doesn't last forever. Eventually, we are born out the other side. Birth is our ultimate beginning, the first initiation of life. As we go through our collective rite of passage to experience a cultural rebirth, it is essential to understand the archetypal dynamics of our original birth. Here lie important roots for our future survival.

Biologically, birth comes through the mother. Archetypally, it is the Divine Mother, the original matrix of nature, from which we emerge. Just as you cannot expect a plant to grow tall when it's cut off at the roots, we cannot deny our roots and sustain the journey. They are the springboard, the sustenance, and the stability that allow us to receive light and blossom into beauty. Earth is the ground we push our roots into in order to reach the stars.

In the chakra system, we begin our long climb upward toward the heavens at the first chakra, located at the base of the spine, often called the *root chakra*. This chakra forms the foundation for the whole chakra system. Its Sanskrit name, *muladhara*, literally means both foundation and "root support." Its archetypal element is *earth*, our holy and sacred ground of being. Roots are also the place we come *from*, and therefore they symbolize our origin and our past, as in family roots or the root of a problem.

Digging into the ground of our distant past, archaeologists have pieced together evidence of an ancient Goddess that reveals our earliest mythological framework. We have forgotten Her many names, even that She was once considered divine, but nearly all cultures remember Her as Mother Earth or Mother Nature. Even though our planet hardened into substance from expanding stardust, this earthy ground is the archetypal Mother of biological life. She is the Divine Mother of us all, the enveloping field that nourishes us as we grow, the foundation of life, and our shared, common ground. Her loss lies at the root of many of our problems today.

Few of us remember our infancy, so it is not surprising that memory of the Divine Mother archetype has faded to the point of nonexistence in our modern world. We mentioned earlier how our "client" Western Civilization rarely talks about his mother and has likely forgotten she ever existed. He probably didn't learn about her in school and no longer remembers what it was like in his infancy when he frolicked freely upon her body, suckling her breast. There are few temples to the Divine Mother today, and almost none in the Western world, whereas the Father is everywhere, with churches, synagogues, and mosques by the millions. Our client might even reply that he didn't have a mother, or he might point downward, shrug, and refer to Mother Nature, but few see her as a living goddess, equal in divine stature to the commonly worshipped masculine God.

And a most beautiful Mother She is. Her verdant hills and valleys, mountains of snow that melt into rivers, abundant tapestries of color and grace, to say nothing of Her unfathomable complexity, are proof enough that She is divine. Her infinite diversity, abundance, and continued innovation astound even the most casual observer. As advanced as our science has become, there are still mysteries to Her miraculous coordination of life that we have yet to understand. How did life begin? How do ecosystems balance themselves? How is such beauty and grace created naturally, without human interference?

After birth, the mother is our first experience of love. Just as it would be important for an individual who had no mother to heal this psychological wound, so it is for our culture. Her loss represents unconscious wounds that continue to perpetuate suffering. So let us explore the birth of culture through nature as the Divine Mother, and examine the role She plays in establishing a new ground for our future. For She is the primal beginning, the sustaining middle, and the holy ground that reabsorbs us all when it is time for the end.

Survival: Our First Task

We shall draw from the heart of suffering itself
the means of inspiration and survival.
—*Winston Churchill*

After the child is miraculously pushed out of the womb, the first order of business is simply to stay in the game—in short, *to survive*. This is life's primary rule. It must be met for evolution to occur. Survival instincts, handed down from mother to child, and from our ancestors through the ages, are deeply embedded within our nervous system and have been honed through millions, if not billions, of years of evolution.

In *Eastern Body, Western Mind*, I describe how the *muladhara*, or root chakra, awakens at birth, when the first task of consciousness is survival and embodiment.[3] Survival instincts are the basis of the collective unconscious—that shared realm of awareness of which we are mostly unaware. They are hard-wired into everything with a nervous system—or even without one—if we consider the way bacteria mutate to resist antibiotics. Called *innate releasing mechanisms* by Joseph Campbell, survival instincts appear as inherent tendencies in the psyche that form the fundamental building blocks of consciousness. They are what makes newly hatched chicks bond to their mother, rabbits hide when hawks fly overhead, or a newborn seek the breast. Such instincts cannot be erased. They can, however, be dominated. The cost is putting ourselves at odds with both Mother Nature and our own inner nature.

Survival instincts are the ground of consciousness, the foundation, and the roots of our being. They are the expression of nature's powerful urge to *continue,* for unless something can establish itself and exist through time, it has no hope of evolving. This is true for an organism, for a relationship, for a species, for an ecosystem, and for a culture.

Survival was the prime directive of the earliest humans, so it is here that we look to the ancestral beginnings of our culture. Having taken the daring step of walking on our hind legs, we humans entered a dangerous world. We could survive only in cooperative groups or clans. To be cast out from the group meant certain death. To work cooperatively with others in the task of survival necessitated a particular development of consciousness. It required skills, tools, language, and rules.

Earth dictated these rules of survival. They were absolute. To live in the severity of Ice Age conditions and hunt dangerous animals was to understand the unequivocal power of Mother Nature. She was the Mother that provided everything—but Her rules were not to be trifled with. Breaking the rules could threaten the tribe's magical relationship with its surroundings, and hence its survival. Mother was all-giving and all-powerful, but She could kill as well as bring forth life.

The Infancy of Culture

The basis of all primate social groups is the bond between mother and infant. That bond constitutes the social unit out of which all higher orders of society are constructed.[4]
—*Richard Leakey*

The infant phase of human culture corresponds to the Upper Paleolithic, a time when glaciers up to a mile thick covered the northern part of Europe, Asia, and North America. This era lasted from about 80,000 to 10,000 years ago. Our present human iteration, *Homo sapiens sapiens*, began far south of the ice, originating in Africa more than 100,000 years ago, as descendants of the first proto-humans, who walked on their hind legs four to six million years earlier. It was only about 40,000 years ago that our ancestors migrated into Europe, though the frigid climate may make us wonder why. Surviving the long winters at the edge of the ice would have forced our ancestors to direct their developing intelligence toward cooperative survival skills—skills that became fundamental to the foundation of culture.

It was during the latter part of this last Ice Age—some 30,000 years ago—that there occurred a proliferation of prehistoric art, seen in numerous small sculptures of mother figures found all across Europe and Asia, and later in elaborate cave paintings such as those at Lascaux and Altamira. This is described as a mysteriously revolutionary period of history during which there was an explosion of symbolic thinking and creative behavior that revealed widespread mythological beliefs. In parallel to the beginnings of individual human life, the primary focus of this earliest art was on images of animals and the Mother archetype. Elaborately painted animals danced on the walls of caves, deep in the womb of the earth. These images signified the sacredness of the hunt and were probably part of an initiation rite for males, where the cave signified a womb or birth canal.

Taking us back through 30,000 years of dust and ashes, images of the Great Mother, with her round, pregnant belly, remind us that deep within our collective consciousness was another time, another reality, characterized by a sacred regard for women's role in the creation of life. At more than 3,000 archaeological sites, scattered across more than a thousand miles, from Western France to central Siberia, some 30,000 sculptures of clay, marble, bone, copper, and gold have been found, all attesting to an apparent reverence for the Divine Feminine as a fundamental aspect of the miracle of life. While these figurines are not identical, they all share common characteristics: they are small and portable; they are three to six inches high; and they have featureless faces, accentuated breasts, bellies, and buttocks, and pointed legs that could be stuck in the ground. It is obvious that these are not individual likenesses but are symbolic. Nor are they limited to a single tribe or area; they represent a widespread sacred symbol of worship.

These figurines—and the narrow passages to the painted caves—would have been part of the initiation rites of humanity's first religion, the veneration of the Great Mother, which began at least 30,000 years ago and extended up to the advent of writing and civilization, approximately 5,000 years ago. Her fertility and abundance was linked with that of the earth itself—the plants that return each year, the young animals that are born in the spring, and the renewal through pregnancy from the all-too-common presence of death during a time when life expectancy was less than 30 years. There is a reason why we speak of the earth as Mother Nature. Archaeologist Marija Gimbutas, a pioneer in this realm, states,

> It was the sovereign mystery and creative power of the female as the source of life that developed into the earliest religious experiences. The Great Mother Goddess who gives birth to all creation out of the holy darkness of her womb became a metaphor for Nature herself, the cosmic giver and taker of life, ever able to renew herself within the eternal cycle of life, death, and rebirth.[5]

The Static Feminine as Our Primal Thesis

The infantile fusion-state is indeed a type of "paradise," but it is one of pre-personal ignorance, not transpersonal awakening.
—*Ken Wilber*

As with the individual child whose primary world is the mother, our original embeddedness in nature represents a state of collective consciousness completely centered around the archetype of the Great Mother: mother as environment, mother as food, mother as birth giver and life taker. This ground of nature forms our collective primal thesis, the original backdrop of human existence. It forms the fundamental ground of human evolution: the participation mystique,[6] or fused identity, that links culture and environment with the same inseparable bond as mother and infant child. Just as early humans could not escape the narrow confines of nature's rule, an infant child cannot survive on its own outside the realm of a mother or nurturing caretaker.

This original thesis of infant and mother—whether for an individual child or a primitive culture—can be called the era of the *Static Feminine,* the first of four archetypal valences that we will visit in our journey through time. Gareth Hill writes about these archetypal dynamics extensively in his book *Masculine and Feminine: The Flow of Opposites in the Psyche,* where they are applied to the individual.[7] My presentation of the Static and Dynamic Masculine and Feminine in this work is my original extrapolation based on these terms but applied to the evolution of culture. I include it here because I see the dance of masculine and feminine archetypes as an essential piece of healing the wounds of our past and creating a balanced and integrated future. We cannot enter the realm of the heart where one gender, representing half of the human race, is subordinated, suppressed, or forgotten. In fact, such a system negatively affects both men and women, holding us all back from true integration, collaboration, and union.

Gareth Hill symbolizes the Static Feminine as an enclosing circle, a limit that is simultaneously cyclic and eternal. We can see this symbol as the original wheel of life onto which we climb with each birth, the primordial first chakra of physical existence. There are many examples: a cell with a nucleus and membrane; the sun surrounded by a planetary orbit; the cycles of nature, beyond which survival is not possible. An infant cannot go too far from the mother and still live. The circle represents that boundary.

The circle is the most basic and universal symbol we have. It is the unified field, the undifferentiated whole, sometimes correlated to Uroboros, the primordial serpent that bites its own tail. As such, it represents what philosophers and psychologists have called a prepersonal, undifferentiated consciousness, that sleepy realm of awareness that has not yet awakened to the possibilities of an individuated self or even to the concept of difference at all. The circle is the symbol of ultimate wholeness, the original perfection, the place where we begin. It is the original unity of opposites, the self-contained completion, without begining or end, the original cell. More literally, the circle is the roundness of the pregnant belly, the nourishing breast, and the gentle curves that are so characteristically feminine. The circle is the cycle of seasons, the self-renewing generative force that brings us birth, life, death, and birth again, in its eternal cycle.

The boundaries of the circle represent the natural limitations of the field of life. Early humans could not transcend light and dark with the flick of a switch. They could not transcend distance with an airplane, nor shield against cold with thermopane windows and push-button heat. Rarely do we escape the gravity of Earth itself. We are still bound to this mortal sphere for our survival.

Though Gareth Hill mentions only the form of the circle itself, I see each circle as defined by a center. For the breast, it is the nipple; for the child, it is the mother; for the solar system, the sun. For our ancestors, it would have been the clan mother. Each one of us is the center of our own circle, expanding outward to the edges of our bodies, relationships, and communities. If we are bound by fear, our circle remains small and closed. If we are too expansive, the energy becomes diffuse. Some of us keep those boundaries closer than others, inviting or withstanding limitation, depending upon your point of view.

It is this circular boundary that defines both the positive and negative aspects of the Static Feminine. The positive aspect of the Static Feminine is that it is nurturing, containing, generative, and maternal. It fosters life, and it keeps and offers protection. It is stable, solid, and familiar. Respect its boundaries and you will be nurtured and safe. Sustainability requires that we respect these limits of a finite world.

The negative aspect is that the circle is *static*—stable but limiting, solid but unchanging, familiar but stagnant. Things in stasis cycle just as they always have, without much innovation. Limiting oneself to the cycles of the Static Feminine can be boring, repetitive, and menial. In a woman's life, it is that stage when she is bound to her infant, cooking, eating, cleaning, feeding, changing diapers, cooking, eating, and cleaning again.

The Static Feminine occurs for men as well. It is found in the work of a farmer, always cyclic, bound to the fixed seasonal timing of sowing and reaping along with the many repetitive chores involved. It is found in most menial jobs, where one follows a parental boss without question, sticking to the rules without much room for creativity or expansion. In social groups, the Static Feminine psyche can be seen in fundamentalism—the need to conform exactly to the beliefs and behaviors defined by the group. It could be argued that denial of our fundamental ground in nature creates the shadow form of religious fundamentalism today, an attempt to find the comfort of the Static Feminine values of family and simplicity.

There is little freedom or change in the realm of the Static Feminine. Biology is destiny. Its rule is, as Sam Keen has stated, "Never do anything for the first time."[8] If each age is characterized by an act of heroism, then the ability to uphold tradition and remain totally faithful to the laws of nature is the heroic act of the Static Feminine. This forms the basis of our traditions and our unquestioned assumptions. It rears its head in those all-too-common statements "But we've always done it this way" and "That's just the way it is."

In every person's life, there are times of beginnings: a new job, relationship, family, or business. It is essential during these times to find elements of the Static Feminine to nourish and support these tender beginnings. This can be found by going to conferences, universities, ashrams, health retreats, a therapist's office, or any other place where one can enfold oneself in a kind of maternal matrix or womb. The limitation of this support, however, is that all too often we are required to mimic the party line and forfeit the ability to think critically. Cult mentality, religious or political fundamentalism, or the enforced conformity dictated by group identity all make up the shadow side of what is initially a drive toward nourishment, support, and safety. We suffer from arrested development if we cling too tightly to this support, much as a child fails to grow up if it cannot differentiate from its mother and gain independence. Yet we weaken our roots, hence our vitality, if we move too far from this essential foundation.

When the Static Feminine is denied, the result is insecurity, rootlessness, anxiety, and fear. Without the enclosing circle, we lose the cohesiveness of being held together, bonded by a common ground. Earth becomes exploitable for commerce. We no longer feel safe. Where we deny this first-chakra connection culturally, it is no wonder that we have environmental crises, economic crises, and health crises—all of which are first-chakra issues. Attempts to replace this lost container can be found in fundamentalism and exaggerated defense mechanisms.

To be bound by the Static Feminine, however, leaves us in a kind of infantile stasis: dependent, naïve, powerless. We have long outgrown this container, yet we failed to keep it in our foundation as we grew beyond it. We will see, as we explore our cultural development in the ensuing ages, how this flaw in our foundation has affected everything we have built. It is interesting that many people refer to an impending or possible "collapse" of our current civilization. Collapse, by definition, moves downward, toward the earth.

The deep ecology movement rightly stresses the need to return to the obedience of nature's laws—or reap the consequences. Yet today's culture has moved so far beyond this state of simplicity that returning to it en masse is literally impossible and would certainly kill much of the population. We cannot go back to the breast and suckle an unlimited supply of mother's milk. We have long outgrown our infancy, with our needs having grown beyond the Mother's ability to provide. It is not likely that humans will give up cars, airplanes, or technology. But we can embrace the sacred ground of nature as the fundamental value of a healthy society.

The Psychology of Nature

The Tree of Eternity has its roots in Heaven above
and its branches hang down to Earth. It is the pure
immortal spirit upon which all worlds rest.
—*Katha Upanishad*

Our future survival is not just a matter of "saving the earth," even though that's essential. More deeply, it depends on understanding how the natural world affects consciousness and health. Our bodies were designed for a world we no longer inhabit. Our physiology is *designed* for the natural world in the way our eyes focus, the way chemicals run through our system when danger threatens, the way we breathe and metabolize, and what we do with our attention. Now we go to the gym and work out on exercise machines, just to keep our muscles in shape after spending our days sitting at a desk. We wear glasses to see small print and take pills to digest processed food, then play recordings of babbling brooks in order to relax. We are evolving new survival mechanisms, yes, but without understanding this original ground of our being, we will fail to correct the overshoot of survival instincts that feeds into trillions of dollars of defense spending, a rapacious economy, and dogmatic beliefs run by fear.

Richard Louv describes this problem as a *nature-deficit disorder*.[9] He illustrates how being in nature employs all of our senses. Sitting at my computer, I use my mind and eyes, without receiving much input of sound, scent, or touch. If I go outside, nature immediately greets me through all my senses. It is a whole-body experience, necessary for a holistic consciousness. Louv quotes study after study showing how contact with nature helps our bodies to heal more quickly, helps our minds to think more clearly, and helps our emotions to become more balanced. This ground of being is vital for our psychological as well as physical survival.

The Static Feminine is an essential part of our heritage and our wholeness. It is where we began, the primal thesis from which we emerged. We must embrace it to be whole, but strike a balance between respect for nature as our innate ground of being and the ability to transcend its limitations. We may be the only species capable of embracing this balance—but we have yet to achieve it.

In the world of the Paleolithic, it was men who hunted the large game and women who gave birth. Both are essential acts, critical to the survival of the tribe. Both aspects were regarded as sacred roles. Yet their duties were distinctly different: one centered around birth, the other around death, even though both were providing food for the tribe. This basic difference is important—not that one was good and the other bad, but that both are necessary elements of survival, mirrors of the essential unity of the circle. As Michael Meade has said, "Death is not the opposite of life, it is the opposite of birth. Both are aspects of life."[10]

We stand at a time when creation and destruction rest equally within our hands. If evolution is "the Gods' way of making more gods," as I suggest at the beginning of this book, then we must come to understand the essential balance between life and death. Indeed, these are the forces of the Gods, and to become godlike, we must learn to wield both wisely. Both are essential elements in the continuation of any successful species. Both are constantly occurring in nature. To create life without limits on population is to court massive death. To wage war without limits or to render forests and species into extinction is to curtail life. As we move forward in time, we will witness the continuing cosmic dance of life and death in the unfolding drama of our evolutionary mystery play.

7 WATERING THE SOUL

The Neolithic

Change can erupt like a river, undammed
from the shifting of psychic ground.
—*Michael Meade*

In the initiatory process, there are both masculine, fiery initiations
and watery, feminine ones. The masculine initiations mature a boy
into a man through trials, challenges, ordeals, and intimidations.
The initiate then conquers fear, discovers his power, and develops
the confidence and bravery necessary for adulthood. This is essential
for both men and women, but traditionally, in the ancestral world
of the hunt, such stoic courage was a necessity for the men. A man
would be a liability for all concerned if he couldn't be counted on to
keep his wits and perform in the face of danger.

The watery initiations are of another order indeed, for they are
the initiations into beauty, pleasure, emotion, and, most of all, into
mystery. The watery initiations bring us to the heights and the depths
of experience. They too inspire heroic deeds—but through devotion
rather than fear. Fiery initiations teach us strength and courage.
Watery initiations open us to feeling and love.

To move from the first to the second chakra is to move from one
to two, from singleness to duality, and from the element *earth* to the
element *water*. Where earth is still and predictable and quantifiable,

water is moving, ever changing, and elusive. It falls from heaven in infinite droplets, flows ever downward in passionate streams, collects in lakes and oceans teeming with life. Following the path of least resistance, water flows through grooves created by a prior journey. In this way, water is passive and surrendering. Yet it has great power: the power to sculpt mountains and carve valleys, to tumble sharp stones into smooth cobbles, and to produce an entire ecosystem from the soil it carries downward from the fiery peaks of volcanoes.

Today, water may be our most precious resource and our most threatening instability. Overpopulation drains aquifers upon which millions of people depend for survival. Climate change contributes to droughts and floods, damaging food supply and requiring billions of dollars to remediate. Rising temperatures increase wind, which dries out soil and farmland, requiring even more water for crops to grow. Dry forests, exacerbated by hotter temperatures, are more likely to burn, requiring even more water to put out the fires. Melting polar ice caps will raise sea levels, which could force hundreds of millions of coastal inhabitants to migrate inland; increasing carbon acidifies the ocean, diminishing fish and plankton. If global warming is a symptom of too much fire and heat, then perhaps we need more connection to the water element.

As a symbolic element often representing the soul, water is the liquid medium that cools, nurtures, and cleanses. It carries the molecules of emotion from inner experience to outer expression. It cools and tempers the fires of anger; it releases the grief of underlying wounds. Before we can truly open the heart, our wounds must cleansed and healed by the waters of the soul. To the soul, water nurtures, cleanses, and renews. It carries the molecules of emotion from inner experience to outer expression. It cools the fires of anger and releases grief from underlying wounds. Water has long been associated with healing. To awaken the global heart, we must begin healing our deep cultural wounds and restore the waters of our collective soul.

Water is connected to the feeling function described by Carl Jung—that mysterious bridge between mind and the body that connects conscious and unconscious. Feelings arise of their own accord, unbidden, from the unconscious. We feel angry, depressed, or afraid, regardless of whether or not we desire these states. Yet the mind has ways of covering over feelings and shutting off watery emotions when they are unpleasant or deemed inappropriate. Such feelings do not die; they are merely suppressed and buried, yet the waters of the soul no longer flow freely.

Feelings bring us joy and the texture of our experience. Without feeling, there is no ground for empathy or compassion, essential values of the heart. Without feeling, we lose our moral compass, and relationships can be callous or shallow. Experience becomes meaningless, while we simultaneously seek to balance this suppression through violent movies, sensationalist gossip, drugs, or sex. Jung suggested that our values emanate from the feeling function. What feels good, we value; what feels bad, we avoid. With our emotions denied, we become valueless, apathetic, and disconnected.

When the mind chooses to block emotions, they are still carried by the body. We may think we're not afraid, but our belly knots into a hard ball. We may try to deny our anger, but our jaw clenches. We grind our teeth at night during those times when the unconscious holds the upper hand. Our feelings come though our senses, whether of pleasure or pain, enjoyment or disgust. Denying our feelings makes us behave senselessly. Such things as drive-by shootings and aerial bombings occur without any contact through the senses—they are senseless acts. By honoring our senses, we become *sensible* instead of *senseless*.

Beauty is an essential but unsung spiritual value. In a harsh world, our senses become dulled. In a world of beauty and sensuality, the senses are nourished. One of the hallmarks of the divine—so evident in the natural world—is its remarkable beauty. The silhouette of mountains against a luminous sunset, the scent of a forest after rain, the abundant display of wildflowers on a hillside, the sound of a bubbling stream, all reflect the divine beauty that abounds in the natural world. We set aside the great treasures of our national parks because of their exquisite beauty. Beauty awakens our inherent erotic nature and stirs the soul.

If we are to build a world of the future—one that truly opens the heart—we must pay attention to creating beauty as much as functionality, to courting the senses as well as the mind, to healthy pleasures as an antidote to pain and suffering. True beauty reminds us that we are close to the sacred and invites the heart to love. For beauty's sake we will treasure and care for our world.

Eros and the Sacred Other

The intellectual history of humankind reads like a gigantic effort to avoid the theme of Eros, to play it down, to trivialize it, to deny it, and yet to go on living.
—Dieter Duhm

Eros is an ancient god. As the universal principle of attraction—that which brings things into relationship—he is the instigator of the heart's longing for another. To the Greeks, he was the force of desire born from the split between Heaven and Earth, as Chaos and Gaia.[11] In Hindu mythology, he is called Kama, referred to as a supreme deity. In the Artharva Veda, among India's oldest set of texts, it is said: "Kama was there first. Neither gods nor ancestors nor men can equal him."[12] He is the god of beauty and youth, the force of creation, springing from the heart of Immense-Being (Brahma) and from the primeval Waters.

Once we have tasted the bliss of Eros, first-chakra survival is not enough. We must satisfy an equally compelling urge for pleasure, touch, and connection—the urge to merge with another, both emotionally and physically. This brings us into an encounter with difference—as any other soul is certainly different from ourselves. Such an encounter is its own initiation. One does not fully grow from boy to man, girl to woman, or child to adult without an initiation into beauty and discovering the incredible power of the archetypal *Other*.

The pleasures of sexuality are the perfect seduction into this second level of initiation. Just as survival consciousness forms the primary challenge of existence, the sexual drive of the second chakra multiplies that existence and extends it beyond ourselves. Through evolution's innate wisdom, the insistent pull of the erotic calls us to release, to join, to bond, to spawn, and to experience ecstasy—all part of the watery realms of the second chakra. Without the waters of pleasure, life is dry, boring, and stagnant. Water helps things to flow; it makes life juicy. Without watering the roots so carefully planted in the first chakra, there is no growth and no sweet fruit to eat. Pleasure, beauty, and erotic allurement invite the heart to open.

But the realm of Eros has been pointedly repressed, with a cost to the soul. Functionality often trumps beauty, evident in most workplaces. Emotion is often considered weakness, so we shut down our feelings and then wonder why we lack compassion. Sexuality is heaped with judgment—it's called immoral, dirty, even evil—and we repress one of the most basic biological urges in nature, the experience of pleasure and bonding. An essential element of human nature, the waters of sexuality find their way around the dams of repression with priests who molest children, sex trafficking, pornography, and a multibillion-dollar advertising industry telling us how to be sexually attractive.

There's a reason for this. Desire is both sweet and dangerous. Eros brings us into duality: self and other, pleasure and pain, satisfaction and frustration. When we reach for another, we risk rejection; when we unite, we risk loss. One friend said of this emotional risk, "There's no such thing as safe sex."

The Psychology of Eros

*We know now, in a very practical manner, that man's cruelty
is directed mainly against what he most longs for.*
—*Wilhelm Reich*

As an infant child grows into her toddler stage, her consciousness gradually extends beyond total immersion with her mother. As she finds security in her own ground, she begins to expand outward. As a child explores, her first distinctions are binary: hot-cold, light-dark, pleasure-pain, good mommy–bad mommy. This extends to her sense of self, through the feedback of love and rejection, where she learns that she is a good girl or bad. Such distinctions are essential but incomplete. Most things in life are not quite so black and white; they contain many shades of gray. With greater maturity, we learn how to make subtler discriminations.

She is starting to move from the nipple at the center of the breast to explore the outer confines of the circle of the Static Feminine. Yet she is still unable to survive on her own, so she runs into limits. The natural urge of a toddler in this stage is to expand, yet the naïve child does not know where the limits should be. Until that is internalized, the mother must say no and enforce those limits. With this powerful word of negation, the first experience of conflict arises. As desires awaken, they meet the frustration of limits imposed by others.

Here we come to the dilemma that psychologists refer to as the archetypal split between Good Mother and Bad Mother. The Good Mother is the one who feeds us, picks us up when we cry, and satisfies our every need with kind, patient nurturing. Through her we develop trust, safety, security, and the feeling of being loved.

The Bad Mother is the one who says no, who slaps our backside for running into the street, who takes away the candy or the toy. She is the one who feels too tired to pay attention to our needs, who is unavailable or angry. She is the mother bird that pushes her baby out of the nest to force it to fly. She is the disciplinarian that makes you do your homework. She is the edge and the limit that may appear cruel, uncaring, or selfish, but whose ultimate nature is also to protect. In fairy tales, she appears as the crone or hag who threatens to cut off your head. As older women face the loss of their youth and beauty, they often receive projections of Bad Mother and are shunned.

To a child, who is still developmentally in the realm of the Static Feminine and totally dependent on its own mother, this presents an agonizing choice. Who will appear if I do this or that? The Good Mother or the Bad Mother? This experience of *choice* provides the foundation for developing the *will*. Once we choose, the will then acts upon that choice, and we are launched into the third chakra to accomplish it.

Later, when we're adults, sexuality (also associated with the second chakra) is equally charged by the binary conflict between biological imperative and cultural taboos. Not only do we face the possibility of rejection when we reach out to another, but for many the pull of the body involves "going against the rules" set down for us, verbally and nonverbally, since we were first old enough to reach our own genitals. Conditioning goes deep, biology even deeper. To go against the rules of conditioning is to risk exile, but to go against the self is to enter a deeper abandonment. Here we find a universal struggle.

This conflict promotes yet another level of awakening. To form relationship, which is the warp and woof of the heart chakra's tapestry, we must first be able to encounter difference and endure conflict. Sexuality is a realm in which this is bound to happen, for the Sacred Other is most assuredly different. As anyone in relationship knows, merging with another inevitably produces some kind of conflict.

The introduction of difference, and its tendency to create conflict, is the next essential element of evolution, following the challenge of survival. Without difference, nothing will ever change. We will remain in the same groove forever, without evolving or moving forward. Yet the inertia of the Static Feminine runs deep. In the eternal stability of the Static Feminine era, what caused us to break that bond with the Mother and create something new?

Entering the Neolithic

When men and women emerged from the uroborus
[primal unity], they emerged as magicians.
—*Ken Wilber*

To answer that question, we now move forward in time from our nomadic ancestors of the Paleolithic Era to the settled agricultural villages of the Neolithic. This change occurred as the last vestiges of the most recent Ice Age melted away, approximately 10,000 years ago, resulting in a revolution that transformed the culture of humanity and its relationship to nature.

For several million years—since the begining of our species, really—we were helpless to do anything but follow Mother Nature in her many moods. We followed game wherever it roamed; we ate well or starved according to the times. We lived in caves when we could find them; we collected grasses and plants where they naturally grew. If game was sparse, if winters were hard, if plants were insufficient, there was little we could do about it.

Then we discovered the miracle of the seed.

Here began the first steps of taking destiny into human hands. Where nature's whim could provide or withhold, our ancestors found a means to provide for themselves. Where families had been nomadic, now they could stay in one place, building homes, temples, and villages. Where once we hunted free-running game, animals could now be kept in captivity. Close to home, animals provided eggs, milk, and meat. They were bred and slaughtered as needed, without the dangerous hunt, and without taking husbands and fathers away from home for days or weeks at a time. With planting, we took a step away from our dependence and enmeshment with nature as mother—and took a step toward our power—one that forever changed the fabric of life on Earth.

Since it is likely that it was women who gathered the plants and tended to the hearth and cooking while the men hunted, it is conjectured that the mystery of the seed was first discovered by women. Preparing the food and making the gourds to carry water, the women would have nurtured the fertility of the fields as a natural part of their duties and of their association with fertility in general. The mystery of agriculture would have been a natural extension of women's earlier mysteries of birth, life, and death. This does not mean that men were left out of the picture—far from it—especially once the principles of farming and animal husbandry were established. Still, the cycles of sowing, cultivating, and reaping were intimately connected with the round of the seasons and the many moods of the Great Mother, and therefore they were still part of the Static Feminine. She had, after all, been the central supreme deity of human consciousness since our ancestral emergence from the apes. Such archetypal icons of the psyche are not easily vanquished.

With the melting of the ice around 10,000 BCE, the Neolithic flowered as a true springtime for humanity. While farming may not have lightened the workload, it nonetheless eased the struggles of survival from the uncertain conditions of nomadic life, allowing a more stationary existence. With permanent dwellings, our ancestors could acquire possessions and build houses and temples.

As it is today with climate change, melting ice in the early Neolithic produced a dramatic rise in sea level, another aspect of moving from the element of earth (first chakra) to the element of water (second chakra). We built ships and traveled by water, which enabled tribes to expand their horizons by making contact with people different from themselves, stimulating consciousness, as well as by trading possessions that increased their wealth and skills. With this geological movement of water across the land, along with the conscious act of irrigating fields, the roots of civilization were well watered. They burst forth into life, which spread especially along the banks of great rivers and the shores of the seas. It may be that early myths of flooding waters were a metaphor for both the rise in sea level and the flood of irrigation that occurred at this time.

When people acquired the means to provide food and shelter, the harsh conditions of survival softened considerably. Fewer babies died, and life span increased. Population expanded, and people began to stay in one place. From 10,000 BCE to 3000 BCE, the global population grew from 5 million to 100 million,[13] with the larger Neolithic settlements, such as Çatal Hüyük or Jericho, housing 7,000 to 8,000 people—very different from nomadic tribes that kept their numbers in the low hundreds, hiving off when they grew too large.

The Great Mother had children, and her children grew up to have more children—both daughters and sons. The greatest blessing of the gods at this time was fertility: to have abundant crops, fertile animals, and many children. The Great Mother, now accompanied by her divine children, was no longer a monotheistic deity. Her children would eventually grow up to become gods and goddesses in their own right, reflecting both masculine and feminine archetypes arising within the psyche. Our morality was based on keeping the gods happy, whether through rituals and sacrifice, or socially sanctioned behavior.

The original thesis was still anchored in the Static Feminine, with its Great Mother archetype, yet it evolved to reflect that of Mother and Child, and eventually Mother and Son. We were no longer infants in the primal garden but more like toddlers. We could travel by foot and by sea, but we didn't travel far. We couldn't yet read or write, and our understanding of the world was naïve and superstitious, filled with magical projections. Yet we lived in harmony with our surroundings, as there was literally no other choice. Our technologies, if you can even call them that, were meager farm implements, and our numbers were too small to dominate nature.

From Mother to Son

The release from the Mother is one of the most important
and most delicate problems in the realization of personality.
—*Jolande Jacobi*

Riane Eisler and others have suggested that the culture of the Neolithic was peaceful and agrarian.[14] Weapons were not featured in Neolithic art, nor were the villages of this time fortified with the defensive walls that would soon appear in cities across the land. Burial remains reveal that women and men were equally respected. Both shared in the business of life, working together cooperatively. But did they share equal status in their view of the divine?

As time passed and culture developed, the male aspect of the divine—as both as lover and son—began to appear. In the heart of the Neolithic, around 5000 BCE, we begin to see not only goddess statues but gods as well. However, as with any new trend, the god figures were fewer, smaller, and younger, often in postures of submission. While it was clear that the Son was gaining entry into the collective consciousness, he still had a long way to go to equal the stature of the Great Mother, who, after all, had single-handedly occupied the center of the psyche since the dawn of human awakening.

Where did this leave men, we might ask? If women were keepers of the mystery of birth, and the Great Goddess was still the primary object of worship, what, then, was the sacred role for the male?

Hunting and gathering were the two essential parts of survival, each with its own mysteries, challenges, and rewards. Providing meat through the hunt had given men sacred status during the Paleolithic times. But as culture progressed into farming and domestication of animals, the importance of the hunt diminished. Yet the realm of birth and the eternal cycles of nature, so connected to the feminine, still held sacred prominence. This produced what Mircea Eliade called a crisis in values, where the sacred relations with the animal world were supplanted by the mystical solidarity between humans and vegetation.[15] He went on to state that this raised women and feminine sacrality to the first rank:

> Since women played a decisive part in the domestication of plants, they become the owners of the cultivated fields, which raises their social position and creates characteristic institutions, such as, for example, matrilocation, the husband being obliged to live in his wife's house.[16]

This erosion of equality would have occurred so gradually as to be hardly noticed, taking some 5,000 years while the mystery of the hunt slowly retreated to forgotten realms of the past or was delegated to small, select groups. Social inequalities are always unstable, and sooner or later they breed countermovements. If men had lost their original sacred role, it would not be long before that primal imbalance would rise up from the collective unconscious to be addressed and corrected.

In the archaeological remains of Old Europe, between the sixth and seventh millennia BCE, the goddess figurines showed a more phallic neck and egg-shaped body, or statues appeared with one side male and the other female. The masculine appeared in the image of a horned animal or phallic serpent, or a figure of half man, half beast. Later myths from Sumer, Egypt, and Greece dramatize the bull as the son of the Mother Goddess, with an actual bull often sacrificed as the symbol of the Son returning to the Mother for rebirth.[17] In other sculptures around this time, the god was shown as a full-grown man in various postures: seated with erect phallus, holding his head like

Rodin's *Thinker*, or with his head bowed in mourning. What was he mourning? we might ask. Was it the loss of innocence? Was he crying for the Mother Goddess or from his own loss of importance?

As time went on, the phallic sculptures of the masculine would grow ever larger in the megalithic uprising of stones, which began to appear sometime after the fifth millennium BCE. These standing stones reflected important solar or lunar events. With astounding precision, they required considerable skill in engineering, mathematics, cosmology, and long-range planning—often taking place over the course of many generations and revealing a capacity for abstract thinking and an expanded sense of time. Stonehenge is the most widely known of these megalithic monuments and is presumed to have been built over a period of 1,300 years[18]—a true testament to intergenerational planning. France has more than 5,000 megalithic sites, while 900 have survived in Britain and over 500 in Ireland.

So we see that in the cradle of civilization, the young god was slowly emerging and asserting himself. Still a child of the ancient and primordial Goddess, he became her lover long before becoming her master. But soon the tables would turn, as we will see in the next act of the human drama: the dawning of the Age of Power.

IGNITING THE FLAME OF POWER

The Dynamic Masculine

The need for many to act as one required
the one to control the many.
—*Andrew Bard Schmookler*

Since civilization began, the leading edge of culture has always been at the meeting point of land and water. It is no surprise, then, that the dawning of the third-chakra organizing principle first arose in the valley between the Tigris and Euphrates Rivers of ancient Sumer (now known as Iraq). Alluvial valleys fertilized by annual spring floods were natural places for agriculture to prosper, while the coastline offered fishing and safe harbors for trade. With ideal conditions for abundant food supply, humanity grew like cells on a petri dish. It was here, in the "cradle of civilization," that Mother Earth rocked her exploding population of toddlers into their early childhood.

In 8500 BCE, the valley between these rivers was a dry, dusty plain, sparsely dotted by a few humble villages. By 3000 BCE, bustling cities sparkled along the riverbanks, glittering like white jewels set among miles of green, irrigated fields. Massive temples towered the plains, and people thronged in the streets.

As the Sumerian civilization spread across the Fertile Crescent, Egyptian culture flourished across the desert to the west. While the Nile River rose and fell, so did the many dynasties of the Egyptian Empire, with an overall continuity that spanned 2,500 years. Farther to the east, along the Indus River, village settlements grew into sophisticated cities, such as Harappa and Mohenjo-Daro; and by 1500 BCE, there were complex cities along the Yellow River in China.

These cultures rose up more or less concurrently yet independent of each other. With successful farming and trading, their populations grew rapidly. However, the fertile valleys of the Tigris and Euphrates, Nile, and Indus Rivers are all areas of circumscribed land, bordered by desert, sea, or mountains. Held by these natural barriers, expanding populations converged upon each other, heating up the evolutionary soup in a melting pot of cultures, languages, and customs. With a rapidly increasing population and exposure to cultural differences, our ancestors faced a new level of challenges.

Vast irrigation projects, with a surplus of grain to be stored and distributed, gave birth to writing and mathematics. With a greater percentage of the population freed from farming to develop other pursuits, labor began to specialize. Some people made pottery, others wove cloth, while still others built houses, worked as scribes, or presided over the distribution of grain. Palatial estates were built for the gods and the priests who served them, from which governance emerged. Around these temples grew cities, where life burgeoned with a new complexity and sophistication. Here began the first civilizations, a word whose root is *civitas*, meaning city-state.[19]

The invention of writing and mathematics and the development of crafts and architecture all mark this time as expansive in every way. Like the experience of a child now going to school, these new horizons were milestones in our maturation process from cultural infancy and toddlerhood into early childhood. These achievements formed the bedrock of modernity, making possible all that we take for granted today.

How to feed, govern, and coordinate growing masses of people stimulated the awakening of the next cultural era: the third-chakra phase of power and will, out of whose bloody clutches emerged the heroic, ego-identified, individuated self. To move from an obedient infant and toddler culture, where power existed outside oneself in the unequivocal rules of Mother Nature, to the birth of individual power was a necessary step in the process of maturation. Without the awakening of personal power, we would have been destined to flow in the eternal cycles of the Static Feminine forever. No doubt the environment would have fared better, but the human race would have remained in an infantile state, unfulfilled in the potential made possible by our forebrains and opposable thumbs.

We are inheritors of a power paradigm that has been the central organizing principle for the entire period of written history—the last 5,000 years. It began at a time of humanity's immaturity, past toddlerhood but akin to preschool—a time when few could read or write, and no one had the technologies for communication, transportation, and labor that we take for granted today. Like a family with many young children, this immature population needed strong governance. Elite members at the top, originally associated with the priestly class, became the rulers who coordinated the vast evolutionary shift that was taking place.

The Dawn of the Third Chakra

Autonomy is essential for personal responsibility. If
we cannot see ourselves as separate beings, we
cannot take responsibility for our actions.
—*Anodea Judith*

Fire is the element of the third chakra, located in the solar plexus. Often called the power chakra, it sparks the awakening of personal power and will, the metabolism of food into energy, and the capacity for purposeful action. With our will, we have the capacity to rise above instincts and emotions (chakras one and two) and move in a new direction. To say "I will" is to create the future, as in "I will cook dinner tonight." If evolution is the Gods' way of making more gods, then free will is an important element in the developmental process. And while many argue over just how much free will humans really have, there is no doubt that we have more capacity to determine our fate than any other species. Realization of that power comes with tremendous responsibility. We are, after all, the only animals to control fire.

Developmentally, the third-chakra phase of childhood, age 18 months to three years, is a trying time, as any parent will attest. The increased motor development of toddlerhood allows the child to move outward, gradually "hatching" from the fused symbiosis with the mother to explore the external world—yet the child knows so little about the world that his exuberance is met with frequent confrontations and limits. But through this exploration, a child discovers his personal will.

It may begin with a chance action such as breaking a lamp while playing in the living room. His mother rushes in, saying, "What have you done?" The child stares at the result and knows—perhaps for the first time—that something within him caused this pile of shattered glass. In this moment, he gains an inkling that his actions affect the world. Thus begins his awakening as a causative agent. He spends the rest of his life learning how to control or enhance that influence.

The realization that we can make something happen with our will becomes like a new toy. We delight in throwing our peas off the high chair and making someone pick them up. We find new power in the way our screams and cries influence the adults around us. When frustrated with a new toy, we find satisfaction in throwing it across the room or stomping on it until it's broken. No wonder this age is called "the terrible twos." The typical child actively rebels against the mother in most every way possible. If she says, "Yes!" the child says, "No!" If she says, "No!" the child will test his limits and do it anyway. Psychologists call this *differentiation*—the act of differentiating from what has been in order to create and define something new. It's an essential part of our development—and of evolution. For without it, we would never have the courage to do something new. From this struggle we develop personal autonomy and will.

Viewed in terms of Gareth Hill's schema of masculine and feminine valences, this rebellion against the mother corresponds to the awakening of the Dynamic Masculine stage. The masculine urge to rebel against the static limits of the mother shoots outward to explore new worlds. Its symbol is a linear arrow moving beyond the limits of the original circle, the sign we now use to denote the masculine, as well as the fiery planet Mars. The arrow is different from the circle in every way, shifting from cyclic to linear, static to dynamic, contained to boundless.

Mars

Human children have an exceptionally long period of dependence, compared with other animals. This creates a strong bond between mother and child. It takes a great deal of confidence and inner strength to overthrow this bond and claim one's autonomy—a strength gained, in fact, by a solid bonding with the mother as an infant and toddler. In the same way that we need firm ground to jump high, this early support forms a firm foundation that makes the child feel safe enough to push away from the mother and develop will and autonomy.

Girls are more likely to imitate their mothers as they grow up—especially in a culture where the feminine is held as sacred. Even though girls differentiate, they have less need to do so to define themselves. Boys, however, *must* differentiate from the mother in order to develop their own masculine nature.

What happens when an entire culture enters this stage of rebellious differentiation? *It falls to the masculine to carry the initial differentiation from the mother culture.* In this way, the awakening of the third-chakra era of power was coupled with the emergence of the Dynamic Masculine impulse to rebel against all that preceded it.

History's Great Reversal

Our object is not to restore the primordial goddess, but to emancipate ourselves from the effects of a culture based on emancipation from her.
—*Catherine Keller*

Imagine the strength required for a culture to overthrow the Great Mother! Her numinous presence had been the central archetype of worship since the dawn of human consciousness. Her power would have deep roots in the psyche. She was the very land that people lived upon, the field that gave them life. It would take a potent force indeed to overthrow such a power, one that would have to be equal in strength yet profoundly different. What was this ominous power?

The first act of differentiating is one of negation. The mother provides a primal ground, the basic thesis of embeddedness in nature. The differentiating masculine forms an antithesis to that basic thesis, and its values and dynamics turn into their opposites. As it occurs in the child, it also occurs in cultural shifts. Alfred North Whitehead put it bluntly when he said, "Each new epoch enters upon its career by waging unrelenting war upon the . . . gods of its immediate predecessor."[20] Joseph Campbell simply called it history's "Great Reversal."[21]

But it was a long, slow turning. It took thousands of years for this initial rebellion against our primal thesis of nature to crystallize into its own thesis, for the power of the archetypal Mother holds strong. The primacy of the Great Mother extended from the first glimmerings of spiritual worship, anywhere from 200,000 to 30,000 years ago, to the period in which this reversal began to dominate the more peaceful agrarian societies. Marija Gimbutas correlated this to the first Kurgan invasions, which began around 4400 BCE and continued in three successive waves over the next millennium.[22] Kurgans, named for their style of group burials in pits, moved down from the northern steppes of what is now Russia, invading the more peaceful valley civilizations. As horsemen, they were mobile, aggressive, patriarchal, and hierarchical. Another marker is the beginning of the Bronze Age (3150 BCE), when we began to use fire to smelt copper and tin into weapons. The Dynamic Masculine period extended into the Iron Age (1200–550 BCE), when the blacksmiths forged in their fires the tools and weapons that men wielded from horses and chariots as they rode across the land and imposed their ironclad rule.

At this time, earth mysteries were replaced by the worship of sky gods, whose power thundered in the heavens with threats of angry retribution. Cultures that had been peaceful began training armies for defense, protecting themselves with walls and fortifications. As civilization became militarized, death was glorified, contrasting the power of the birth-giving mother.

As humans traveled across the land and seas, it is easy to see how the sun and stars traveled with them while Grandmother Mountain or a sacred spring was left behind. Thus, worshipping the sun and celestial energies was more fitting at a time when travel and trade expanded horizons and stimulated new questions about our origins and values.

The overthrow of the mother, singly or collectively, represents a powerful act of rebellion against everything that came before it. We need only look at the influence of a religion like Christianity, just 2,000 years old, to imagine how powerfully the archetype of the

Great Mother might have loomed in the collective consciousness of our ancestors. It was only the ability to provide for our own survival that made this risk possible. By taking nature into our own hands, through successful planting, harvesting, and building of shelters, humanity gained enough freedom from nature's absolute rules to create a new set of rules.

At its beginning, an instinctive rebellion is immature and often destructive. New movements take little care to preserve what precedes them and focus instead on establishing their own values, even at the cost of destroying the base upon which they stand. Like the action of a frustrated toddler with a new toy just beyond her abilities, social behavior was still shaped by primitive instincts. Just as a child at this stage doesn't understand how difficult he might be, the early awakening of the third-chakra era was a movement that knew not where it was going. An inner imperative simply reached out for power against the helplessness of its infant dependence.

With the advent of writing at the beginning of the Bronze Age, we have for the first time a record of the myths and laws that allows us to witness the archetypal meanderings of history. Whatever conjecture we might make from the burials and artifacts of the Neolithic, written language has the ability to portray a detailed story. The Bronze Age was a transitional time; its myths tell of the passage of power from Mother to Son, myths that were no doubt passed down orally for many generations before they were written. Here we find stories of initial separation and the eventual triumph of one part over another. These involve the separation of the World Parents, the slaying of the Mother, and the rise of the Hero, all of which set the stage for a unified Father God, who provides salvation from the suffering and chaos that result from this tumultuous and violent period of human history.

Myths of separation also represent the ability to make distinctions, a primary aspect of a budding intellect. The first elements to be separated were the Earth and the Sky—archetypally, the earth *Mother* and the sky *Father*. The separation of the World Parents represents the first division of masculine and feminine, the archetypal divorce from which, metaphorically, we all became children of a broken home. Many mythologies reflect this archetypal divorce: the Egyptian star goddess, Nut, and the earth god, Geb, who are separated by their son, Shu; the Greek goddess Gaia and the heavenly chaos of Ouranos, whose separation brings forth Eros, or desire; the Japanese sun goddess, Amaterasu, who is sent to a cave by her mate, Susanowo; the separation of the Maori Mother Papa and Father Rongi. In Babylonian myth, Marduk cuts Tiamat in half and separates her body into sky and earth. The Sumerians told how Enlil, the son of the sky god and the earth goddess, separated his parents and then married his mother, repeating the motif of the Great Mother and her son-lover, long predating Oedipus:

> Enlil, who brings up the seed of the land from the earth,
> Took care to move away Heaven from Earth.
> Took care to move away Earth from Heaven.[23]

Here we see a repeated theme of the original unity breaking into duality, with the offspring, usually a son, standing triumphantly between them. In this way, a single male entity, be it a god or a man, *achieves the heroic task of creating differentiation and then order.* In this separation of the World Parents, consciousness makes a clear distinction between basic polarities: heaven and earth, above and below, spirit and matter, father and mother, light and dark, male and female.

Erich Neumann, in *The Origins and History of Consciousness,* suggests that this original separation created guilt and loss, a feeling of isolation that happens whenever we separate from a source of love and protection. We can see how this suffering and loss was then projected outward to the next set of "separation" myths, which feature a grieving goddess, separated from her child or consort, who wanders the earth in a kind of exile, searching for her loved one. These wanderings eventually take her down into the abyss of the Under-world, where she enters the forgotten realms of the collective uncon-scious while her son takes center stage as the carrier of light. From this dynamic, the male is often equated with light, representing the realm of awakened consciousness, while the feminine is associated with the darker, unconscious realm of the soul. In the Sumerian myth of Inanna, which we visited in chapter 5, there is both separation and a shift in power. Inanna is forced to marry the shepherd, not the farmer—perhaps a man from the invading tribe rather than her own agrarian community. After she enters the last of seven gates to the Underworld, she finds her sister, Ereshkigal, giving birth in a sweaty, dirty bed. Meanwhile, Inanna's consort, Dumuzi, celebrates royally in her temple above, having taken over her abandoned throne.

In Greece, the story differs little. The grain mother, Demeter, loses her daughter, Kore, to Hades, god of the dead, a deal made behind her back by the all-father Zeus. In Demeter's grief and rage against the power of Zeus to make such a deal without mother or daughter's consent, Demeter halts all growth. Here we see the ancient goddess of agriculture raging against the sky god's triumphant power to alter the normal chain of events. Whereas a rightful passage may have been for the daughter to assume her mother's divine station, as queen of agriculture, she instead becomes queen of the dead.

In Egypt, Isis loses her brother and consort, Osiris, who is cut to pieces by his dark brother, Set. As a result, Isis must search the countryside, looking for the pieces to resurrect her mate. Even mother Mary of biblical myth loses her son, Jesus, to the crucifixion and weeps powerlessly. A mother archetype without a child to love is a bereaved goddess indeed. But it gets even worse.

In other myths of the time, the child who has separated his parents now faces the task of slaying the monster of his past, which often appears as a dragon or serpent. The monster, larger than life and replete with animal characteristics, is said to represent the terrible aspect of the Great Mother, whose anger has been incurred by the rebelliousness of her child. She now represents the darkness of the prepersonal unconscious, which will douse the light of the emerging ego at the slightest lapse of attention, therefore requiring constant vigilance. But perhaps this monster is also the chaos that one faces when the established order has been turned upside down in the battle for power. For to keep that power, the chaos must be vanquished.

Meanwhile, peoples of the Bronze Age spread across the land, separating themselves from the lands and communities they knew. They struggled with the constant strife of invading tribes, competing pantheons, and the rule of expanding empires. To the Assyrians, one of the bloodiest of ancient peoples, conquest was a divine mission of their kings—the initiatory challenge of the rich and powerful. From the Hebrews and the Aryans, one can follow a path of destruction that moves outward from the Fertile Crescent into the Indus Valley, North Africa, Greece, and Northern Europe, violently fragmenting the fabric of civilization, even as it was just being built.

Walling Out Nature

We build too many walls and not enough bridges.
—*Sir Isaac Newton*

As populations multiplied in the circumscribed valleys of the first civilizations, they inevitably began to enounter disputes over land and water. Over time, what began as local skirmishes escalated into larger and bloodier forays until, centuries later, whole armies of men were waging all-out wars in a relentless compulsion to expand and conquer the territory around them. As these wars escalated, the archaic instinct of survival, once oriented to the challenges of Mother Nature, became directed instead into defense against *human nature*. Survival became militarized, forging divergent personal wills into singular collective entities of power and might.

The escalation of military skirmishes was coupled with the construction of strategic defenses. Villages that had been embedded in the natural world began surrounding themselves with fortified walls, something that was rare before 3000 BCE. The city walls were like a cell membrane that sheltered its people within and defended them from invasion without. The administrative intelligence of each city served as the cell's nucleus, which emanated from its temple complex.

Within the boundaries of these fortifications, cities grew large and dense. People lived along narrow streets, in simple mud brick houses piled on top of each other. In Mesopotamia, for example, the city of Uruk crowded a population of 50,000 people into a mere 1,000 acres. Toward the end of this era, Babylon was the first city to sport a population of 200,000, diverse in customs and language—hence the origin of the term *tower of Babel*.

The erection of a wall represents an accomplishment as well as a defense. The accomplishment is the triumph over nature and the defense against enemies. Symbolically, it represents the ability to make distinctions, something commonly associated with the masculine psyche. As a defense, however, it cuts two ways, just as defenses do in our psyches: while they protect, they also deny. To be walled away from potential enemies was to be separated from nature as well, and here lies an important and often overlooked shift, one that I believe is possibly as significant as pushing seeds into the ground.

With walls around us, we were no longer immersed in nature as an everyday experience. The primary images of consciousness were no longer fields and forests, birds and beasts. Though many people still worked the land to provide food and hunted the forests outside, the evolutionary edge of culture took place within the walls of cities, much as it does today. Consciousness within these cities became focused then—*as it still is now*—more upon a social order created among humans than upon the organic order that exists in nature.

This human departure from nature's limits brought us instead to the nature of human limits. Young and naïve as we were, those limits were many. We knew little about the larger world. Survival instincts gave us a basic distrust of the unknown. We entered the uncharted territory of large-scale, cooperative living, where people with different gods, languages, or traditions converged upon each other. Like a child whose world shifts from family to school, we moved from the *intimately personal village* to the *vastly impersonal city.*

Without the most basic technology we take for granted today, the feeding and governing of 50,000 people in a limited space, walled off from nature, posed an enormous challenge of coordination—far beyond anything our ancestors had previously encountered. Initially, there were no myths for this kind of living. The maternal challenge of producing enough food having been mastered, the next set of problems—housing, distribution of goods, and defense—did not find their solutions in the natural world.

With walls around our cities and new challenges to face, the realm of the Great Mother was rapidly losing relevance. Though she would remain strong in the ancestral unconscious for millennia to come, her ways were fading with each successive generation born and raised within city walls. While anarchy may have worked well for the smaller villages of the previous era, it was unworkable in the larger cities. When the mother retreated, a new organizing principle was needed. It was time for humanity to ignite its cultural third chakra.

The Son Rises

The innate and necessary stages of psychic development require a polarization of the opposites, conscious vs. unconscious, spirit vs. nature.
—*Edward Edinger*

It was into this vacuum of social governance that the age of power awakened. A new force was rising—that of the heroic Son, whose growing feet stepped decisively into the footprints of the disappearing

Mother. Those with an awakened will could amass enough power to provide effective leadership and coordinate converging populations into some kind of social cohesion.

Yet every light has its shadow. Along with the quantum leap in intellectual horizons grew the darker forces of warfare and slavery, wielded by tyrannical young kings, drunk on their power. For even though leaders were rising up to meet the challenges of a populous civilization, they were nonetheless young and naïve. (Alexander the Great, for example, was only 19 when he started his career.) Their conquests were often fueled by ego. The Mesopotamian ruler Ur-Nammu, for example, built the largest ziggurat of his time and made sure that every brick was inscribed with his name. At Abu Simbel in Egypt, Ramses built statues of himself 30 feet tall, cut 180 feet into a cliff. The fuel for feeding this imperial ego was the sweat of slaves and the blood of conquered people. As Hari Meyers states, "Empire is the collective expression of personal aggrandizement."[24]

A leader's job was to maintain order, coordinate production of resources, and provide protection. This fell to people who had both the passion and the ability to wield that kind of power. As women were busy bearing and suckling their many children, it fell more naturally to the men to take leadership roles as well as to defend their village when attacked. An unexpected attack, with its attendant slaughter, needed to occur only once to inspire the men to train each other as soldiers in preparation for the next time. Such training was essential to survival, yet it diverted time and resources from domestic life into developing weapons and strategies for defense. As warfare escalated and spread, it took men away from the homestead, away from their wives and children, and thus began the separation of masculine and feminine that typifies the middle childhood of our collective story, when the two genders play in their separate realms.

Since women had been representatives of the previous *natural* order, it was men who became rulers of the new *social* order. This new order had to coordinate individual wills into a cohesive and powerful group force. In the early childhood of our civilization, this occurred through dictatorial parental rule, handed down through a pyramidal hierarchy of one man's might over another. The social anarchy of an earlier time became hierarchically stratified, with the few ruling the many. If nature had been a harsh taskmistress in the past, the ever-growing presence of violence and warfare was harsher still.

As tribes and city-states invaded each other, seeking to expand their power and prosperity, an unholy choice was forced upon any cluster of humanity that wanted to maintain its ways: *adapt to militarism or disappear into oblivion.* In his insightful book *The Parable of the Tribes,* Andrew Bard Schmookler describes four possible outcomes for a society invaded by militant marauders, paraphrased below:[25]

1. *Destruction.* They can be destroyed completely, with the invaders taking over their city.
2. *Absorption.* They can surrender and be absorbed into the ways of the invading culture.
3. *Withdrawal.* They can run for their lives, with many dying in the process, leaving their homeland behind to be taken over by the invaders.
4. *Imitation.* They can develop a militaristic society and become just like their attackers.

Each possibility leads to the same outcome. Whether by destruction, absorption, withdrawal, or imitation, the area invaded becomes militarized. This is not to proclaim that war is inevitable but to say that it is self-propagating. Violence begets violence.

Those who failed to develop militarily were simply killed, leaving the aggressive victors to rape the women and dominate the gene pool. Throughout history, the horsemen dominated the farmers, the chariots beat the foot soldiers, iron weapons triumphed over bronze, and the guns and cannons wiped out those with arrows and spears. The horrendous culmination of this trend in the atomic bombs of

Hiroshima and Nagasaki provides an enormous imperative to avoid what happens next. In applying this reasoning to our future, Schmookler states,

> Doubtless, part of our present problem is that the nuclear arms race is an atavistic attachment to a strategy that is no longer adaptive. . . . Our means of self-protection have become a source of our own endangerment.[26]

Those who survived these attacks, and lived long enough to become our ancestors, were the ones with the best weapons, the biggest armies, and, most important, the *organizational ability to wield them with single-minded purpose*. For an army would fail if its actions were disorganized. These actions needed to be meticulously coordinated, even while adapting to new and dangerous situations. Smaller bands could be democratic, but larger armies required absolute obedience. Larger groups had more power and were capable of greater domination. They became the victors who called the shots, wrote the history, and shaped the world from which we came.

The old adage of divide and conquer shows the importance of a unified front. Dissenters were dangerous. They could undermine the group's resolve and were therefore branded as traitors, ostracized, or executed—which gives us some insight into why pacifists meet such hostility during times of war. If a soldier argued for peace or rebelled against his commander, he could undermine his group's ability to act as a single-minded force. Fear and doubt were liabilities, as they could spread contagiously among the troops. In the face of battle, men were forced to deny their fear, as well as any sentimentality for the wives or children they left behind. To deny fear, love, longing, and need is to deny feelings in general. Instead, war was glorified, with heroes defined by the number of bodies massacred.

This denial of feeling made it possible for people to commit acts of brutality and oppression without sensitivity or compassion. The softer emotions were ridiculed and associated with the "weaker" sex—an insult to one's masculinity. This habit of repressing emotions still plagues men today as they struggle to recover their authentic inner life.

To repress emotion, then, would have been a requirement in the militarized male world. Emotional repression also requires a denial of the body, in which feelings and sensations occur. To live among violence, one has to suppress fear, compassion, and disgust. Yet to suppress these feelings is to allow violence to continue unabated. Internal repression creates a wall around the heart—a psychological parallel to the defensive walls around cities at the time. But here we were building walls within ourselves against our own nature.

The ordeals of battle have been a kind of initiation for men for a very long time. Living far from home and community, relying on strength and endurance, facing death on a daily basis, being among men only, and encountering new worlds never seen before—these were all experiences that were believed to turn a boy into a man. It was the most common path at the time for a man to become a hero.

The Hero's Quest

Instead of clearing his own heart, the zealot tries to clear the world.
—Joseph Campbell

From the birth of the many, and the need to control them effectively, came the power of the one. This one became the Hero—a single male whose fantastic and often fanatical deeds shaped the fate of his people and the course of human history.

If a society was organized through the maintenance of large, cohesive power structures, then this cohesion needed to be forged by some kind of singular purpose. Such privilege and responsibility fell best to a single individual whose personal power was potent enough to command huge numbers of men to leave their homes, wives, and children and face hunger, discomfort, and death on a daily basis. This required enormous charisma and organizational abilities. In addition, this ruler needed to be able to round up enough resources to support his armies on the campaign, feeding, clothing, and protecting tens of thousands of men while constantly on the move in unfamiliar enemy territory.

As an example, imagine this: Alexander the Great had to procure 52,000 tons of provisions to feed 87,000 soldiers, 18,000 horses, and 52,000 workers—for a mere four-month period during his 13-year campaign.[27] And this had to be accomplished with the meager technology of the fourth century BCE! It required immense personal power and charisma, with exacting commands carried out through strict obedience.

As the shapes of the Egyptian pyramids and the Mesopotamian ziggurats might imply, power was seen as emanating from a single source on high that ruled in hierarchical fashion: from God to sacred king, then successively to the ruling bureaucrats, merchants, peasants, and finally slaves. As fighting escalated and civilizations became embroiled in hostilities, war forced a change in the ruling theocracies. In early Sumer, for example, before 2800 BCE, decisions were made by councils of elders. However, in times of crisis, such as a war, the council appointed a single leader, called a *lugal*, which literally means "big man." Eventually, as the lugal retained his hero status during peacetime and ruled over community life, this word came to mean "king."

So the institution of kingship grew out of a military structure superimposed on an older, religiously based political system. The absolute authority of a commander over his army served as the prototype for the king's authority over the city. And king he remained, passing his rule to his male heirs and assembling all others into his kingdom. From his subjects, he took tributes, increasing his wealth. With slaves captured in conquest, he built palaces and temples.

Ken Wilber puts this in perspective in this passage from *Up from Eden:*

> Still seen as a god by the pious, but with the appetites of any other idiot, the "divine" king was in a position to fulfill the wildest fantasies of the Atman project: power, immortality, cosmocentricity, omnipotence. And with a rapidity that is astounding, the basic mold of the standard political tyrant was set. The warrior kings, in short, cut themselves off from subservience to community. Instead of serving society, they arranged the reverse: a replacement of social sacrifice with undiluted personal ambition.[28]

As consciousness shifted from the world of nature to the world of humans, the locus of power shifted from the Great Mother to the absolute rule of a single man whose status was elevated to that of a god. The protection and survival of his people depended on his sole power and wisdom. Through his rule, the disparate elements of a culture were homogenized into something that could at least live in peace with itself, if not with its neighbors. But this peace was bought at the price of dictatorial rule. It was to the king's will that his subjects surrendered their own.

Humanity's first forays into power, then, were wildly unequal. If we consider the growing great gap between rich and poor in the world today, we need only look back at the ancient kings, who lived in luxurious, palatial estates with tens of thousands of slaves, to know that this economic gap is a vestige of a very old story. The Egyptian pharaoh Amenhotep had as many as 90,000 slaves. Later, in ancient Rome, emperors could have 20,000, while the wealthy might have only 4,000, and the merely comfortable as many as 500.[29] The complete disregard for the basic human rights of these social underclasses is utterly appalling. Often slaves were castrated to become eunuchs, murdered at the drop of a hat, or punished mercilessly. Even in the more rational periods in Greece and Rome, slaves were tortured, crucified, or forced to wear "gulp preventers" to keep them from eating food that they handled. Human life was abundant, bought and sold as a commodity, with little regard for the interior experience of others. With the realm of feeling denied, how could there be compassion?

A narrowing hierarchy of power dominated the masses, which meant that most people were powerless. The only way for them to achieve freedom was to emulate those who had power. They might become heroes themselves, striving to evolve their own will and strength to dominate others as a way of overcoming their own oppression. The more brutal the leader, the more brutality would be seen as the way to overcome their own violation and achieve freedom. *Here begins the great love of power.*

This age brought forth the archetypal theme of the Hero's Quest—the initiatory journey to find inner power and exaltation through heroic deeds. Most of the myths echoing this theme were allegories of how the light of male consciousness triumphed over the dark, unconscious feminine. The positive side of this quest was that it awakened individual power within the people who embarked upon it. A hero was one whose third chakra—with its attributes of power and autonomy, assertiveness and confidence—had been ignited. A hero could explore new territory, create something that had never before existed, and bring disparate people together under one rule, fostering the social cooperation that formed the ground of civilization. The heroic deeds of our ancestors were the evolutionary drivers of their time. They were the people who dared to stand out from the rest, to move in a new direction, to make important discoveries, and to lead the triumph of "good over evil." Surmounting challenges and ordeals was their form of initiation.

A shadow side of the Hero's Quest, however, is that it's inherently based on conflict. Heroes are created because they *triumph* through conflict, whether internal or external, meaning that some kind of conflict is necessary for one to become heroic. It may be a conflict between old and new ways of being, between reason and instinct, or between one country and another. A man gains hero status only by engaging in some kind of battle and emerging victorious. Heinous crimes have been committed in service of the battle between "good and evil" to the point where it is hard to tell which is which—as we will witness later in the Dark Ages. The general plot of most adventure movies involves a protagonist hero who triumphs over the "bad guy," a character who seldom gets rehabilitated.

The glory of the Hero's Quest has become one of the dominant myths of our time. In contrast to the watery initiations of love and beauty, these fiery initiations create strength and confidence. But when stripped of their sacred context, the fiery initiations develop traits of dominance and aggression, war and miltarism. When stripped of initiatory elements, they show up far too often as the passion to become rich, famous, or powerful—purely for the sake of the ego. Separated from the feminine balance of beauty and love, this shadow side of the fiery third chakra is burning up our resources and dominating our world.

At its deeper levels, the Hero's Quest follows all the steps of an initiatory journey: separation, loss, confinement, revelation, transformation, and finally return. It is an archetypal journey for the evolution of consciousness—both individually and collectively. Joseph Campbell, in his classic book *The Hero with a Thousand Faces*, describes both its light and dark sides in a way that looks all too familiar in our present world. On the positive side, he states,

> The effect of the successful adventure of the hero is the unlocking and release again of the flow of life into the body of the world. The miracle of this flow may be represented in physical terms as a circulation of food substance, dynamically as a streaming of energy, or spiritually as a manifestation of grace.[30]

Campbell also points out the shadow side: the overextension of the quest, its dissociation from everyday life, and the abuse of the powers gained. Campbell's description of King Minos, one of many mythic heroes of the past, is all too reminiscent of economic heroes today:

> The figure of the tyrant-monster is . . . the hoarder of general benefit. He is the monster avid for the greedy rights of "me and mine." The havoc wrought by him is described in mythology and fairy tale as being universal throughout his domain. . . . The inflated ego of the tyrant is a curse to himself and his world—no matter how his affairs may seem to prosper.[31]

The wielding of power clearly relates to the issues of the third chakra, sometimes called the navel chakra because of its location. Campbell goes on to state,

> The World Navel, then, is ubiquitous. And since it is the source of all existence, it yields the world's plenitude of both good and evil.[32]

Thus the Hero has both a light and a dark side. As he amasses power, he can choose to serve either good or evil. To act wisely on that choice requires strength of character. The maturing of our heroic power requires that we realize our acts are capable of both good *and* evil—sometimes at the same time. Wonder drugs can produce bacteria resistant to treatment. Supplying people with what they need at any cost can also contribute to climate instability, which endangers us all. Genetically modified seeds may produce pest-resistant crops, but they also may have damaging effects on the health of animals and people and further crop yields.

The final step in the Hero's Quest is the return home. This is when the fruits of the quest, the elixir of healing, or the wisdom gained from the quest is applied to healing the community. Our heroic technologies can now address our environmental crises; our heroic medicine can now address the healing of the whole person. Our heroic quests for higher consciousness can now manifest through enlightened actions that change the world for the better.

Evolving the Third Chakra

No human being can stand the perpetually numbing
experience of his own powerlessness.
—*Rollo May*

The social development of power brought tremendous gifts, yet they came at a price. The conquests of tribes and city-states forged vast empires, capable of great wealth and great works. This era coordinated larger populations and spread common languages, customs, and crafts, spawning developments in writing and mathematics, architecture and agriculture. The great monuments and palatial estates constructed during this era were triumphs of the ancient world.

Yet this power became increasingly impersonal, often brutal, with an economy built on conquest and slavery. Defensive walls shut away the natural world. Constant warfare and strife robbed people of a safe ground and in that way separated us from our common ground. It separated men and women for months or years at a time and suppressed the feeling function that kept us in touch with ourselves and each other. We became warriors against each other and against ourselves.

Schmookler points out that our reality now "selects" for power. This means that our choices are based on the maximizing (or love) of power, rather than on the increase of love, peace, or well-being. Because power is equated with survival, it appears that the only choice is to choose paths that lead to more power. We "choose" to support the military at the cost of social programs—saying it is a matter of "survival." We get passionate about the patriotism of war, rallying to support the troops, right or wrong, sublimating our own sense of powerlessness with a militant nationalism. Avenging deaths becomes more important than solving the problems that caused them. In a further twist, many believe that giving up our liberties will bring us liberation and that this kind of power will bring us the very peace, love, and freedom that it denies.

In order to maintain the new ground of separation from all that preceded it, the Dynamic Masculine eventually became the *Static Masculine,* instituting a set of values, customs, and beliefs that institutionalized the split from our original thesis. These values have carried culture from the early Greek philosophers to the present day. If we are to outgrow the rigidity that holds our culture in its destructive patterns, we need to understand the Static Masculine valence as we encounter the Greeks and Romans and explore both the light and dark sides of Christianity and science in the next four chapters.

9 FROM ARCHETYPES TO IDEAS

The Static Masculine

Only the free mature male is able to think rationally.
—*Aristotle*

As populations grew within the walled cities of ancient times, the organic roots of our past were paved over with cobblestoned streets. Daily activities swarmed within a dense array of dwellings, civic plazas, and temples. Pride of workmanship provided elegance and sophistication in architecture, sculpture, and murals, resulting in pride in one's locale. Ships gathered in glistening harbors bearing goods from afar, and merchants traded goods in bustling markets. City populations expanded from tens of thousands to hundreds of thousands, creating a new level of complexity. With the influx of new ideas from exposure to different cultures and beliefs, people began to question, debate, and reflect.

The Greek settlements in Asia Minor led the way for a new social organization—the *polis*—an independent, self-governing city-state. Each polis had a distinct identity with its own dialect, religious traditions, and customs. Within the polis, people gathered in large public squares called *agoras* for assemblies, events, and conversation. Freed from the tyranny of outside authority, the people within a polis gained an increased sense of independence. They debated ideas with passion, giving birth to philosophy, metaphysics, and even rudimentary scientific inquiry. These were pivotal contributions of the Axial Age, a worldwide renaissance of wisdom teachings that extended from 800 BCE to 200 BCE.

Within the polis, civic participation was considered vital, a participation that in turn vitalized the city. As people's pride grew for their polis, so did a new identity. They started to see themselves as *citizens*—participants in the creation of their own sociopolitical reality. Citizenry offered a new personal identity, inspiring deeds out of willingness and passion, not just blind obedience to a monarch. The welfare of the polis was considered more important than individual lives. The willingness to fight for its dignity was mandatory. (In fact, the English word *idiot* comes from the Greek *idiotes,* meaning one who keeps to himself and doesn't participate in civic life.) Yet, paradoxically, Greek idealism pushed personal evolution to a new height. The Olympic games lauded beautiful bodies and physical skill. Artistry advanced a new standard of beauty. Intellectual rigor and the ability to debate were highly respected marks of sophistication.

Class distinctions still existed, ranging from rulers to slaves, with the elite at the helm, but a middle class of merchants was emerging, fueled by the profits of seafaring trade. Councils of elected citizens gradually replaced the monopoly of hereditary kings, giving birth to the first democracy around 550 BCE in the city-state of Athens. Only males could be voting citizens, and at first this was limited by heredity to an elite class. Over time, citizenship expanded to include some commoners and foreigners, even emancipated slaves—but never women. Thus it was a democracy made entirely of men.

Freed from the rudimentary chores of survival by the labors of women and slaves, the masculine elite had more leisure to contemplate the nature of the world. Their ideas began to undermine the bedrock of religious beliefs. Myth and rationality flowed into a heady philosophical ambrosia that awakened a new conciousness. "The Greeks were the first to see the world as a question to be answered," quips Richard Tarnas in *The Passion of the Western Mind*.[33] "These were the first stirrings of thought and research ever made by free individuals, without any priestly coercion or religious interference," writes Jacob Burckhardt in *History of Greek Culture*.[34]

Human civilization was maturing. The personal ties of family and clan expanded into an increasingly impersonal urban life. Though the Gods and Goddesses still bound the psyche to mythic archetypes, they were beginning to lose their power and influence. Just as it is with maturing children, the mother and father's influence was still very present but less central. Instead, laws became the regulators of human behavior, impersonal codes that could be written, preserved, and applied to all.

Early Socialization in the Heart Chakra

To love rightly is to love what is orderly and beautiful
in an educated and disciplined way.
—*Plato*

Most of us can remember a time from our childhood when we were humiliated for some unfortunate display of immaturity. Maybe we were teased for being a "crybaby," punished for being out of control, or ridiculed by the big kids. These experiences form the unconscious background of our social programming. Boys, teased for being a sissy if they cried, learn to put away their tears and become little men. Girls learn to be "sugar and spice and everything nice," repressing their aggression. As a child, I was a brainy kid who wasn't fully anchored in her body. I was teased about being clumsy, and this goaded me into an intense study of gymnastics and later led me toward yoga.

As children gain enough verbal and physical maturity to spend time away from their parents, the social world becomes their central focus. This happens when they go to school and leave the known and relatively safe world of the family for a less personal, but no less important, social milieu. Until a child has some degree of impulse control gained in the third-chakra stage—being potty trained, for example, or controlling his aggression—he cannot be admitted to the larger social world. It simply won't accept him. But once there, the child has to navigate a new set of codes and conditions in order to get along.

Still immature, however, the child fashions his behavior through a combination of established rules and social cues. Adults set out the rules, while the other kids let him know what's acceptable. Where identity was wholly ego centered in the third-chakra phase of our terrible twos, we now begin to develop our social identity. We adopt roles to become more likable or accepted: we become the helper, the clown, the leader, or the performer, for example.

This early socialization is the beginning of the heart-chakra developmental stage. Of course, all children want and need love from the moment they're born. But until they've developed impulse control, there's not much they can do to secure that love. They cry or they wet, and somehow nature has it that in most cases, they're loved anyway. As children gain impulse control, they can shape themselves to please others. They do so automatically and unconsciously, splitting off from their "baser" needs and behaviors in order to be accepted into the social world.

It's a good thing, too. You need only visit a child-care center at the end of the day, before the parents show up, to see chaos ready to reign. Patience dwindles and tempers flare, while noise levels climb to piercing heights, each child vying for her own selfish interest. If we grew into adult-sized bodies without controlling our immature aggression, humans would probably have gone extinct a long time ago. That there are still parts of the world, armed with technology, that have not yet tamed these instincts is of grave concern.

Our greatest need at this budding fourth-chakra stage is just to belong. When we find it, we often fuse our personal identity with that of the group. Until we've done the deep searching to discover who we are as unique individuals, we may never grow past this identity, no matter how old we are. The power of the group then becomes the substitute for our own sense of personal power. We define ourselves as Republicans or Democrats, gay or straight, feminists, right-to-lifers, Christian, Jewish, or Neo-Pagan—the list is endless. Part of the adult work of healing the heart chakra is to shed these layers of false personae and discover the authentic self that dwells within. Only by intimacy with our own interior can we develop true compassion for the interior experience of another—a key task of the mature heart chakra.

For children, the institution of rules provides a safety that allows them to prosper in their early social interactions. Now that they have language and simple reasoning, the most common question children ask at this stage is "Why?" They want to understand the rules of how things go together so that they know how to fit in. "Why does the sun come up in the morning?" "Why do we brush our teeth at night?" "Why does Jimmy get to stay up later than me?" "Why is Daddy angry?" Knowing the reasons behind things allows life to proceed more sensibly.

Held within a structure provided by the adults in charge, a child can relax. He knows how to behave and can instead focus on his playmates. Great power is given to the maker of these rules, power that is put outside the self. For a child, too young to know how the game works to make his own rules, this is entirely appropriate. But the safety associated with externalized power becomes a factor in the love of power that may be lifelong.

While I submit that the development of the heart chakra begins here at this stage of childhood (age four to seven), its full opening

---

takes the rest of our lives. From the social world of the family to the larger world of school and beyond, our frame of reference continually expands as we grow. Our lessons of love come in myriad forms, from the excitement and heartbreak of our first romance to the birth of a child, from the long-term partnership of marriage to engagement with one's community or nation, from rejection of our authentic self to its eventual reclamation. Our pains and losses teach us compassion; our joys guide us to our future.

The parallel here is that the convergence of populations in the social world of the polis is like the early socialization of a child going to school. The institution of laws created social order and at least internal peace, even if warfare and conquest were occurring at the borders of these lands. Acceptance of laws laid the ground for larger, more diverse groups to live together peaceably enough to create new levels of organization and higher states of consciousness. As it is with a child, the elite makers of these laws held a numinous power. Even as democracy was giving more power to citizens, it held a thread of the love of power, still evident today in the way we trade personal freedoms for national security.

From Dynamic Masculine to Static Masculine

At his best, man is the noblest of all animals; separated
from law and justice, he is the worst.
—*Aristotle*

Whereas the Dynamic Masculine seized power in the previous era by overthrowing the Great Mother, the next task of this new ruling paradigm was to maintain and expand that power. Such power was, by definition, everything opposite to the values that preceded it, so the original wholeness had to be resisted—walled off, both literally and psychologically. In this way, the Dynamic Masculine forces that had established their dominion over the Static Feminine matured into the *Static Masculine*—an organizing system that held power through the principles of reason and logic, laws and conformity. While the more third-chakra characteristics of force and coercion were still present (as they are even today), the institution of written laws enabled a more cohesive order, less subject to the whim of tyrants and more applicable to voluntary complicity. Gareth Hill's symbol of the Static Masculine is the equal-armed cross. We can see how the cross represents distinctions: two linear lines divide above from below and left from right. Later the cross would become a ubiquitous symbol of the Static Masculine era.

The Static Masculine holds things in place. Its purpose is stability, but unlike the Static Feminine, whose stability is cyclic and grounded in instincts, the Static Masculine is linear and grounded in logic. It focuses on distinctions: it discerns, divides, and regulates. Static forms do stabilize, but they also create rigidity, which is essential for maintaining a larger sovereign unit or empire, especially one that extends thousands of miles without modern technology. Rigid rules forged the chaos of converging populations into a homogenized cultural soup. They provided a common ethic for the social world, which was slowly finding stability in the hum of urban life.

Conquered lands required governance to maintain order and economic flow. Laws were propagated by the written word and enforced by society's elite members who could read. Written laws could reach across distances and establish universal social prinicples. Written words are static, unchanging. Literal truth was, quite literally, a *written* truth, frozen into stasis at the time of its writing.

From Myth to Logic

*We ought to fly away from earth to heaven as quickly as we can;
and to fly away is to become like God, as far as this is possible;
and to become like him is to become holy, just, and wise.*
—Plato

The golden age of Greece burst forth, laying the intellectual foundations of Western civilization, establishing new fields of inquiry such as medicine, history, geometry, science, rhetoric, and philosophy. The focus of consciousness shifted upward, becoming more cerebral than material, transcending the instincts and urges of the lower chakras and surging toward a reign of logic and rationality.

As civilization became more complex, it also became more ordered. It is no surprise, then, that men turned their attention to the mythic realm and attempted to find order there as well. Homer had long ago created his famous epics, *The Iliad* and *The Odyssey*, where the gods intervened directly in the lives of men. Hesiod's *Theogony* ordered the entire pantheon of divine archetypes into a kind of family genealogy, in which Eros, god of desire, is born from the separation between Gaia, the Earth Mother, and Cronos, chaos or time.

As always, new ways of thinking clashed with the old. Logical discourse diverged from the myths and legends of the past. The Greek gods and goddesses of nature were now worshiped in man-made temples, their stories reflecting irrational antics that played whimsically with human fate. Sacrifice became a means to appease their whims, with many thousands of bulls, goats, and pigs slaughtered as offerings to increasingly distant and angry gods. A philosophical tension ensued, and the mythic and the rational began to diverge.

Logical discourse began with the Pre-Socratic philosophers, to whom we owe the first division of the cosmos into the essential elements of earth, water, fire, and air. These various schools proposed many other fundamental distinctions that led to the first rudimentary forms of metaphysics—an advance for Western civilization.

Socrates built upon this earlier tradition by teaching that the key to happiness was the development of a rational, moral character. He introduced the idea of *ethical rationalism*—an ethics based on logical sense rather than the antics of the gods or the authority of the state. He felt that to know the good was to do the good—that humans, when given educated choices, would naturally choose moral behavior. Socrates was a prominent supporter of gender equality and held fast to the passion of personal dialogue, eschewing the written word. Unfortunately, his habit of deep questioning and independent thinking marked him as a troublemaker, resulting in his public trial and forced suicide in 399 BCE. In his final act of passionate dedication to the truth, he chose to drink poison hemlock rather than recant his subversive views. He was remembered as saying: "I was really too honest a man to be a politician and still live."[35]

Socrates's student Plato carried on the inquiry for an even deeper order. He believed that appearances were deceptive and that the senses couldn't be trusted. Using the analogy of firelight casting shadows on the wall of a cave, he saw the known world as but a shadow of a hidden, divine flame, which emanated from a world of perfection, beauty, and abstract forms. These ideal forms led the mind upward, toward transcendence. The material realm, which had once been the ground of our being, took a step backward in Plato's philosophy. Instead, nonmaterial ideal forms generated the changeable, physical world. These ideals were eternal, while matter was temporal. Human instincts were seen as base, compared with the awakened rational mind.

To Plato's student Aristotle, the reverse was true: ideas rose out of existing physical forms. Both Plato and Aristotle were addressing the relationship between spirit and matter, recognizing that they influenced each other—the question was how. Later, a famous

Rennaissance painting by Raphael, called *The School of Athens*, depicted Plato pointing upward and Aristotle pointing downward, highlighting their philosophical differences. Thus, mind and matter began their separation, along with myth and reason. The value previously attributed to the material world shifted to the mental world of ideas. As spirit and matter diverged, there began a polarization of archetypal elements that became infused with the cosmic battle between good and evil.

Nowhere does this split make itself more apparent than in the philosophy of Manichaeism, in which we see the irrevocable division of the cosmos into Good and Evil. The roots of Manichaeism are found in a Zoroastrian myth of separation, this time between two brothers. As the story goes, Father Time (Zurvan) sacrifices for a thousand years to give birth to a son and comes to doubt whether his actions will ever bear fruit. At last, two brothers are born. Ahura Mazda, the brother of light, is born from the merit of his sacrifices, while Ahriman, representing darkness, is born from his doubt. Ahriman, knowing that the privileges of kingship will go to the firstborn, rips through the womb to be born ahead of his brother. To keep his sacrificial vow, Father Time has to grant the dark brother kingship for 9,000 years, when it will at last be his brother's turn to reign. From this myth, we see how evil, or darkness, is derived as the first condition, but with the intervention of time, good can prevail in the end. In this myth, evil is born from doubt. (Notice the absence of any feminine figure in this myth concerning womb and birth.)

The dialectical battle between good and evil is an underlying theme of the Static Masculine era. It still rules our culture today, in nearly every adventure film or novel, in the fanaticism of religious wars, and in the divisiveness of politics. While we could argue that this ethical dualism invites us to rise above evil and evolve our actions toward the good, such atrocities as the Inquisition, the Holocaust, two world wars, and countless other genocidal events—as well as racism, poverty, and the destruction of the environment—attest to the fact that we still have a long way to go toward the triumph of good over evil.

From Macedonia to Rome

There is nothing impossible to him who will try.
—*Alexander the Great*

Alexander the Great was Aristotle's student, schooled in Greek ideals in a direct lineage from Plato and Socrates. His father, Philip II of Macedon, was a powerful ruler whose ability to unite Greece in 338 BCE greatly inspired Alexander. Upon his father's murder, two years later, the 19-year-old Alexander set out to unite the rest of the known world. In a mere 13 years, he conquered the Persian Empire and united the lands from Greece to India. Though fierce as a fighter and mighty as a general, he was humane to his enemies, allowing them to keep their ways, while infusing his own. As a result of this respect, he was able to spread the rationality of Greek ideals, language, and customs across the lands of diverse people. Even though his death at age 33 fragmented his extensive empire, the flavor of Greek culture had deeply influenced the immense cross-cultural maelstrom that he had ruled. Alexander's Hellenic legacy provided a way of life that was masculine, rational, and humanistic.

Alexander had also met Jewish tribes on his forays through Persia, where Cyrus the Great had freed them from captivity in Babylon 200 years earlier. These were yet another people organized by Static Masculine principles. They lived by a strict written moral code, keeping a sacred covenant with a single, all-powerful male deity. By accepting the divine commandments of Moses recorded in the scripture known as the Torah, they allied themselves with a fierce god who could save or damn, punish or reward. Imagining themselves to be God's "Chosen

People," they believed that they were divinely summoned to bring the spiritual light of peace and prosperity to the promised land. This would come about through a future messiah who would demonstrate divine powers and lead his people to the realization of that promised land. After their centuries of brutal existence, including enslavements in Egypt and Babylon and decades of wandering the desert in search of a homeland, one can imagine how important it would have been to the Hebrews to obey the commandments of their powerful god, Yahweh, to the letter of the law.

After Alexander's death, his empire fell to the quarrels of his generals. The pinnacle of Hellenistic society—along with its democratic organization—politically declined. Culture needed a new center of stabilization. With their sense of *carpe diem*, the Romans seized the opportunity and took on the massive task of coordinating an even greater number of people in a single empire. While the Greeks had debated their ideas and somewhat democratically elected their rulers, it was Rome that institutionalized those laws, with a backbone of rigidity. Dominated by an imperial spirit more than the fresh independence of Greece, Rome took the next step in the Western world's social coordination.

The Early Roman Empire

Great empires are not maintained by timidity.
—*Tacitus*

Rome was a sizzling cultural stew—a city of squalor and wealth, terror and grandeur, savagery and sophistication. It was ruled by a masculine oligarchy that owned most of the land. Its large public buildings allowed huge numbers to gather: one Roman bath could accommodate 3,000 people,[36] while the Circus Maximus could seat 150,000, possibly more. At its largest expanse in the second century

CE, the Roman Empire ruled over 60 million people. Its territory spread across two million square miles, from northern Europe to the upper edge of Africa, from Spain to the Levant. If we compared the Roman Empire at its height to a map of today, it would include all or part of 48 different modern countries.[37]

Roman governance became a mix of third-chakra political ambition and ruthless militarism combined with a fourth-chakra ability to embrace many diverse peoples and customs. This acceptance engendered a sense of belonging for those males willing to acknowledge Roman authority—and crushing domination of those who weren't. As Roman conquests expanded the empire's borders, the Roman world became wealthy, bringing back booty for imperial palaces and slaves by the thousands.

Despite the Roman talent for law and order, killing and enslavement were still commonplace throughout Roman society, even for sport and entertainment. The famed Colisseum could seat 55,000 spectators; there, on a single day, thousands of animals might be slaughtered, or hundreds of gladiators might fight to a grisly death amid the cheers and growls of spectators having a good time. Members of the Senate murdered each other with little attempt to hide their actions. Avenging murder was a duty whose avoidance led to humiliation. Unwanted babies were thrown on the village dung heap, where the poor might rescue them to raise as slaves. No room for childishness here—life was brutal.

However, the Romans cared greatly for art and beauty, in part because of their assimilation of Greek culture. They built palatial homes for the rich and engaged in elaborate rituals for all occasions, complete with ornate statues, altars, and temples. Their genius for laws and social contracts created consistent standards for conducting business and amassing wealth and power. Extensive roadways enabled people to travel more easily. They spread far from their homelands, no longer supported by their native social customs.

Men and women led separate lives in both the Greek and Roman worlds. Even though the Divine Feminine was still worshipped through various goddesses, she was much reduced in stature. The Great Mother figure of Hera/Juno (her Greek and Roman names) was now a jealous bitch, whining about her husband's antics. The romantic passions associated with the goddess of love, known as Aphrodite/Venus, were seen as a wicked curse that induced madness. Mistress of the animals and wild places, Artemis/Diana became a murdering maiden protecting her nakedness. Medusa's head full of snakes turned men to stone with a mere glance. Hardly an appealing sense of the divine for any of them! Even the legendary founding of Rome by the children Romulus and Remus was pointedly devoid of a mother, as the abandoned twin boys had to be suckled by a wolf instead.

In the mortal realm, women in both Roman and Greek societies held the legal status of slaves. In Roman law, the *pater familias,* or eldest male, held the power of life and death over his wife and the rest of the family. Daughters lived by the absolute rule of their father, wives by the rule of their husband. Women were largely confined to their house, regarded as property, and expected to be obedient. The society of men set the tone for the civilized world.

Along the edges of the Roman Empire, border wars were constant, vestiges of the Dynamic Masculine continually forging out into new territory. The Romans relentlessly conquered and looted their neighbors, bringing back continuous supplies of slaves to build their extensive palaces, streets, and aqueducts. Sometimes 10,000 slaves would come through the gates of Rome in a single day.[38] In the city of Rome itself, up to 40 percent of its one million inhabitants were slaves.

Yet the Roman Empire maintained an internal peace, known as the *Pax Romana,* into the first few centuries of the Common Era. This allowed Greek polytheism and Platonic ideals to meet with Jewish monotheism and early Christian idealism to weave their disparate fibers into a single myth that would eventually become the state religion. Rome's inner stability, wealth, and extensive road system gave it the power to amplify new ideas throughout its vast empire. Members of this massive cross-cultural world were ripe for a new story that would give them more stability, social cohesion, and lasting peace. This was the field that gave birth to the next major guiding myth of humanity.

10

LIKE FATHER, LIKE SON

Early Christianity and the Biblical Myth

Gods are mortal men and men are immortal gods.
—*Heraclitus*

The biblical story of the life, death, and resurrection of Jesus has had a greater effect on the shape of Western civilization than any myth in our collective history. Approximately one-third of people in the world today define themselves as Christian, with estimates as high as 73 percent in the United States.[39] Regardless of your religious orientation—whether you're a true believer or an atheist, a Buddhist, a Jew, a Muslim, or a Pagan—Christianity dominates the spiritual airwaves throughout much of the world. In the West, the assumptions and beliefs of Christianity influence every facet of our civilization: education, health care, population control, environment, economics, sexual mores, women's rights, and politics.

Countless volumes have been written about Christian theology, and bloody wars have been fought over its interpretation. What I attempt to present here is but a broad sweep, comparing its original heart-chakra vision of higher consciousness and a loving community with the way that vision played out in a culture still caught in the third-chakra imperialism of the Roman Empire. My purpose is neither to defend nor to denigrate Christianity, but rather to illustrate—

within the limits of the next two chapters—both its brilliant light and its equally dark shadow. Only by bringing both polarities to consciousness can we come to the wholeness necessary to integrate Christianity's heart-based message and create a new paradigm.

The Times of Jesus

In one way or another one "lives" the myth, in the sense that one is seized by the sacred, exalting power of the events recollected or re-enacted.
—Mircea Eliade

When Jesus was born, Galilee was an idyllic place: a self-sufficient land of natural beauty, dotted with small villages, hot springs, a rolling river, and plenty of food. Though ruled by Rome, it was a land set apart from the whirlwind of political intrigue that categorized Roman governance. Its population was of mixed races, sophisticated in Greek culture and faithful to Jewish law. The people of Galilee had a way of life worth protecting. They lived peacefully with their environment and each other. Because they were far from Rome and lived largely unto themselves, they were difficult to command. Around the time of Jesus's birth in 4 BCE, King Herod's son Archelaus had assumed the crown, but it was said that he was cruel and incompetent, causing Rome to direct its attention toward subduing the region. This was the land and the political climate that gave birth to what has become the central myth of the Static Masculine era.

Christianity is based on the story of a humbly born man whose gentle presence taught his followers a new way to think about life and community. Jesus the Nazarene[40] (the latter word meant "initiate") was a radical visionary, a prophet, and an avatar of the heart chakra. His central message of love stood in radical contrast to the aggressive and dominating values of the time. He taught his followers to love their enemies, to turn the other cheek, and to practice forgiveness against trespassers. Where ancient kings had been distant and authoritarian rulers whose power was forged in conquest and whose wealth was built with the sweat of slaves, here was a prophet with a different kind of story, ripe with new hope and meaning. Like the Buddha five centuries before him—whose wisdom had not yet migrated to the Western world—Jesus modeled compassion over judgment. He collapsed the stratifications of a classist and sexist society into a new community of social equality. Few of us today realize how radical these ideas were at the time.

In the myth that grew out of his brief, 33-year existence, Jesus was the product of an immaculate conception between a Divine Father and a virgin, human mother. As a result, he was regarded as both human and divine, an issue that was hotly debated in the centuries that followed. He even claimed his own divinity with the statement that "I and the Father are one" and told his followers that they too were gods.[41] The archetypal son was maturing; the boy-become-man was now merging with the Father archetype as a symbol of divine consciousness. If evolution is the Gods' way of making more gods, then this was part of Jesus's message: we are all divine—and our source can be found within as well as without.

Women had long been reduced to the status of a daughter—submissive, invisible, and obedient to husband and father. Jesus's father was divine, while his mother was mortal—certainly not a relationship of equals in the literal sense. (A deeper reading of the Virgin Mother who mates with God harks back to the Pagan myth of the virgin Earth that brings forth life as a result of penetration by the radiant sun.) Over the centuries since the Nativity, Mother Mary has been both fervently worshipped and strictly forbidden. As the mother of a child who was both human and divine, her status has been hotly contested. To the patriarchal mind-set, Mother Mary was only a vessel, a passive recipient, stripped of sexuality and free will. But if she was merely mortal, how could Jesus be divine? The only other feminine figure in the popular Jesus myth was Mary Magdalene, who may have been a priestess at the time and later reduced to the status of a prostitute. With the mother reduced to a maiden, and the maiden seen as a whore, the natural trinity of Mother, Father, and Divine Child from Pagan myth was replaced by a masculine duality—Father and Son—with the Holy Ghost to be added later, a neutered "spirit" in place of what was once a Divine Mother.

Masculine and feminine archetypal dynamics had now turned completely about. The Great Mother archetype, so central during the Static Feminine era, had long ago been overthrown by the priests and kings rising up in the Dynamic Masculine era. Now, in the Static Masculine era, the son was stepping into the shoes of the Father, with women holding the status of powerless young girls. The motif of the all-providing Mother with her son/lover shifted to its opposite: the omnipotent Father and his daughter/wife. It would be nearly 2,000 years before women would begin to rise up from this oppression, during which time conditions would get far worse before they started getting better.

Revolutionary Spirituality

You cannot serve both God and money.
—*Matthew 6:24*

Jesus was a rebel who challenged the values of his time. He flouted Jewish law by working on the Sabbath. He broke social taboos by associating with tax collectors, lepers, and whores. He decried the greed of the money changers. He preached that spiritual salvation was available to anyone, Jew or gentile, rich or poor, slave or master. Even women were welcome to participate as equals, a radical act at the time.[42] In a hierarchical world of haves and have-nots, where social status was absolute, he leveled the playing field with a kind of equal-opportunity spirituality. His philosophy did not require wealth or status. By contrast, his preachings invited the poor to join in and break bread with those of higher classes, a practice that went against strong social taboos.

Jesus required only faith and love—faith that the individual would find salvation in the Kingdom of God, and love as God's divine gift, to be shared unconditionally. His followers believed that he performed miracles as a demonstration of his love and his divine powers. Scarcity turned to plenty; water turned into wine. Diseases were healed, eyesight was restored[43]—even the dead could be raised! It's easy to see the appeal that this egalitarian, spiritual utopia would have had in the ancient world. It was an exhilarating social experiment: a belief in a world free of suffering, the tantalizing promise of a sane society.

The Jesus story mirrors the process of initiation. Its elements combine the myths of the Greek mystery cults with the Jewish prophecy of the savior-king, creating a natural fusion of the two cultures. Jesus's baptism or purification, the period of isolation in the desert that followed, and his crucifixion and resurrection reflect the stages of initiation through which a deeper, divine reality is revealed. If evolution is the Gods' way of making more gods, Jesus was a shining example of evolution's possibilities, a living ideal of a human whose advanced consciousness demonstrated powers beyond anything known. His teachings were mystical clues about how to evolve our own consciousness and wake up to the miraculous power of the divine within. However, his evolutionary vision was not limited to individual consciousness, but was centered around a radical social vision of community that broke down the barriers of hierarchical status, redeemed the poor and dispossessed, and sought to harmonize the tensions between Jews and Romans.

A central vision of Jesus's teachings was that the Kingdom of God was accessible right here on Earth, available to anyone. This radical idea addressed the previous separation of the World Parents, reversing the archetypal split between heaven and earth and regarding humanity as one expanded family. Early Christian communities transcended the old boundaries of clan, tribe, and race by calling each other brother or sister. Priests were called fathers. Later, the word *pope* would come from the word for "papa." It was a radically adventurous movement that created, through love, the unity that the great empires had tried to forge through warfare. Jesus's initiation in the desert enabled him to see a more inclusive union. What had been archetypally divided was beginning to come back together. Unity—of the archetypal realms of heaven and earth, Father and Son, masculine and feminine, and one tribe with another—was the social message of Jesus's new story. It offered a grand synthesis to a fragmented world. These were rich ideas that infused the early communities with a spiritual passion that spread across the land. As the gospel spread westward through the Roman Empire, Jesus's teachings were taken as literal fact to be believed, rather than clues to an initiatory experience.

The Roman world, however, was ruled more by power than by love. To keep the downtrodden masses from revolting, the Romans maintained a strict reign of terror. Crucifixion was one of the ways they displayed their power. The Jews, believing that their covenant was with the land they lived upon, rather than with the distant city of Rome, resisted Rome's taxation. The historian Josephus told of a field of 2,000 Jews crucified near Galilee in 4 BCE for taking part in a rebellion, their corpses left on the crosses as an example to others.[44]

By contrast, Jesus did not force or manipulate. Unlike the kings of his day, he was not born of wealth or political privilege, as his humble birth in a manger implies. Early Christianity was a grand experiment carried out by social revolutionaries high on the energy of a new vision. They recognized each other as members of a new society, brothers and sisters in a common cause, inspired and held together by their love for each other and for Jesus as their teacher. He was the intermediary to a spiritual realm that could be joyfully shared by all.

When, just 33 years after his birth (and only three years after he began teaching publicly), Jesus was brutally murdered, the blow to his followers must have been monumental. With his untimely death, Jesus's message of hope and love risked becoming obscured for eternity. The movement was young and still unformed. Very little had been written down. Many still doubted his authority.

But death followed by a story of resurrection made his life miraculous. His teachings were preserved and revered as the word of God. No longer a simple prophet with a progressive vision, Jesus became a figure of immortality, the Christos or Messiah. Whether his resurrection was real or symbolic was a subject of controversy between the Gnostics, who saw his life as an allegory for spiritual initiation, and the orthodox Christians, who interpreted the events literally.

As birth was the numinous mystery of the Great Mother, death had been perhaps the ultimate male mystery. It was death through war, and the fight against death through immortalized tombs and palaces, that propelled human behavior into the obedience of the Static Masculine paradigm. And whereas the ancient mystery religions had commonly celebrated the cycles of life, death, and rebirth in their rituals, the death and rebirth of Jesus made this mystery into a concrete reality, one that could be shared by all, symbolically ritualized again and again. While the sacred king of ancient times was, on occasion, sacrificed for the good of the land, the sacrifice of Jesus was for all time and all people. The death and resurrection of the Christ echoes an older cycle of the Pagan god of the harvest, such as Dionysus or Osiris, who is cut down annually to arise again each springtime.

Death being the powerful motivator that it is, the horror of the crucifixion and the miraculous story of Jesus's resurrection inspired an extraordinary zeal to redeem Christ's death by propagating his message far and wide. The cross then became the dominant religious icon for spreading his message in the Christian West, an image ubiquitous to the present day.

Christianity after Jesus

God became man so that man might become a god.
—Athanasius of Alexandria

Jesus wrote very little while he lived. Most of what has come down to us about his life and death was written after he died. Those who followed Jesus when he was alive had no need for scripture—they had a living experience. Many were poor and illiterate. But as Christianity was Romanized, it became a religion of an imperial state. Not that the religion had no passion, as we shall see, but over a period of 400 years, what began as a minority cult was increasingly fused with Roman politics, laws, and institutions until it dominated, and essentially wiped out, the older Pagan beliefs and practices.

The prolific apostle Paul, who lived in the first century, shaped much of Christian theology through his writings. A product of his times, Paul was a Roman citizen, a Pharisaic Jew, and a Greek by education. He never met the living Jesus, but he was converted by a vision he received on the road to Damascus—a journey he had begun with a firm intention to put a stop to the growing Christian cult! As the Greek mentality was already grounded in the mystery cults celebrating death and rebirth, the Greeks of Corinth saw the resurrection of Christ as cause for celebration to be accompanied by ecstatic rites. From letters written at the time, it seems that Paul felt uncomfortable with the spirit of celebration. Adhering instead to the notion of the Greek noble death and the ideal of martyrdom, he stressed the need for seriousness. According to Paul, Christ's obedience unto death exemplified the proper spiritual attitude for the Christian community.[45] This death was the ultimate sacrifice for the love of God. Though Jesus had originally preached about salvation from sin, later Christianity became infused with the idea that *willingness to suffer* demonstrated moral character. The cross was the perfect symbol to remind Christians of this.

The cross, as I have mentioned, is Gareth Hill's symbol for the Static Masculine. The lines of the cross create distinctions, boundaries, and walls. The horizontal line of the cross draws a division between above and below, heaven and earth, mind and body. The vertical line divides left from right, rational thinking from intuitive, male from female, good from evil. In this sense, the divisions that had already been created by the Dynamic Masculine—the separation of heaven from earth, masculine from feminine, mind from body—were now given a symbol that expressed, maintained, and institutionalized that division.

If we place a human body against a cross, the lines intersect at the heart. Though Jesus was a prophet of the heart who preached a message of love and unity for all people, the cross upon which he was crucified was firmly planted in the soil of a paradigm that was anything but loving. The ground of Roman soil did *not* unify men and women, spirit and body, or civilization and nature.

Yet the divine kingdom that Jesus prophesied was not another dominant empire, but rather a promise of human redemption in a world of blinding paradoxes and acute spiritual hunger. Unfortunately, an empire ruled by force and obedience was the social structure of the time. It's no surprise, then, that as Christianity spread through the Roman Empire, it was co-opted by the imperial values that ruled that empire. The divine and timely message of love, no longer renewed and updated by its living founder, was instead spread by messengers whose cultural milieu was institutional, authoritarian, and oppressive to women, minorities, and the poor. As Joseph Campbell said to Bill Moyers in *The Power of Myth*, "The power impulse is the fundamental impulse in European history. And it got into our religious traditions."[46] As Christianity was Romanized, it became a servant of imperial values rather than the original Christian ideas of love, charity, and service. As the fourth-chakra vision was planted as a seed, it was carried by a third-chakra imperial structure. Yet the seed went underground and continued to grow.

Christian Martyrs

For it is plain that, though beheaded, crucified, thrown to wild beasts, chains, and fire, and all other kinds of torture, we do not give up our confession; instead, the more such things happen, the more others—in even larger numbers—become faithful and worshippers of God through the name of Jesus.
—*Justin Martyr*

Early Christians were not immediately accepted in the Roman Empire but remained fringe members of society in the first centuries of the Common Era. As a result, they kept largely to themselves in those early years. Their unwillingness to accept the Roman emperors as gods and make sacrifices to their divine cults was seen as politically contemptuous. In fact, their refusal to honor the old gods got them labeled with the term *atheists,* or nonbelievers. Such refusal was considered dangerous to the social and divine order. What if the gods got angry and sought retribution by sending pestilence or drought? Before the gods could act, Roman officials took the upper hand and persecuted some of the Christians instead. How much this was motivated by religion and how much by politics is hard to say. Brought before tribunals, Christians were asked to renounce their faith—or face public execution. Many chose martyrdom, finding more freedom in death than in life. Even in the face of torturous deaths, the martyrs believed that their acts demonstrated strength of faith and were the highest calling they could aspire to. An unexpected consequence was that this proved to be an effective marketing tool for Christianity—for what kind of God could inspire such zeal that people were willing to suffer and die for its cause?

A decisive turning point came in 312 CE, when the originally Pagan and immensely influential emperor Constantine received a vision. He saw a large cross in the sky, emblazoned with the words "In this sign, thou shalt conquer." As if in answer, he won his next battle miraculously. Ostensibly, Constantine knew little about the Christian religion at the time and struggled with how to align his victory with the fact that the God of Christ was not a God of war. Yet he took this omen as a sign to solidify his power and unite the multiethnic Roman Empire under a single set of beliefs. He did an about-face on the persecution of Christians and instead began rewarding them with money, tax exemptions, and prestigious positions. By this act, he cleared the way for all church dignitaries to serve his imperial rule. In the century that followed, the number of Christians grew from 5 million to 30 million.[47]

With this unification of church and state, political rulers were allowed to influence church doctrine. Constantine presided over the first ecumenical council at Nicaea, in 325 CE, where the issue of Jesus's divinity was debated. Was Jesus mortal or divine, a man or a god? The council eliminated any possibility of a logical trinity composed of father, mother, and child, and replaced it with the Father, the Son, and the Holy Spirit. All forms of Christianity, other than the form we now know as Orthodox, were banned.

After Julian, the last Pagan emperor of Rome, died in 363 CE, the entire pantheon of the old gods and goddesses dissappeared—along with all their colorful diversity and messy passions—into a wholly masculine monotheism. In 388, the Emperor Theodosius ordered the Pagan statues beheaded and temples destroyed.[48]

Any traces of the initiatory tradition of the Gnostics were destroyed.[49] Orthodox Christianity became the official state religion, a means of bringing spiritual unification to the Roman Empire. In 391, the Altar of Victory in the Roman Senate was destroyed, and 410 brought the sack of Rome from northern barbarians, which some identify as the fall of the Western Roman Empire. To the east, the Byzantine Empire continued into the Middle Ages with periods of peace and prosperity, eventually falling to the Turks in 1081.

What was brought under the umbrella of unity in this early Christian period was all that was above ground: religious dogma, behavioral codes, and the sociopolitical world of men. What was left out of this unity were the feminine and the attributes of the first two chakras: the sacredness of the earth, the body, sexuality, and pleasure. Repressing our lower chakras, we reached upward, to the heavens.

It seems the world was not ready for the fourth-chakra message of love. Instead, the heroic impulse of the power-seeking third chakra was projected onto the figure of Jesus. He was the new Hero, and the common man was relieved of the journey, at least in the outward sense. The heroic impulse now took place on the inner planes, as reason and logic battled with our more archaic passions and instincts. In a divided world, the teachings of union could not yet be realized. Whereas the mystery religions, such as the Eleusinian rites of Demeter and the rites of Orpheus, were about finding wisdom through a personal descent, Christians believed only in ascension, with the high being mightier than the low. The gap between heaven and earth—for which Jesus had proposed a synthesis—grew wider.

The Twisting of Sex and Power

Women should not be enlightened or educated in any way.
They should, in fact, be segregated, as they are the cause
of hideous and involuntary erections in holy men.
—*Augustine of Hippo*

If sexuality had not received enough of a blow from the ascetic attitudes of early Christianity, its final throttle came from one of Christianity's most influential thinkers: St. Augustine, Bishop of Hippo. Born in Thagaste, North Africa, Augustine was the son of a Pagan father and a Christian mother—a splendid setup for wrestling with the contradictions of his time. His father, Patricius, was known for his frequent affairs and encouraged his son to pursue his passions, as fathers tend to do. As a young man, Augustine lived well. He fathered a child out of wedlock, cohabiting with his concubine, whom he apparently loved for many years. He was strongly drawn toward the dualistic teachings of Manichaeism, with its eternal battle between good and evil, in which the human body, like all matter, was considered evil. Despite nine years of study, he never officially joined that faith, yet it clearly influenced his thinking and teachings throughout his life. This posed quite a contradiction between his beliefs and his lifestyle.

Augustine's mother, Monica, was emotionally enmeshed with her son, apparently suffering greatly when he did not live according to her expectations. Deploring her husband's infidelity, she begged Augustine to curb his desires and pressured him to leave his concubine for a woman of higher status. To further that goal, she saw to his education. As a learned man, he developed a talent for rhetoric that made him one of the most prolific writers of his time—including the first deeply introspective autobiography, *Confessions*, which is how we know so much about his inner process.

While Augustine struggled internally with the clash of values within and around him, Monica prayed fervently that he would see the error of his Pagan ways and convert to Christianity. Her prayers were answered when, at age 30, Augustine encountered the writings of Plato and experienced the preaching of St. Ambrose. One day while meditating, he heard a child's voice inside his head that said repeatedly, "Take it and read, take it and read." He randomly opened the Bible to the following passage in Paul's epistle to the Romans:

> Not in reveling and drunkenness, not in lust and wantonness, not in quarrels and rivalries. Rather arm yourselves with the Lord Jesus Christ; spend no more thought on nature and nature's appetites. (Romans 13:13–14)

This passage spoke directly to Augustine's inner struggles. Here he found integration of his Manichaean roots, his Platonic aspirations, and his spiritual longing. He could at last make peace with his suffering mother, who promptly found him a suitable marriage and sent his concubine back to Carthage. His fiancée was only 10 years old at the time, and a year later he broke off the unconsummated engagement. Though his heart still suffered from the separation from his concubine, he chose to follow Christ and lead a celibate life—or at least he tried.[50]

But old habits die hard; his sexual passions did not succumb to his will, and he quickly took up with another concubine. He was unable to control his desire, a major subject of his *Confessions*. Because he could not *will* his desire away (his phallus rose and fell without his conscious control), he concluded that free will was something that the original Adam may have possessed but he himself did not.[51] In fact, even having sexual desire was to Augustine proof of original sin. Extrapolating from his own experience, he decried that humanity was enslaved to sin. Through long and tortuous reasoning, he came to believe that the original sin of Adam's copulation with Eve was passed down through the generations in the substance of semen. Therefore, all descendants of Adam—meaning everyone, Pagans, Christians, and Jews alike—were guilty of original sin from the moment of conception, having been contaminated by this vicious substance for the whole of their lives. Beginning life in sin, and stripped of the free will to do anything about it, humans couldn't do anything *but* sin. Elaine Pagels, in *Adam, Eve, and the Serpent* states,

> Augustine believed that by defining spontaneous sexual desire as the proof and penalty of original sin, he has succeeded in implicating the whole human race, except, of course, for Christ. Christ alone of all humankind, Augustine explains, was born without libido—being born, he believes, without the intervention of semen that transmits its effects. But the rest of humankind issues from a procreative process that, ever since Adam, has sprung wildly out of control, marring the whole of human nature.[52]

Augustine further declared that Adam and Eve's sexual desire—and all the trouble it caused—was the result of their disobedience to God. Therefore, obedience to church and imperial authority alike was the only way to counter this sin, as a sign of obedience to God himself. He believed that the dictatorial authority of the church was the only force that could liberate men from their evil nature and was therefore necessary for governing a peaceful state. As time passed, Augustine became increasingly authoritarian. He supported the institution of fines and penalties, the denial of free discussion, and the use of physical coercion to maintain order. Giving up his sexuality seems to have made Augustine a very rigid man. Ever since Augustine, original sin has been the official doctrine of the Catholic Church.[53]

One might wonder why the people of the fourth and fifth centuries would accept such convoluted reasoning. The answer, Pagels argues, is that espousing the belief that people were incapable of self-control and therefore of self-government was highly advantageous to the command of imperial authority. Augustine's beliefs made it a religious duty to submit to imperial rule. This was a convenient philosophy for the few who wanted to rule the many. Church and state, utterly intertwined, need not separate their authority. Pagels explains:

> Augustine's theological legacy made sense out of a situation in which church and state had become inextricably interdependent.[54]

Free will—the contentiously complex element of the third chakra—was now culturally and scripturally suppressed. Without free will, there was no spark, no fire, and no evolution. Sexuality, passion, and the pageantry of the old rituals were now defined as sins. Innate sexual desire, and even the emotions of longing for connection with another, were traits to be chastised as people were asked to be chaste. Intimacy between men and women went into further decline, widening their separation. With this loss of passion came a loss of heart.

Augustine was a complex character whose writings reflected the battle between power and love. Like Jesus, he believed that love existed to help the poor and needy, and that love of God was humanity's highest ideal. Yet he was caught in the power paradigm of the Roman Empire at a time when Christianity was gaining a foothold and desperately needed the continued support of the government. While history is always a complex weaving of many people, deeds, and events, it is perhaps here that some of humanity's heart-chakra development became arrested. Denial of our basic urges put us at war with our innate nature. Further separation between men and women did not foster empathy or caring. Jesus's original message of love and spiritual enlightenment became mired in the imperial struggle to maintain order and consistency throughout a bloated empire held together by rigid control.

Despite six centuries of internal peace, power, and prosperity—as well as its assertion of holding the high moral ground—the Western Roman Empire fell into political and moral corruption and collapsed. The factors deemed responsible, we might note, are all present in various forms today: rapacious expansion, ambitious generals, barbarian incursions (read terrorism), power struggles between church and state, sustained inflation, moral decay, and epidemic disease. With the fall of the Western Roman Empire at the end of the fourth century, its people were plunged into turmoil. Like traumatized children desperately trying to survive difficult times by pleasing an authoritarian father, Western civilization entered the ensuing Dark Ages wearing a straitjacket of moral restrictions lashed to the psyche with fear. The period that followed was a dark and depressive spiritual wasteland.

SHEDDING LIGHT ON THE SHADOW

The Dark Ages

> One does not become enlightened by imagining
> figures of light, but by making the darkness conscious.
> —C. G. Jung

With passion and free will diminished, the Western world entered a dark time. The archetypal mother long forgotten, we were left with a stern father whose countenance grew ever stricter as he single-parented humanity through its formative centuries of childhood. Social order was based on unquestioning obedience, with error punishable by death, damnation, or torture. Death, as a means of control, grew ever more menacing. Bishop Clement of Rome, as early as the first century CE, stated that whoever disobeyed the divinely ordained authorities had disobeyed God himself and should receive the death penalty.[55]

Under this kind of severity, social morale was greatly subdued. Religious experience was no longer direct, as Jesus had suggested, but occurred through mediating priests, who doled out blessings in exchange for supporting their massive hierarchy. The Father's rules were written in books that became law, though only the elite had access to these books. Morals and ethics were dictated by those who lived celibate lives in stone monasteries, removed from daily life and familial love. These codes had less to do with the establishment of a sane and egalitarian society than with strict adherence to the Static Masculine values of the day. Suffering was viewed as just punishment for sins.

All that had been rejected in the Great Reversal that overthrew the Static Feminine—the body, sexuality, passion, pleasure—was relegated to the shadow. The divine earth was seen as a material trap. The Great Mother and her wide pantheon of nature deities were obliterated from memory: statues, temples, and artwork were destroyed. Christian churches were erected on Pagan holy sites and superimposed the new order. Rituals to the Goddess were declared heresy. The Divine Feminine archetype was sent deeper into the Underworld, along with emotions and free will. Repressed feelings were shoved into the shadow and denied, not to fully resurface until the early 20th century, on the psychoanalytic couches of Freud and Jung.

The old mythology of a divine order based on nature was replaced by a new belief: that Christianity had lifted society from an archaic primitivism, and that warfare, hierarchy, and male domination had always existed and were therefore natural, even part of God's plan. Where the old gods had held properties of dark and light within a single archetype, the Christian God was seen as completely pure. Shadow aspects were projected outward, onto nature, women, and heretics—and inward, against one's instinctual drives. The physical world, once a divine, magical creation, was now the province of the devil, an archetypal repository for all that was rejected. A righteous spiritual path was marked by disengagement from the physical world—an impossible task, since we are, in fact, mortal creatures.

The divine realm was now otherworldly, accessed through disengagement, asceticism, or death itself, which would hopefully lead to a heavenly afterlife. People drew inward toward the daunting task of managing their inner world, shaped by the decree of priests and the certainty of scripture. The exuberant spirit that had sparked the spread of early Christianity became mired in judgment, dogmatism, and resignation.

Yet we were willing to sell our souls for this stability, along with its promise of salvation. It even carried a sense of grandeur, as we learned how to build taller and higher, with elaborately arched cathedrals drawing our attention upward. They stood in stark contrast to the humble, dirt-floor hovels in which the common people lived. Religious services provided comfort and safety in dark times, with angelic choral singing and the most elaborate works of art to be found. With Gothic arches, stained glass windows, and sculptures and paintings depicting celestial scenes of cherubic angels adorning the haloed figures of biblical myth, Christianity continued to spread, offering a strange mixture of oppression and inspiration.

The Middle Ages and the Crusades

Deus lo volt!
—Battle cry of the Crusades

As the exquisite cathedrals rose up from the ground of the Middle Ages, so did their cost. The church had to amass wealth in order to maintain its elaborate hegemony. Church properties were free of taxes and composed up to a third of the territory of Western Europe, with vast estates that produced abundant income.[56] Imperial rulers made contributions, much as special-interest groups do today. People could obtain forgiveness for their sins simply by giving money to the church (a process called *selling indulgences*). The wealthy could buy eclesiastical offices—called *simony*—while the church confiscated the property of anyone deemed a *heretic,* a word that comes from the Greek *haeresis,* meaning "choice."

The pope's power was now unlimited. He could proffer land deals with entire countries and rule over kings. The pope could even declare war, as did Pope Urban II, who launched the First Crusade in 1095, when word had come to Rome that infidels in the East were preventing pilgrimages to Jerusalem, a practice that had been peaceful for hundreds of years. With a common enemy to rally against, the dispirited imperial powers came together with religious zeal. In a wide appeal to all of Christendom, Pope Urban II promised complete remission of sin to any who would join the Crusade and make the long and treacherous journey to the East.

The initial response was a passionate cry of *Deus lo volt!* ("God wills it!"). Crusaders took a public vow of military service, with resulting grants of indulgences and even land should they be lucky enough to return. Ostensibly intended to defend the Holy Land, the Crusades became a war against anyone who was not Christian, namely Muslims and Jews. Those who were attacked were astonished at the ferocity of the invaders. Entire villages of men, women, and children were slaughtered. A chronicler, Raymond of Aguilers, illustrates the glorification of death in his description of a scene in Jerusalem as it fell in 1099:

> Wonderful things were to be seen. Numbers of the Saracens were beheaded. . . . Others were shot with arrows, or forced to jump from the towers; others were tortured for several days, then burned with flames. In the streets were seen piles of heads and hands and feet. One rode about everywhere amid the corpses of men and horses. In the temple of Solomon, the horses waded in blood up to their knees, nay, up to the bridle. It was a just and marvelous judgment of God, that this place should be filled with the blood of unbelievers.[57]

Had the world gone mad? Had we lost all moral ground? The Crusades, in various bursts, went on for approximately 200 years, killing hundreds of thousands of men, women, and children, all in the name of a supposedly moral God. What was the lasting value of this killing spree? Though it did increase the wealth of Italy, lands that were invaded were not permanently gained. Rather, the permanent effects were the heightening of animosity between Christians and Muslims, increased anti-Semitism, and a deepening of the schism between the Latin Christians of the West and the Greek Christians of the East.

Though the Middle Ages was a dark time, a long, slow process of awakening was occurring. Through increased literacy, people were learning and questioning the absolute authority of the Catholic Church. Yet each heresy or revolt only increased the punitive authoritarianism of the papal hierarchy.

In 1231, this exceeded all previous limits with the establishment of the Papal Inquisition by Pope Gregory IX. Formed as a separate tribunal, independent of bishops and prelates, it was a totalitarian regime. From village to village the inquisitors roamed, with their black robes and cowls, their stern faces, and their terrifying power. Unsuspecting peasants, mostly women, were captured without notice, removed from their homes, and confined in rat-infested prisons whose cost was exacted from their families. The accused had no recourse to defend themselves. Often they never even knew the identity of their accusers or the nature of their crime. Yet they were brutally tortured until they confessed to heresy or condemned another. It was a miserable choice: humiliating public penance and possible life imprisonment for those who repented, or death by hanging or burning for those who would not.

Though whole villages were massacred during the Crusades, the Inquisition was pointedly focused on cruelty. It was a movement not just of conquest but of pure sadism. Steven Pinker, in *The Better Angels of Our Nature: Why Violence Has Declined*, minces no words in his description:

> Medieval Christendom was a culture of cruelty. Torture was meted out by national and local governments throughout the Continent, and it was codified in laws that prescribed blinding, branding, amputation of hands,

ears, noses, and tongues, and other forms of mutilation as punishments for minor crimes. Executions were orgies of sadism, climaxing with ordeals of prolonged killing, such as burning at the stake, breaking on the wheel, pulling apart by horses, impalement, disembowelment, hanging . . .[58]

The rest is too gruesome to mention.

The Inquisition was also highly lucrative. The Church amassed wealth as it systematically confiscated the property of the victims. Inquisitors required local communities to pay for their trials, and they took bribes from the upper classes in exchange for protection. The result was a culturally instilled terror that repressed the urge to speak or even think creatively. This instilled a fearful mistrust of one's own community.

Why would anyone agree to participate in such atrocities? In the dualistic view of the times, anyone not joining the vengeance of the righteous was guilty of heresy. Defending friends or family could bring death. Priests who objected could be tied to the stake if they refused to participate in the grisly atrocities. Neighbor was pitted against neighbor, child against parent.

As fear prevailed, resentment toward the Church went underground, silent and festering, while religiosity dominated all facets of society. Only the truly faithful were safe, so intelligent people retreated into monasteries, withdrawing from everyday life. As if this were not enough to subdue the human spirit, the spread of the Black Death that began in 1348 cut across all classes, striking the pious as well as the commoner. The Church seized upon the plague as a demonstration of God's punishment for people's sins—not its own, of course—and used it as further proof of the need to obey Church authority. As medicines proved useless to stop the plague, the practice of medicine became suspect as well, including herbcraft and midwifery, often the domain of women. Instead, the evil within was believed to be purged through bleeding, a barbaric practice that killed tens of thousands each year.[59]

A Break in the Clouds:
The Italian Renaissance

There are three classes of people: those who see; those who see when they are shown; those who do not see.
—Leonardo da Vinci

It is amazing that out of this cultural depravity, with all its suppression of wisdom, compassion, and creativity, there could even be a Renaissance, yet the human spirit continually transcends its circumstances. During a time riddled with pestilence, economic depression, and ignorance arose a miraculous rebirth of intellectual discovery, creative expression, and spiritual exuberance, unparalleled since the Axial Age of the Greeks. If we have any doubts today about rebirthing humanity into our next era, we need only look to the Renaissance for inspiration. Here's a brief summary of the factors that led to this awakening.

In the early 14th century, while the southern city of Rome was declining as the center of commerce, cities in northern Italy were busy intersections of trade routes for spices, dyes, and silks from the East, and wool, wheat, and precious metals from the North. Extensive imports of food and goods shifted wealth to the cities, breaking the hold of the feudal system, ruled by the landed nobility. Similar to the polis, this new wealth allowed cities to be more independent, fostering a spirit of independence in general, with a new freedom to question the intellectual tyranny of medieval Christianity. Prosperity gave rise to a banking industry with Florence at its hub.

Paradoxically, the massive deaths that occurred from the Black Plague, which wiped out over a third of Europe's population, resulted in labor shortages, hence increased wages. As the plague passed, new births created new demand for services. Increased flow of money gave rise to a sophisticated banking system, with loans, stocks, and investment opportunities. In 1345, the king of England's inability to pay his debts (run up by the rising cost of his military) crashed the major banks of Florence. This left investors wondering what to invest in—and the result was a flow of money to the arts.

Francesco Petrarch (1304–1374), a poet with a passionate love for classical Greco-Roman texts, commenced a grand project for the reeducation of Europe. His romantic poetry heralded the ideal of an autonomous individual with an interior emotional life, giving new meaning and value to one's existence. Scholars uncovered texts from Greek antiquities previously forbidden in the suppression of Pagan works as heresy.

Petrarch is sometimes called the "father of humanism," an optimistic philosophy that saw humans as essentially good, rational, and sentient, with the ability to think for themselves—a sharp contrast to the Christian view of sinners in need of redemption. He believed that God had given humans their intellectual and creative gifts to be used to the fullest. We were no longer inconsequential pawns stripped of free will, but contributors to a society of our own making. He wrote poetry to an idealized feminine in the figure of Laura, which perhaps gave a sliver of room for feminine appreciation, though women were still subject to their husband's rule and expected to remain in the background. Some, however, worked alongside their husbands, and others found ways to educate themselves by becoming nuns or courtesans.

Another influx of ancient knowledge came from the Greek scholars who migrated to Italy as a result of attacks by the Ottomans in the eastern Byzantine Empire. Their influence helped found academies in Florence and Venice, bringing about a renewal of scholarship. The rediscovery of architecture, literature, painting, and sculpture from the past inspired Renaissance artists to reach for new heights of creativity. Guilds formed, and with them a politics of the people desiring more self-determination of their fate. The dawning of civic humanism fueled citizens with a pride and passion to create the most beautiful cities and sophisticated works of art. Leonardo da Vinci, Michelangelo, and Raphael produced their astounding works. Clothes became colorful, music joyful. Passion for life found new forms of expression.

Unprecedented accomplishments launched the first shoots of modernism into the world. The printing press, patented by Gutenberg in 1454, spread literacy and education, feeding a long-latent hunger for learning. The magnetic compass enabled easier navigation and travel. Columbus discovered the New World in 1492, expanding our horizons. Mechanical clocks now allowed society to coordinate itself more precisely and gave rise to new models of mechanics. The suggestion that the Earth revolved around the sun turned the geocentric theory of Ptolemy on its head, undermining the credibility of Church doctrine. Leonardo da Vinci bridged science and art. Shakespeare penned his famous tragedies and comedies. Music combined multimodal harmonies, as life itself found a distinct new coherence of independent cities living in peace and prosperity with each other.

Cultural Fifth Chakra: The Rise of Literacy

Art is literacy of the heart.
—Elliott Eisner

Despite humanity's arrested development in the heart chakra, and even regression to third-chakra tyranny, the Renaissance can be seen as the start of a cultural fifth, or throat, chakra, oriented toward self-expression, communication, and creativity. The advent of the printing press enabled collective communication as never before, with the slow spread of literacy, albeit through the upper classes. The printing press made the Bible widely available. Parents sat in on their children's lessons, learning how to read. Questions were asked, opening new inquiries into the order of things. Printed books that were identical made it possible for a body of knowledge to be stabilized, built upon, discussed, and explored, much as the Greeks had in their polis through conversation. But the printed word allowed ideas to spread more widely across the land, translated into different languages, founding academies of study.

Once a child masters reading in early elementary school, prodigious learning occurs through the realm of communication. In individual development, I have delineated this period as spanning approximately ages 7 to 12. Not that learning or communication ever cease, but this age opens to a wide influx of information, expanding our understanding of the world. Young minds are sponges of curiosity, aptly able to incorporate new information, learn languages, and delight in discovery. Safety, security, and independence allow a freedom of thinking that fosters inquiry.

This can be a child's most creative period, if he has the necessary freedom and security to support his expression. Arts and crafts, playing an instrument, dancing, drama, writing, singing—these are activities of delight as a child develops her self-expression and creativity. Ideally, in this time of relative innocence, we have not yet developed the inner critic that constricts our confidence or the adult belief that the arts are frivolous expressions of childhood that interfere with making a sensible living.

The burst of creativity in the Renaissance, along with the invention of the printing press, heralds a further step into our cultural fifth chakra. Not that we had left behind third-chakra dynamics by any means, nor had we completed our fourth-chakra development. Instead, humanity moved forward in its capacity for communication, knowledge, and wisdom, even as other aspects of our development lagged behind.

While the Greeks may have been the first Western society to question and self-reflect, the Renaissance of the 15th century was perhaps the first *self-conscious* period in history, meaning that people recognized and named the changes they were experiencing *while it was happening*. It came to birth within a span of 30 years, spawned by perhaps a thousand people, with none of the technologies we take for granted today. If we compare the accomplishments of the Middle Ages with those of the Renaissance, and then compare these with the innovations of our own time, where we have telephones, radio, television, computers, and the Internet, we realize that we are once again at an unprecedented horizon of possibilities.

Unfortunately, the Italian Renaissance was short-lived. Even while lavishly exploding with great works of art, the Catholic Church played a dual role of both benefactor and oppressor, gradually kindling a collective resentment into a smoldering fire. While the average citizen was waking up, both intellectually and spiritually, the Roman papacy was reaching new depths of corruption. Italian states surrounding Rome became mired in political battles in which greed, murder, and duplicity exceeded all reason. Pope Sixtus IV, for example, appointed relatives with no religious training, even children, as bishops and cardinals, giving them huge sums of money, which they spent on lavish lifestyles. As successive popes squandered the Church's massive wealth, they exacted more and more funds from the peasants, through taxes and the sale of indulgences. One could even pay ahead for sins not yet committed, or pay for the deeds of deceased relatives to release them from purgatory. Such out-of-control recklessness was bound to create a backlash.

Social Protest:
The Protestant Reformation

Faith must trample under foot all reason, sense, and understanding.
—Martin Luther

While the Catholic hierarchy in Rome was falling further from grace, religiosity continued to grow in Northern Europe and elsewhere in Christendom. In the harsher climate of the North, piety and poverty lived in stark contrast to the opulence in Rome. When at high noon on October 31, 1517, a monk by the name of Martin Luther posted his "Ninety-five Theses" on the door of a German church, the smoldering resentment toward Catholicism flared into the blazing fire of the Protestant Reformation. Luther's refutations of papal indulgences and many other corrupt practices were the spark of the "protest" after which the Protestant Reformation was named. Within just a few decades, these reformers broke the thousand-year rule of the Roman Catholic Church as the only religious authority. This "protestation" spread throughout Europe and marked the beginning of the rebellion against the Father—as it was perhaps the first hint of our budding adolescence.

Protestantism was a movement that shifted the locus of power from church to state and from priest to layman. It opened the way for new ideas and empowered the individual. It sought to rectify the Christian mission through a return to Christianity's original values as stated in scripture. Yet it painted over the colorful joy of the Renaissance with a very dark brush. In contrast to the excesses of Catholicism, Protestants took on a religious severity.

Unlike the Catholic Church, with its ostentatious cathedrals and elaborate rituals, Protestantism was simple: it relied on faith, grace, and scripture alone. Luther believed that the individual should be able to connect directly with God, without having to deal with a priest or the Catholic Church, which he felt had strayed too far from Christ's original message. Therefore, scripture was the way to restore sanctity to the Christian lifestyle. Like Augustine, Luther believed that humans were doomed to sin. He did not believe that sins could be bought off with indulgences or even "worked off" by good behavior; they could be redeemed only through God's grace as revealed in the Bible. Sins were merely a symptom of a deeper malady, which only faith could cure. Initially, he deplored the acts of the Inquisition and the rampant racism against Jews, Turks, and Moors, but it wasn't long before the Protestants came to commit equally heartless crimes against humanity.

Since Luther's interpretation of scripture did not accord divinity to Mother Mary, he discouraged her worship and banned mother-son images of Mary and Jesus. The apostle Paul saw women as the weaker vessel and stated in 1 Timothy 2:11, "Let a woman learn in silence with all submissiveness." As declared in the works of Paul, Augustine, Tertullian, and Luther, the blame for sexual desire landed squarely on woman as the devil's gateway. In the second century, Father Tertullian wrote, "Women are the gate by which the demon enters . . . it is on your account that Jesus died."[60] In the sixth century, the Council of Macon took a vote as to whether women even had souls.[61] Thomas Aquinas, whose 13th-century philosophy valued nature as the perfection of the divine, left women entirely out of the equation. He said, "Nothing defective should have been produced in the first establishment of things; so woman ought not to have been produced."[62] And in the very town of Wittenberg, where Luther first tacked up his 95 refutations, there was debate over whether women were even human beings.[63]

While the Catholic Church had forbidden priests to marry—some say to keep property from descending to potential heirs—Luther reversed that practice and eventually married and raised six children, some of them girls. Nonetheless, he said, "Take women from their housewifery and they are good for nothing. . . . If women get tired and die of childbearing, there is no harm in that; let them die as long as they bear; they are made for that."[64]

When Pope Leo X issued a papal bull for Luther to withdraw his protestations, Luther simply burned it. The Catholics responded in a variety of ways, some positive, some negative. The Jesuits, an elite priestly order, stepped up the education of the young, founding hundreds of educational institutions throughout Europe. Yet more bloody wars ensued. Civil wars between Catholics and Protestants took the lives of hundreds of thousands, as a religion divided against itself killed over disputes in interpretation of scripture and the sources of spiritual authority. These battles were as bloody as the Crusades. In France, on St. Bartholomew's Day (August 24), 1572, as many as 10,000 Protestants were slain.[65] Seventeen years after Luther nailed his objections to the church door, the Catholic Church had lost England, Denmark, Scotland, Sweden, Switzerland, and half of Germany to Protestantism.

Each side entered an ever more aggressive competition for religious certainty. The Protestants reacted by adhering even more strictly to scripture, with increased judgment for any deviant behavior. Protestant mobs destroyed images and statues of Christian saints, much as the Catholic Church had destroyed Pagan art throughout the Roman Empire 1,200 years earlier. Protestant sects fragmented, and each argued that its interpretation of scripture was the right one.

As the shadow aspects of human consciousness descended even deeper into the unconscious, the belief that humans were inherently flawed hardened into the bedrock of assumptions. Jesus's message of love and glory on earth was obscured, while the emphasis on his suffering and sacrifice was augmented. Both Catholics and Protestants became even more severe in their rejection of the physical body and sexuality, to the point where in some cases, even bathing was regarded as a sin. A Sorbonne prior and doctor wrote,

> You must regard every kind of touching of your own and others' bodies, every liberty, as the most serious of sins; although these lewd acts may indeed be secret, they are loathsome in God's sight, who sees them all, is offended by them, and never fails to punish them most severely.[66]

Skin itself was considered a spiritual liability. Clerics decreed that the female body was to be covered in dark clothing at all times. Home furnishings became austere. Pleasure of all types was frowned upon, even public celebrations, theatrical productions, and the simple activities of children, such as swimming or sledding.

The God of love that had fueled Christian passion in the early days of the Jesus movement had become a God of fear. Luther proclaimed,

> This is the acme of faith, to believe that God, Who saves so few and condemns so many, is merciful. . . . He seems to delight in the tortures of the wretched, and to be more deserving of hatred than of love. If by any effort of reason I could conceive how God, who shows so much anger and iniquity, could be merciful and just, there would be no need of faith.[67]

It didn't get any better with Luther's successor John Calvin, a Frenchman, whose mother had died during his infancy. Like Luther, Calvin believed that humans were a sorry, sinful lot, with women at the bottom of the heap. He ordered church elders to spy on families and denounced all dancing, singing, playing cards, and boisterous behavior. Sex before marriage was punishable by death. Even his own stepson and daughter-in-law were executed, along with their lovers. Any single woman found pregnant was instantly drowned. Even a child was beheaded for striking his parents.[68] Since Luther had proved that print was such a powerful medium, Calvin's regime controlled the press, with any criticism punishable by death.

Meanwhile, as the Italian Renaissance came to an end, the Spanish Inquisition, which had begun in 1481, continued to torture and murder thousands of victims. By 1570 it had established independent tribunals as far away as Peru, Mexico, and Goa, India.[69] But punishment for mere heresy wasn't enough to demonstrate religious purity. In Spain, King Ferdinand and Queen Isabella launched a vicious campaign forcing first Jews and then Muslims into exile, killing thousands of those who resisted. Pope Innocent VIII declared in 1484 that witchcraft was a central threat to the Christian world. He commissioned a manual for eradicating witches, called the *Malleus Maleficarum*.[70] Aided by the invention of the printing press, this heinous torture manual spread rapidly throughout Europe, fueling an epidemic of insanity whose cruelty knew no bounds. Estimates of people—mostly women—who were tortured, hanged, or burned vary from 30,000 to possibly hundreds of thousands.

If this was not enough to turn the Great Mother into a wild beast, Christianity changed the ancient horned and goat-footed god, Pan, who had been a symbol of the life force in nature, into an image of the devil. The devil was equated with everything that was opposite to Christianity. He was believed to work his evil by reversing all values and supposedly could be summoned by saying the Lord's Prayer backward. Worshippers of the devil were said to fly or stand on their heads. Women, in particular, were accused of cavorting with the devil. Under pain of torture, they even fabricated confessions to that effect, supporting the delusion. All that was magical, mythical, or connected with nature was associated with witchcraft, until it became a heresy *not* to believe in the evil deeds and presence of witches.

As religion took on the exacting task of subjecting divine spirit to the rigor of the written word through the Bible, the newly emerging scientific community was about to make provable discoveries that contradicted the word of the Church. Soon the worlds of matter and spirit would take another step away from each other, during the Enlightenment period of the 17th and 18th centuries.

FROM FAITH TO REASON

The Enlightenment

 It is surely harmful to souls to make it a
heresy to believe what is proved.
—*Galileo Galilei*

We have seen how Christianity was a heart-based teaching born in
the soil of a paradigm still organized by third-chakra power-over
principles. Christ's seeds of compassion, acceptance, forgiveness,
and love were carried on the winds of a patriarchal mind-set that
demonized nature, sexuality, the body, and women. The brief
awakening of the Renaissance set the stage for new possibilities
by warming the intellectual climate through the rise of literacy
and a renewed spirit of independence from Church authority. New
intellectual inquiry made possible the next flowering of humanity.

As cultural children, we were growing up. We were properly
socialized and knew how to behave. We played our roles dutifully.
With our passions somewhat tamed, life proceeded more predictably.
We were ready for the next leap forward. For the first time since
the invention of writing, some 2,500 years earlier, the printing press
eventually enabled the spread of literacy to more of the population.
While literacy was unevenly distributed toward the upper classes, it
was slowly trickling down to the masses, bringing new possibilities
for knowledge. Though estimates vary widely, about half of the men

and a quarter of the women could read and write by the end of the 18th century. Like children moving from elementary to middle school, we were able, by mastering the basic arts of writing and arithmetic, to explore the vast territories that these skills made possible.

It was out of this climate that the shoots of the Scientific Revolution began to sprout. At the height of the witch burnings—an irrational collective psychosis if ever there was one—science offered a sane alternative: rational, empirical study. With Christianity monopolizing the realm of spirit, the world of matter lay rejected—evil to some, inconsequential at best. Not only was the Divine Mother stripped of her divinity; she was all but forgotten. This gave us enough separation from nature to regard her objectively, to examine matter as an inanimate thing, devoid of spirit.

The Sky Father had long ago replaced Earth Mother as the central deity. As if in parallel, Copernicus suggested that the Earth was not the stationary center of the cosmos but actually orbited the sun—a revolutionary idea in every sense of the word. From his first realization of this fact, in 1514 at the height of the Renaissance, it would still be 20 years before he dared share it with the pope, who initially approved. Still, Copernicus waited until the end of his life to go public with his theory, holding his printed manuscript for the first time just one day before he died in 1543.[71] His ideas, however, did not die, but continued to push against the vehement repression of scientific reason.

Copernicus was not alone in his heliocentric belief, nor was he the only one to fear persecution. Half a century later, in 1600, Giordano Bruno was burned at the stake for his heretical ideas, among which was daring to agree with Copernicus. But truth cannot be hidden forever. When Galileo's telescope provided visual proof, 10 years after that, it would seem that the proper order of the heavens was obvious. Yet even Galileo, who enjoyed great respect for his scientific observations and mathematical scholarship, faced persecution for his findings. At the ripe age of 70, while in poor health, he was abducted from his home, taken to Rome, and forced to recant his views before a Catholic tribunal. In an attempt to keep his views quiet, he was confined to house arrest for the last eight years of his life. His *Dialogue Concerning the Two Chief World Systems* (1632) remained on the Church's Index of Prohibited Books as late as 1835.[72]

When Johannes Kepler published his laws of planetary motion in 1609, the idea of a mathematically sensible movement of heavenly bodies fell into place. Yet the Catholic hierarchy chose to support scripture instead. As time passed and the enlightened view of the solar system became more widely accepted, a dividing line was crossed. The church lost respect, and science gained it. Faith and fact diverged.

Yet the precision with which the heavenly bodies moved through the cosmos was seen by many as proof of God's perfection. How else could something be so exquisitely designed? As scientific explanations replaced mystery, God's role in influencing the present was diminished. God was now seen more as a distant father, a divine architect, who had designed the universe and then abandoned the kids to raise themselves. Divinity was no longer accessible through faith or deeds; but like a carrot dangling before our eyes, it just might be found through scientific discovery. By cracking the codes of creation, we, too, could approach godhood. Excitement grew with each mystery solved. The world became rational, explainable, and potentially controllable. Discovering the secrets of matter held a glimmering possibility of finding new power. As science became the new religion, scientists became the new priests.

Among them was Francis Bacon, often touted as the founding father of modern science for his establishment of the "scientific method." In 1597, while other men of his time were torturing witches for their devilish secrets, Bacon suggested that the scientist needed to "torture nature's secrets from her."[73] Nature was a "she" who should be "constrained," made a "slave," and "forced out of her natural state" so that "human knowledge and human power meet as one."[74] In graphic sexual symbolism, Bacon wrote that nature's "holes and corners were to be entered and penetrated."[75] He described this new method of inquiry as a "masculine birth," one that would bring forth a blessed race of heroes and supermen. Man's role was to have dominion over the natural world, and scientific knowledge was the means. Bacon wrote of a technocratic utopia, ruled by a scientific priesthood that would make decisions for the good of the state.[76]

Now, philosophical inquiry examined either the realm of spirit—an invisible force that could be known only through faith or subjective experience—or the realm of matter—the visible, inanimate world, understandable through rational exploration and objective experience. It wasn't until René Descartes's revelation of *cogito ergo sum*, "I think, therefore I am," that science began to consider the *source* of our questioning—*consciousness itself*. Though sages of the East had been talking about consciousness for thousands of years, Descartes popularized the notion that a thinking "I" exists within each one of us as an indelible foundation of being.[77]

Doubt was the gateway from which Descartes's thinking emerged. He realized that if he'd been raised Muslim or Jewish, he might not have believed as a Christian, which raised doubt as to the ultimate truth of Christianity or any other worldview. Doubting everything he could possibly contemplate, he finally realized that the only thing of which he could be absolutely certain was that he possessed an aware, thinking consciousness that was capable of doubting. Even the body could be an illusion, he thought. Only the fact of his thinking was proof of his existence.

Descartes's ideas grew from the ground of a good Jesuit education, in which he was renowned for his brilliance in mathematics. The flower of his thought was that the universe and the human body operated mechanically. Consciousness was the ghost in the machine, much like the driver in a car today. *Mind and body were completely separate*. He wrote, "There is nothing included in the concept of body that belongs to the mind; and nothing in that of mind that belongs to the body."[78] Like Bacon, Descartes believed that the aim of science was the domination and control of nature—plants and animals being simply machines without soul or spirit. He promoted the notion that nature was a mechanical system whose language was mathematics, precise and logical.

Descartes considered this to be a divine revelation, one that could promise certainty in an uncertain world. Cartesian rationalism was needed to cool the fires of the witch burnings, for if spirit and matter were separate realms, then how could someone's magical thinking make the crops fail? As rationalism slowly replaced superstition, the human experiment took a giant step forward. The sprouts of reason were growing into a sturdy tree.

By the time Sir Isaac Newton's apple fell into this garden of rationality, science had congealed into a paradigm that concretized the Static Masculine separation of spirit from matter, heaven from earth, and mind from body. Gravity, not God, was now the force that moved the worlds. Newton's discoveries were hailed as the enlightened triumph of reason over medieval ignorance. Following Newton's publication of the *Principia* in 1687, the enlightened view was that the universe was made of material particles that moved according to mathematically predictable laws and principles. It was a purely mechanical system. That which could *not* be seen or measured was given little, if any, importance. Though Newton had been a deeply religious man, his theories explained much that had been attributed to God and further divided science and religion. Newton's mechanistic view of nature dominated scientific inquiry for the next 300 years.

These ideas made fertile the garden of the Enlightenment. An explosion of understanding lifted us out of the Dark Ages of superstition, persecution, and church hegemony into a period bursting with information and understanding. It took power out of the heavens and brought it down to "man." Long-held mysteries were solved, with a promise of increasing freedom for all. Given the brutality of the Dark Ages, we can imagine the relief and appeal that such rationalism would have had.

Cultural Sixth Chakra

The only thing worse than being blind is having sight but no vision.
—*Helen Keller*

The sixth chakra, located in the brow area, is related to the element of light, the root word in *enlightenment*. Here, deep in the center of the head, where the pineal gland descends downward, lies what is known as the third eye, the center of wisdom, insight, intuition, and vision. The sixth chakra is the entryway into visionary consciousness—and indeed even the realization of the existence of one's own unique consciousness. Its Sanskrit name, *ajna,* means "to perceive and to command." It is here where the god Shiva shoots lightning bolts from his third eye, piercing ignorance.

Developmentally, this stage begins when we have gained enough knowledge through the learning and communication in our fifth chakra to assemble a larger picture of the world. Typically, this happens at adolescence, as young teens start to piece together their own worldview, questioning and rebelling against the assumptions of their elders. With this newfound ability to see and question, the role of parental authority is pushed to the background, while peer opinions become of utmost importance. Also at adolescence, the middle-childhood separation of the sexes starts to reverse, as the raging hormones of puberty awaken sexual desire and the opposite gender becomes more interesting. Prodigious energy abounds with this liberation. Certainty, based on a small amount of knowledge, is typical.

The Enlightenment period could be said to be the beginning of our cultural sixth chakra. It would still be some time before the invention of the light bulb in 1879 or the technology for photo images and motion pictures. But here was a period when we were beginning to see through the darkness. We were gaining information that made sense of the world, piecing it together to figure out who we were, what we were made of, and how things worked. Higher education abounded with universities and academies. Blessedly, deaths from wars, homicides, and violence in general markedly declined.[79]

Discovery of Evolution

It is not the strongest of the species that survives, nor the most intelligent that survives. It is the one that is most adaptable to change.
—*Charles Darwin*

While Descartes was the person most remembered in the West for acknowledging the interior dimension of consciousness, it was Charles Darwin who discovered the evolution of species and popularized the idea of biological evolution. In *The Origin of Species* (1859), he examined the way natural selection demonstrated an evolutionary process. To Darwin, evolution was driven by chance and necessity, rather than by external design on the part of a divine architect. Such a view further undermined the belief in God as the noble creator or controller. At the same time, the elite view of humans as the pinnacle of creation was deflated by the revelation that we were just another animal crawling our way up the food chain. The divine, within and without, took another step backward.

Darwin's theory of evolution by natural selection, however, was interpreted through the third-chakra dynamics of struggle and competition, leaving us with a legacy of the idea of "survival of the fittest." A closer reading of his texts reveals that he spoke far more often of such things as love and cooperation as important evolutionary forces, and that it was actually the philosopher Herbert Spencer who coined the term "survival of the fittest."[80] David Loye, a noted scientist and evolutionary theorist, did a word count on Darwin's 900-page original manuscript of *The Descent of Man* (his 1871 sequel to *The Origin of Species*) and discovered, to his amazement, that "survival of the fittest" occurred only twice in the entire text, and the second time was in an apology for exaggerating its importance![81] "Competition" was mentioned only 9 times, "selfishness" 12 times. By contrast, Darwin spoke of love, mind, and brain nearly 100 times each, with additional emphasis on consciousness, intellect, higher morality, and imagination. While Darwin's theory has been taught to school-age children the world round, his emphasis on love, conscience, and moral agency has been pointedly overlooked. The aggressive and dominating values of the time ignored these aspects of his theory for the following century.

Darwin's theory had far-reaching implications for the shaping of society. On the one hand, he dealt another blow to biblical authority by suggesting (as geologists had done previously) that the Earth was indeed far older than had previously been imagined—far too old and complex to have been created in merely six days, or even thousands of years. He also demonstrated the paradox that dynamic change was the enduring principle of creation, challenging the previous view of a fixed and unchanging reality. Despite ample proof, his theory of evolution by natural selection was still banned as late as 1951 by the Catholics and 1967 by some Protestants.[82] The right to teach the science of evolution in our school systems continues to be hotly challenged by some Christian conservatives.

Secondly, the idea of natural selection through competition contributed to an egocentricity that gave every man permission to serve himself above all others. Otto Amman, in 1911, said, "Bravery, cunning and competition are virtues. Darwin must become the new religion of Germany,"[83] a view that contributed to the rise of Nazism. In the United States, William Graham Sumner, a political and social science professor at Yale, claimed, "Millionaires are a product of natural selection. Let it be understood that we cannot go outside this alternative: liberty, inequality, survival of the fittest, not liberty, equality, survival of the unfittest."[84] This attitude can still be seen in economic debates today.

Yet the benefits of this period were many. The fruits of the

Enlightenment gave us not only rational understanding but also a cascade of inventions and discoveries that liberated us from the rigors of survival. It loosened the powers of aristocracy and paved the way for the rights and freedoms of democracy, or what Ken Wilber has called the "dignities of modernity."[85] Through the microscope we discovered bacteria and learned to use sanitation to prevent disease. Along with better nutrition, this discovery increased the human life span. The Industrial Revolution (1760–1840) created machines to extend the power of the body and reduce our dependence on servants and slaves. With great reluctance, the captains of industry distributed more income to the average man, enlarging the middle class. Power was slowly trickling down from God and dominant hierarchies to ordinary individuals.

By the time the engines of the Industrial Revolution began spewing carbon into the air, the mechanical worldview was mechanizing our lives, using machines to fertilize the fields, pave the roads, harvest the forests, and make more machinery. Technology exponentially expanded our powers, enabling us to do more with less. Poverty could be addressed by mass production of goods that created jobs and lowered prices. Traveling, trading, manufacturing, and distributing all became easier, bringing more autonomy to individuals and families while widening our access to the world.

The wheel of progress picked up speed. The promise of a better life made by religion was seemingly delivered by industrialism. The standard of living for most of the Western world rose dramatically in the latter half of the 19th century. No longer did the common people live in dirt hovels. Food and goods were distributed far and wide. We could travel by rail and see more of the world. We may have had to slave away in a factory to pay for our homes, but ownership allowed more autonomy and more privacy from each other. We continually sought to improve our private world with furnishings. A previously missing but essential element of the third chakra began to develop— *the sovereignty of the individual.*

Increasing Individualism

The high destiny of the individual is to serve rather than to rule.
—*Albert Einstein*

Today, we take for granted the idea that each person is an individual, but this was not always so. If we backtrack to Hellenic Greece, we remember that a person who kept to himself and did not participate in the democracy of the *polis* was called an *idiotes*. Jeremy Rifkin, in *Biosphere Politics: A New Consciousness for a New Century*, describes how individualism was not well developed even in the Middle Ages, when a man who wandered by himself was considered effeminate at best, or, more often, insane and ridiculed. Communal living at that time was the norm, with extended families, servants, and even animals sharing a single dwelling. Those with less means lived in one-room houses, where three generations might sleep in one bed. As the economics of communal living shifted toward paychecks for individual workers, privacy became a privilege of wealth and a new ideal to attain.

The walls that first defended our cities in ancient times, and then enclosed us in great halls in the Middle Ages, now divided us even further as we enclosed ourselves in private homes and bedrooms. Rifkin goes on to describe how the increasing privatization led to shame.[86] The Protestants had put an end to public baths, and bodily functions were now hidden from view. Sex, bathing, elimination, and sleeping became more private affairs.

With a mechanical worldview, a social world walled off from nature, and an increasingly impersonal universe, it's no surprise that by 1888, Nietzsche could make the fateful proclamation that "God is dead." Faith in the church had waned; spirituality was at an all-time low; the world was deemed lifeless and mechanical. The Goddess had long been forgotten. We had become spiritual orphans, lost from our mythic ground, abandoned by both Mother and Father, hungry for a new spiritual home.

The Divorce of Matter and Spirit

Matter is spirit moving slowly enough to be seen.
—*Pierre Teilhard de Chardin*

The worldview of scientific materialism, which reached its peak in the 19th century, asserted that only matter and energy were real. Consciousness, spirit, soul, and all nonphysical qualities were omitted from legitimate study because they could not be objectively measured. Objectivity became more important than subjectivity. The world was regarded as an "it" to be manipulated and used for our purposes. Ironically, materialism harks back to our original thesis, of matter as the primal ground, the basic matrix; even the word itself derives from *mater*, or "mother."

Yet, in veiled form, the Divine Feminine realm was beginning to return. In 1854, the Catholic Church decided that Mary, like her son, Jesus, was a product of immaculate conception. Since original sin was passed through semen (remember Augustine?), Mary was declared free of sin and could therefore be worshipped.[87]

As the trauma of the Inquisition retreated into the past, women felt safer to express their opinions. The first shoots of feminism began to sprout. In 1848, the first women's convention was held at Seneca Falls, New York, inspired by the rejection of women delegates to an anti-slavery convention in London. With little promotion and only a few days' planning, 300 women and 40 men drew up a "Declaration of Sentiments" in which they listed 18 "injuries and usurpations." In 1869, John Stuart Mill called upon men to end "the legal subordination of one sex by another."[88] Three years later, Susan B. Anthony pulled the lever in a voting booth, believing that she would survive her subsequent arrest on the grounds that she met the Fourteenth Amendment's qualification for "person." (She lost her case.) It wouldn't be until much later, in 1920, that women in the United States would finally win the right to vote, nearly 2,500 years after the first democracy in Greece. Only one woman from the Seneca Falls conference would live long enough to cast her vote.

As we made our way through the 19th century, the repressed aspects of nature, passion, creativity, began poking up from the ground again. As the feminine gained power and began to grow up from its daughter status, masculine and feminine *values* started to dance with each other again, even if equality between the sexes was scarcely addressed. Thinkers of the time were divided into two camps: those who modeled reality with objective, masculine logic, who followed earlier thinkers like Kant, Hume, and Locke; and the Romantics, who reveled in nature and the more feminine aspects of beauty and subjectivity (such as Rousseau, Goethe, and the poets Byron, Keats, Shelley, and Blake). Whereas the scientists saw the world of nature as devoid of spirit, the Romantics experienced nature as infused with spirit. While scientists measured and recorded all aspects of the outer world, the Romantics turned their attention to the inner world. The scientific community believed in a modern, technology-driven future, but the Romantics resisted modernity, fearing its estrangement from nature, and valued simpler principles. Each stream had its own validity.

As these ideas oscillated between two philosophical poles, technology harnessed polarity in the form of electricity. Even though we had not yet fully awakened the heart chakra on a collective level, we were now advancing further into the fifth chakra with the first means of electronic communications. The telegraph, which began operation in 1844, was the first major leap in communication since the printing press nearly 400 years earlier. Alexander Graham Bell made the first electronic phone call in 1876, and within four years there were 54,000 customers in the network.[89] By 1901, we bridged the Atlantic by radio, and by 1920 we were playing records and going to the movies. Even as we were courting our individuality, the interconnected networks of communication were weaving a collective web, giving birth to new possibilities. The curve of discoveries was accelerating.

In our modern world, it's hard to imagine—save for an occasional power failure—the monumental triumph of the light bulb. Though we had means of transcending distance through travel and the telegraph, it wasn't until New Year's Day, 1879, that Thomas Edison engineered the first commercially viable light bulb. (He didn't like to sleep at night but only periodically catnapped.) Primordial darkness took a giant step backward as the world slowly became electrified and illuminated. The harnessing of electromagnetic forces had expanded the realms of the fifth chakra, enabling telegraph, telephone, and radio, and could now bring light to the sixth chakra with the invention of electric lighting, cameras, and motion pictures. Communication and images brought distant lands a little bit closer. With these tools, our world expanded.

It wasn't long before science moved from the examination of forces to the examination of relationships. After Einstein's special theory of relativity (1905), neither science nor the Bible could claim an absolute point of view. Energy was not separate from matter—they existed on a continuum as aspects of the same thing, its law described by Einstein's famous equation ($E = mc^2$).

With discoveries in quantum physics, we looked into smaller and smaller increments of matter and discovered that subatomic particles move backward and forward in time, joining space and time in yet another continuum. Certainty dissolved as we discovered that photons were both particles and waves, and material substance started to look more like empty space. The subjective domain was reintroduced into science, as we discovered that the observer influenced the experiment. Space and time appeared more relative than absolute. The Static Masculine worldview was losing its rigidity, no longer able to rely on predictability and certainty.

The Inner World

It is impossible to overlook the extent to which
civilization is built upon a renunciation of instinct.
—*Sigmund Freud*

Meanwhile, as the positive and negative poles of electricity illuminated our homes and ran our factories, the budding science of
psychology discovered the rejected pole of our psyche: the unconscious. While Freud wasn't the first to talk about the unconscious
(Romantics such as Goethe and Schiller had named the unconscious
as a source of creativity), he was the first to explore this mysterious
realm with rational analysis. If our selves had become divided, Freud
gave voice to these divisions and named them. The *id* represented our
repressed desires and emotions, and the *superego,* seen as its polar
opposite, represented our conscience and spiritual ideals. The ego
was the intermediary; its job was to manage the id, yet still face the
demands of external reality. In doing so, the ego both defined and
defended the self.

The discovery of the unconscious uncovered the repressed elements of the lower chakras: bodily instincts, sexual urges, and emotional traumas. They were contained by intricate walls erected within
our psyches, called *defenses*, much like the walls that had been erected
around cities for defense, so long ago. We found common patterns
in these psychological defenses and began to name them: repression,
denial, projection, reaction formation, sublimation, displacement,
regression, and dissociation. All were patterns by which the ego kept
unwelcome material out of awareness.

Though saddled with defenses, the ego was the leading element
of the psyche. Like a young shoot, it needed much coddling and
encouragement. Psychoanalysis gave it that attention. People began
to examine themselves and reflect on their behavior, motivations, and
fantasies—some would say to the point of excessive self-absorption.

Most important, people were awakening to a deeply interior "I." It became socially acceptable, even laudable, to make the most of that "I," not only to discover its motivations and feelings but to better oneself—to become rich, beautiful, accomplished, recognized, or admired—a privilege that had previously been limited to the elite. The ego was awakening among the masses.

With this awakening of the interior "I" in the early 20th century came a quest for individual rights. Workers joined unions to fight for their rights in the workplace. Slavery was addressed, viciously fought over, and finally abolished worldwide, at least legally, by 2007.[90] We began to see that all sorts of subclasses, previously ignored, needed protection of their rights. As we moved into the 1960s, this trend blossomed into movements for civil rights, women's rights, children's rights, gay rights, animal rights, and environmental rights. But these rights had not yet been coupled with responsibilities. They were a beginning but did not take us into maturity.

Could it be that one must first awaken the interior "I" to have a true understanding of "we"? Could it be that we need to be in touch with our own pain and inner defenses to understand the defenses of others and make compassionate contact? Could it be that we have to establish the ego—that is, find our own will, autonomy, and power—before we can voluntarily surrender its defenses to another? Here is perhaps one reason why third-chakra development precedes the fourth: we must find our autonomy and interior self before we can truly love.

Yet the ego, as we all know, can be its own trap. It, too, can be insatiable, inflating itself to godlike proportions in order to maintain its illusion of power and separateness. While we think it took prodigious effort to break the hold of the sleepy unconscious and escape the jaws of the primal Mother, we may find that it takes even greater strength to escape the constant demands of the ego. These demands consume both the psyche and our environment in quests for personal empires, larger houses, jewels, clothes, and a multibillion-dollar cosmetic and plastic surgery industry, to say nothing of the lust for money and power. The vanity of the ego can keep us isolated, alienated, encapsulated, and exhausted.

It was necessary to develop a healthy ego in order to transcend it. We needed to discover our own interior self to know that such a self existed in others. We had to find the power to determine our own lives before we could use that power in service of something larger. We needed to learn separation before we could fully create union. Strengthening the ego leads us toward awakening, yet it can also stand as a barrier. It is the vehicle that drives the journey, but if we never get out of the vehicle, we will never arrive at our destination.

Modernism's Light and Shadow

Where there is much light, the shadow is deep.
—*Johann Wolfgang von Goethe*

If we are going to balance polarities, we must embrace both our light and our shadow. Like every age, the modern era has generated both blessings and curses. We put an end to the witch burnings, but later dropped the atom bomb. We solved many of nature's mysteries, yet plundered her resources. We extended the human life span through medical advances, yet we created carcinogenic environments and spread diseases around the globe. We studied and categorized every conceivable life form, yet we are rendering many of them extinct. We raised the standard of living with electric lights, refrigerators, automobiles, telephones, stereos, radios, televisions, cameras, computers, cell phones, and countless other devices; yet the creation of these products pollutes the air, water, and earth while enslaving those who build them on factory assembly lines. We have created transportation that allows us to distribute goods and see the wonders of the world, yet the burning of fossil fuels is changing the climate.

The advances have been staggering. A little over 500 years ago, Europe had just discovered the Americas. Now we can fly to the moon and beyond, and see pictures of Earth hanging in space. Before the invention of the printing press, few people could read or even had access to books; now we have the Internet, a global network of easily accessible information. In the Middle Ages, thousands of people died from the practice of bleeding; now we can transplant hearts and reattach limbs. We've abolished slavery and instituted democracy in much of the world.

The trouble is, we have lost connection to our sacred ground along the way—the ground of the earth, our bodies, and our souls. We have transcended the limits of nature but lost the experience of her majesty. We have risen above superstition but have lost mythic meaning. We have gained privacy but lost community. Many live mechanical lives, out of touch with the inner world of feeling. We live for the moment at the cost of the future. Like adolescents, we have more power than wisdom. Our ability to differentiate from nature and our inner world has brought us to a cultural dissociation, or as Wilber puts it, the "disaster of modernity."[91]

It *is* still possible to address the disasters of modernity and harvest its dignities. The good news is that we can reclaim what we've lost without denying what we've gained—*if, and only if*, we face the adolescent challenge of stabilizing our adult size as a population, remediate our environment, and learn to grow spiritually instead of physically. The great thrust of progress that has brought us our physical infrastructure must now explore the frontiers of consciousness and find mature relationships through the heart.

We have experienced the organic stability of the Static Feminine, the dominating upheaval of the Dynamic Masculine, and the stabilizing rationality of the Static Masculine. The Great Mother with her son-lover has been matched by the Great Father and his daughter-wife. To reach adulthood and enter egalitarian relationships, each gender has had to emancipate itself from the parental projection that results in domination. The masculine rose up and overthrew the Great Mother long, long ago. But the liberation of the repressed feminine is still relatively new. There is one more archetypal pattern that needs to be embraced in order to integrate the full quaternity of these gender valences and reach the heart: the dance of the Dynamic Feminine.

13

SPIRALING INTO ECSTASY

The Dynamic Feminine Awakes

It would appear, as far as the divine is concerned, that we are opening rather than closing, inventing rather than devolving, experimenting and thrusting and whispering new secrets to the moon rather than quivering in the corner, afraid of our own divine shadows, slouching toward death, unaware that our cosmic shoes are untied.[92]
—*Mark Morford*

It wasn't the first earthquake to shake the streets of San Francisco, yet the Summer of Love in 1967 marked a social upheaval that shook the edifice of Static Masculine assumptions and sent ripples throughout the world. Some 100,000 hippies, or "flower children," as they were also called, gathered in the Haight-Ashbury neighborhood of San Francisco, proclaiming an ecstatic movement of peace, community, freedom, gender equality, and exploration of consciousness.

The Vietnam War was raging, and World War II, with its Holocaust and atomic bomb atrocities, was not far in the distance. Thanks to the Marshall Plan, Europe was recovering, while America had retreated into a kind of post-traumatic conservatism, with masculine dominance largely unquestioned. Capitalism was reaching its height, with the pursuit of happiness centered around material success and a stable, "Father Knows Best" kind of nuclear family.

As we progressed through the '60s, higher standards of living and an expanded middle class afforded a new kind of freedom. Movies, radio, and television were now everywhere, offering windows into the rest of the world. Along with ads for brighter detergent and cleaner floors, real-time visuals of the Vietnam War aired in the living rooms of America's neighborhoods, sparking outrage and awakening. A passionate peace movement arose, accompanied by electronic rock bands and enhanced at times by drug-induced expanded consciousness. These mind-blowing experiences had a way of poking through to the seventh or crown chakra, spawning a spiritual revolution, as people sought ways to reach these states of awareness without drugs. The Broadway musical *Hair* proclaimed it the dawning of the Aquarian Age, an age of "harmony and understanding, sympathy and trust abounding" when "peace will guide the planets and love will steer the stars."

As the flower children of the peace movement pushed blossoms into bayonets, police clamped down with their penchant for law and order. Tension between new and old paradigms sizzled once again. The hippie movement bloomed into its full adolescent expression, the philosophical distance between generations growing into an unbreachable chasm. Rebellion against the status quo became the hip thing, and long hair, beads, and bellbottoms were the uniform through which the peaceful revolutionaries could recognize each other. As in all revolutions, everything that was previously established became suspect—including anyone older than 30.

While the popular chant was "All we are saying is give peace a chance," the cry was for far more than that. The hypermasculine, scientific-materialist, military-industrial complex had reached its height of imbalance. The feminine, with its yin softness, colorful creativity, and love for community, was yearning to move out of subservience. Technology allowed ideas to be amplified, and this occurred through the many great songs of the era that protested the old and romanticized the new, from such artists as Pete Seeger to Grace Slick, the Beatles to the Grateful Dead.

Here was a flowering of humanity's heart chakra, burst from the seeds of the first Greek democracies, Buddha's message of compassion and contemplation, Jesus's teachings of love, now with many stems of a literate, educated, scientific, and technological populace that made this flowering possible. Here was a new discovery of the power of consciousness, one that questioned the existing collective assumptions as never before.

Like the Italian Renaissance, the '60s was a brief flowering that glimpsed an ideal possibility but did not sustain it. As quickly as it began, it was shut down by police crackdowns, media propaganda, and the inevitable burnout of a fledgling movement. Yet its values went underground, influencing everything from diet to public policy. These values were passed down to the next generation, who raised their children with philosophies of love, freedom, and egalitarian ideals. Those children are coming of age now. They are awake and aware, technologically savvy, hyperconnected, and facing a dying world ravaged by previous generations.

The Dynamic Feminine

The feminine values are the fountain of bliss.
Know the masculine. Keep to the feminine.
—Lao-tzu

We can now explore the fourth aspect of our gender dance in terms of masculine and feminine valences. After millennia of oppression, the Dynamic Feminine brings a much-needed balance to the preceding eras: to the grounding but limiting primal thesis of the Static Feminine, to the violent overthrow of that thesis by the Dynamic Masculine, then stabilized by the rigidity of the Static Masculine. The Dynamic Feminine alone is not the way of the future, but *when put together with the previous three valences*, we have a wholeness from which we can proceed to our maturity. Later we will look at how these four qualities complement each other. But first we must understand the nature of this arising feminine force.

Where the cross was the symbol of the Static Masculine—rigid and linear, logical and deterministic—the Dynamic Feminine is symbolized by a spiral. Moving out from the center or *heart* of the cross, the spiral breaks down the rigidity and separation of the arms of the cross, moving toward a circular, flowing expansion. But unlike the Static Feminine circle of containment, the spiral has no limits. It is not fixed, permanent, or repetitively cyclic, but nonlinear and ever expanding. In the words of Gareth Hill,

> The tendency of the Dynamic Feminine is undirected movement toward the new, the nonrational, the playful. It is the flow of experience, vital, spontaneous, open to the unexpected, yielding and responsive. . . . In its highest aspect, the Dynamic Feminine is the synthesizing creation of new possibilities and new combinations. It is the insight, awareness, gnosis, that comes only through actual experience. Its effects are the uplifting, ecstatic inspiration that comes from the experience of transformed awareness. Its central value is Eros, not in the image of the arrow shot from the bow of Amor, but that which is awakened by the arrow's piercing. Its attributes are participation and process.[93]

Those who are bringing the Dynamic Feminine to life are not just women, but males and females who seek ecstatic experience though connecting inner realms to outer community. *Ecstatic* means "ex-stasis," or outside the realm of stasis. Raves, Bhakti fests, kirtans, music festivals, yoga conferences, Rainbow Gatherings, Burning Man, multimedia concerts, and Pagan festivals are all examples of individuals coming together for a group ecstatic experience. The spiritual emphasis is on reclaiming the divine ecstasy that had been largely lost among the rules, regulations, and dogma of the Static

Masculine era. Personal practices, such as meditation and yoga, now have less emphasis on the solo journey, as in the contemplative traditions of the past, but are increasingly practiced in groups, combined with music, dance, ritual, poetry, or "prayerformances." While there are always those who show up just looking for a good party, the primary drive of these gatherings is a kind of group bliss: spiritual expansion in connection with others, uniting of the personal and the collective.

The communities that form around these ideas are far from conformist. Their members exhibit blatant individuality, if not eccentricity. Their hallmark is creativity and connectedness, often with a bold recovery of Eros. Both genders enjoy a sex-positive lifestyle, one that celebrates the erotic yet still reflects a sophisticated sense of boundaries and ethics. The adherents of these ideas tend to be fit and sexy, living embodied lives adorned in flamboyant fashion statements.

Where the Static Masculine sought knowledge and certainty, the Dynamic Feminine offers a more inquiring openness, based on the realization of how much we *don't know*. Process is more important than content, the means more important than the ends. A group may spend more time on *how* their meeting is conducted than on the actual content of the agenda. It might take longer to get things done, but people are often happier with the result.

Getting outside the static is not just a spiritual state, however. In science, the Dynamic Feminine can be seen in chaos theory, quantum physics, nonlinear dynamics, and living systems theory—all of which expand the boundaries of the mechanistic, Newtonian worldview. These new dimensions in science are relatively indeterminate, fluctuating, and highly relational, speaking of a dynamic web of relationships more than of things themselves. These forms transcend the determinism of the previous mind-set of scientific materialism, calling us to still-deeper mysteries. In medicine, we find increased interest in alternative healing practices, focused on wholeness of mind, body, and spirit, such as energy healing, acupuncture, hypnotherapy, body-work, prayer, yoga therapy, and meditation.

In the social realm, the Dynamic Feminine is exhibited through the revolution in human and other rights (animal, environmental), nonviolent actions, civil disobedience, participatory democracy, and social networking. All of these represent a peaceful, collaborative way of coordinating large numbers of people around specific issues and information.

Spiritually, this movement could be said to have pushed open the petals of the crown chakra—the highest center, which represents the mysteries of consciousness itself. The movement is reflected in religious ceremonies that are created spontaneously by small groups without leaders, often in people's living rooms, needing no authoritative structure. It also runs through the yoga world, as people find community while honoring the temple of their body.

As a movement, the Dynamic Feminine is inherently tribal, yet keen on organizing and networking with other tribes. The Internet-organized Tribe.net, for example, boasts "member-created groups for every interest."[94] Though people who embody this movement still marry and raise children, the nuclear family is less important than the tribal community, with children known and cared for by many and a trend toward fewer children in general. More people choose not to have children at all—an important step in controlling population and becoming a mature species.

Social interactions are both high-tech and high-touch. Just as the last five centuries since the printing press required people to become literate in order to participate in the larger society, technology has emerged as a new language, whose fluency is required to fully participate in this eco-techno-spiritual awakening. Text messaging, online networking, and digital communications in general are a native language for the emerging generations. As if in balance to the high-tech world, public displays of affection are removed from shame and privacy and can be more easily expressed in public. Hugs replace handshakes. Sexuality is not restricted to heterosexual dyads and is more accepting of gays, bisexuals, and open relationships. There is more comfort with nudity and erotic costume. The body is exalted and kept fit, often decorated, pierced, and tattooed. Races, genders, sexual persuasions, religions, and nationalities work and play together, with far less awareness of their differences.

Self-Reflective Consciousness

Your visions will become clear only when you can look into your own heart. Who looks outside, dreams; who looks inside, awakes.
—C. G. Jung

As the Apollo spacecraft circled the moon in 1969 and relayed the first pictures of Earth from space, we could see—for the first time ever—our reflection as a whole planet. At the same time, a new level of self-reflection began to awaken as people explored psychotherapy and other forms of self-examination: consciousness-raising groups, encounter groups, self-help books, and psycho-spiritual workshops. As we healed our wounds and woke up to a greater reality, we saw new possibilities for our collective potential.

Though the first tendrils of the Dynamic Feminine can be traced back to the Romantics of the 19th century, the movement burst into flower in the '60s through the psychedelic revolution that opened people's minds to the frontiers of consciousness. As drug experiences dissolved the barriers of the ego, a higher order of truth was revealed that transcended rigid belief systems. The outer edges of the ego were not the only thing to dissolve, however, for the psychedelic experience made people more sensitive to their environment, both internally and externally. Heightened awareness put people more deeply in touch with themselves. They discovered that the food they ate, the health of their body, and the degree to which personal issues were resolved had great bearing on the quality of their psychedelic experience. Organic foods and fibers, natural surroundings, and personal practices became valued as contributing to a clear state of consciousness—whether on or off drugs. Mind and body were no longer separate but were mutually influential. Mental health was no longer a quality of the mind alone but now involved the body. By the '70s, body-based therapies such as bioenergetics, Rolfing, rebirthing, chiropractic, and massage of all kinds had emerged. There was a resurgence of such modalities as Chinese medicine, herbology, and homeopathy, to name but a few. Medicine began to recognize the influence of one's psychological state as a factor in health and disease.

A new interest in spiritual teachings developed—one that reached back to the practices of Eastern traditions, as people sought ways to achieve their spiritual high by natural means. People meditated, reflected, practiced yoga, and discovered that they had chakras. Interest in Eastern religions provided balance with important pieces that were missing in our largely Western worldview. Where Christianity had dominated the spiritual airwaves of Western civilization for the last 1,600 years, now attention turned toward non-Christian spiritual traditions, reviving ancient beliefs and practices from around the world: Buddhism, Hinduism, Taoism, and, lest we forget, the rediscovery of the Goddess in the revival of Paganism. Books exploring these many traditions abounded, and a new branch of education sprang to life: the world of spiritual workshops and retreats, along with teachers who were now more like ordinary people than spiritual masters or gurus.

The central vision of this movement was that life is an intricate, living web—all of it sacred. With renewed reverence for nature, accompanied by grief over its loss, the first Earth Day arose in 1970, accompanied by a back-to-the-land movement that spawned urban gardens, wilderness recreation, and the pursuit of deep ecology. If mind and body were no longer separate, neither were culture and planet. A new synthesis had begun, emerging from deep within the soul, as polarities began to recognize each other as part of a larger unity.

Nonviolence was a fundamental value held by this movement toward wholeness. War and corporatism exhibited stark contrasts to the harmonic relatedness that individuals were experiencing—and therefore knew to be possible. A new questioning of morality looked at the shadow side of modernism: racism, sexism, rapacious pollution, and imperial domination. Ethics began to shift from the realms of sexuality and original sin to questioning the values of economic greed, warfare, and militarism.

Rights for All

We don't need a Declaration of Human Rights.
We need a Declaration of Human Responsibilities.
—*Six Nations Iroquois chief Oren Lyons*

As the standard of living and political freedoms continued to grow for much of the population, it became increasingly obvious that they hadn't improved for *all* people. The quest for rights of all kinds became part of the unifying force of the Dynamic Feminine. The Civil War had ended slavery a century before, but the living conditions of African Americans in the ghetto were still deplorable. The civil rights movement picked up where the abolition of slavery had left off, addressing issues of racism and poverty, shadows in the illusion of prosperity for all. Martin Luther King steered the movement toward nonviolence, which slowly began to chip away at the white male hegemony that had always been in charge. Politics, media, academia, sports, and finance began to show more faces of color. The pursuit of other rights followed: women's rights, children's rights, gay rights, animal rights, consumer rights, disabled rights, and the more silent rights of habitats and endangered species. Leonard Shlain, in his book *The Alphabet Versus the Goddess,* suggested that television, which allowed information to be conveyed in images rather than the written word, made possible a rebirth of feminine values, as it employed more of the right brain than the left. Certainly, women's liberation, as it was called at the time, played a huge role in making this movement for human rights possible.

As women in the '60s went to consciousness-raising groups and compared stories, they discovered common themes. Many realized that they were living someone else's life, with values that were alien to their own. They threw away the orange juice cans they tried to sleep on to curl or straighten their hair, kicked off their high heels and pantyhose, and began to dance barefoot in the grass. While their brothers burned draft cards, women burned their bras. A new kind of sisterhood emerged, with its own distinct flavors. Women were finding their own voice, their own style, and along with it, their righteous indignation over centuries of oppression.

Meanwhile, archaeological discoveries brought to light information about ancient Goddesses that had long been buried and forgotten. We discovered that God had not always been a man on a throne with a long white beard and that Goddesses had many forms. We learned that there were once priestesses as well as priests, and that the Divine Feminine was not simply God in drag but something wholly different and equally holy.

Women rebelled against their oppressors, be it their dictatorial fathers, college professors, bosses, or husbands, and set out to make their own way. They left the kitchen and entered the workplace. They set up rape crisis centers and child-care agencies and started their own businesses. Some women discovered the love of other women as they freed themselves from the romantic expectations of men. Women-only environments freed both gay and straight women from the expectation of dainty behavior, perfect hairdos, uncomfortable clothing, and the mask of makeup. Men learned how to make their own coffee. They, too, discovered the sacred in each other and formed men's groups to redefine their identity. Same-sex love, both male and female, cracked open the closet door and began its uphill journey for social acceptance.

Self-reflection through psychotherapy entered the mainstream. People wanted to know more deeply who they really were beneath their gender-specified roles. Women wanted to find their power. Men, though more hesitant, increasingly entered therapy themselves. Self-help groups for alcoholism, drug abuse, gambling, sex, and the enabling of any of these addictions sprung up all over the country. The angry residue of 5,000 years of a dominator paradigm flared into an energized awakening of freedom. Powerlessness became less tolerable.

Though we still have a long way to go toward true equality, we are no longer surprised when women, minorities, or gays hold positions of power. Fewer people tell their daughters that they can't become doctors or tell their sons that they have to go to war to be real men. Gay couples can walk down at least some streets holding hands. We've had our first black family in the White House. Now the fight is legislative: Can gays marry and have the same privileges as other couples? Can women find birth control as easily as men can find Viagra? In an overpopulated world, do women have the right to an abortion on demand? Do the silent animals, forests, and oceans have any rights at all?

If the Static Feminine was our infancy, the Dynamic Masculine our terrible twos, and the Static Masculine our middle childhood, then the Dynamic Feminine can be said to be our full-fledged adolescence. It is the independence rebellion—for better or worse—against the Father and all he represents: institutions, hierarchy, bureaucracy, rules, and regulations. Women and men join together as equals—in relationships, in the workplace, even in politics. Sexuality is seen as a sacrament leading to a spiritual connection. Freedom and self-determination are essential, along with openness and flexibility, meaning and creativity. This movement seeks to transcend limitations in every way.

In its negative aspect, the Dynamic Feminine can be so resistant to structure that it becomes ineffective. It can be indulgently hedonistic, so fully in the moment that it goes nowhere, so bent on equality that no one can lead. New Age platitudes can replace grounded research. Altered states can take you so far into the deep dimensions of the cosmos that you lose touch with reality. This negative aspect results from denying the other archetypal patterns of the past—the steady grounding of the Static Feminine, the focused drive of the Dynamic Masculine, and the structural rigidity of the Static Masculine. Without these tempering influences, the Dynamic Feminine alone is not whole.

The bulk of progressive values reflect the Dynamic Feminine sentiment. In the words of Paul Ray, who coined the term *cultural creatives*,

> The new progressive values planetary rather than national interests, eco-sustainability rather than sentimental environmentalism, feminism rather than Heroic models, personal growth more than personal ambition, and condemns globalizing mega-corporations more than the religious right.[95]

The Dynamic Feminine emerges at a time when technology allows us to transcend the written word with multimedia downloads of high-speed communication. Where reading is inherently static—a slow and linear mental process, building logically from one thought to another—the absorbing of information today is immediate and whole-brain; it comes increasingly through YouTube videos more than books, with people getting their news more from websites or Comedy Central than from newspapers. Rather than staring for hours at tiny text on a white page (as you are doing right now), the reader receives information instantaneously, through sound and images. Channel surfers can watch several programs at once. Cell phones can access the Internet. Computers can talk and listen, remember and perform. The World Wide Web is interactive, not passive.

The Dynamic Feminine movement is still young. We have yet to see exactly where it will take us. We know, for example, that the Dynamic Feminine tends to be highly resistant to structure. On the other hand, adherents of the Static Masculine value system tend to be highly threatened by the freedom, vitality, and audaciousness of the Dynamic Feminine. Whether we resolve these dilemmas and find balance in time to address our mounting crises is an open question. But I argue that without the Dynamic Feminine, we are missing an essential piece of our awakening.

Though the truth and goodness of these ideals of equality are generally recognized in the West, we still have a long way to go before gender balance, racial justice, peace, and environmental sustainability become a global reality. And we have yet to see the larger effects of achieving these ideals. What does a peacetime economy offer when we no longer have a bloated military budget? What happens to collective intelligence when lower classes have better access to education and meaningful work? How is population stabilized when women have power over their own bodies? What happens to politics when it reaches gender balance? What sense of well-being is promoted by a healthy environment? What effects will the Internet have on the awakening of consciousness? How will this movement evolve as the environmental and political situations in the world increase in intensity? In the final section of this book, I offer a vision that attempts to answer these and related questions.

The Dynamic Feminine *alone* is not the way of the future, but it is an essential representation of values necessary to move forward into a truly holistic and fully integrated paradigm. Because the Static Masculine is by nature rigid and unchanging, it becomes outdated in a dynamic and changing universe. Yet as we go through the transition of initiation to the next level of the heart, the Static Masculine, as well as the residual values of earlier eras, is still needed to hold scientific rigor and maintain stability through laws and social customs. In fact, the Static Masculine has been so busy holding things together that it literally *can't* let go until the new organizing principle is mature enough to direct civilization adequately, without descending into chaos. Yet, the horrors of climate change, water shortages, and other environmental disasters will bring their own chaos if not checked.

Seventh-Chakra Awakening

As theology meets science, a new evolutionary conception for the creative trinity is coming in being. Theology itself is evolving.
—*Rupert Sheldrake*

The seventh, or crown, chakra is the portal to pure consciousness, higher wisdom, information, intelligence, and spiritual realms. The cultural opening of this highest chakra is difficult to pinpoint. It has occurred in various ways throughout the ages, through countless spiritual masters, teachers, writers, and innovative thinkers in every culture. Priestesses and priests of the past have been intermediaries to these higher states of consciousness. Enlightened teachers have spread their wisdom, seeding awakening for those who were ready to comprehend their message. Prodigious volumes from India and the East have predated modernity on the nature of consciousness and the means of attaining higher states of awareness. You might even say that all our cultural advancements have been sparked by people whose consciousness was at least more advanced than that of their contemporaries. Avatars of the crown chakra have always been with us, from the writers of the Indian Rig-Veda and the Upanishads to Chinese philosophers such as Confucius and Lao-tzu; from the Greek philosophers to Buddha, Jesus, and Muhammad; from Rumi to more modern gurus such as Gurdjieff, Ramana Maharshi, Maharishi Mahesh Yogi, and Sri Aurobindo; from Mother Teresa to the world spiritual leader the Dalai Lama. This woefully incomplete list demonstrates that seventh-chakra awareness is a perennial phenomenon.

Like fish that don't know they're in water, we swim in a field of consciousness that we take for granted. In the West, it wasn't until Descartes that consciousness was named as a defining facet of our existence. Even then, most scientists ignored this dimension as best they could, as it wasn't quantifiable and predictable. But the awakening of the '60s made consciousness a frontier of its own, worthy of deep study, finally of interest to the general populace. The altering of consciousness through mind-expanding drugs alerted people to the fact that they *had* consciousness and that the state of our awareness made a huge difference in our experience and behavior. We opened the windows of perception and examined everything with new eyes, and a much bigger picture of the nature of reality was revealed to us. Overall, consciousness was turning its attention to the nature of consciousness itself, not just in esoteric communities of gurus and disciples, but as a part of everyday life. Through meditation, we discovered the neutral witness that dwells within and learned how to cultivate its peaceful presence. We found we could examine the contents, processes, and various states and stages of consciousness and began cataloguing them in myriad ways.

The result has been a quiet but extensive spiritual revolution. The wide availability of spiritual texts of all traditions has made multiple faiths more accessible to study. Yoga and meditation centers have sprung up everywhere, the way Christian churches spread in the first few centuries of the Common Era. The Goddess, long buried in the Underworld, has made a comeback, giving women a sense of their own divinity. In the United States, books on spirituality are a high-selling category, with women making up the majority of the market. Retreat centers for spiritual workshops, and the paraphernalia for spiritual practice, from candles to zafu cushions, have become big business. Yet these are all means for people to wake up to a higher dimension of consciousness and possibility.

While we silently tune in to the "inner net" of awareness, the outer Internet spreads ideas across the globe at the speed of light, creating a collective organ of consciousness, often called the *noosphere*. Only 500 years ago, we figured out how to print books. Today, humanity's colossal body of information is available at the click of a mouse to anyone with access to a computer. While this still doesn't reach the majority of the world's population, it is spreading rapidly and exponentially. When the first website was launched in 1991,[96] there were five million Internet users in 12 countries, with 70 percent dialing up (remember dialing?) from within the United States. By 2010, less than 20 years later, the World Wide Web is accessed by one-third of the global population—over two billion users, 90 percent of whom are outside the United States.[97] The highest per capita Internet use correlates with the most democratic and progressive nations, with Iceland at the top, followed by Norway, the Netherlands, Sweden, Finland, and Germany. (The United States is 10th, after Canada, Japan, and the United Kingdom.)[98] Now we can hold more information in the palm of our hand in a mobile phone than was contained in the computers of the previous century that were the size of a city block. Perhaps WWIII has been headed off by the WWW—the World Wide Web—making us collectively smarter. Ideally, increased access to information leads us to wisdom. Hopefully this will be a long-term outcome from the Internet as we mature into our cultural adulthood and continue to develop this amazing tool.

The crown chakra, as the thousand-petaled lotus that is its namesake (Sahasrara), opens to the heavenly source the way a flower drinks in sunlight. That means we reach *upward,* toward the light of transcendence and the "higher" realms of consciousness, as well as drawing heavenly energy *downward,* into the body, to inform our behaviors. For it is not enough to merely sit on our cushions and meditate: the world needs us to take actions that emanate from wisdom and to work together to cocreate heaven on earth. In this way. we take on the daring task of being young Gods and Goddesses in training, embodying the divine in splendor and beauty. Just because we have begun to pierce this chakra from a wider cultural base than just a few spiritual masters, there is a long way to go to raise this consciousness in the masses. The crown chakra does not open all at once; rather, like a flower, its petals open gradually from bud to bloom, fed by sturdy roots in the earth, supported by passion, power, and purpose, and blossoming from the divine power of love.

The Integral Heart

Love is the affinity which links and draws together the elements of the world. . . . Love, in fact, is the agent of universal synthesis.
—*Pierre Teilhard de Chardin*

Our long journey home has taken us from our birth in the primal womb of nature, through infancy, toddlerhood, and middle childhood, into our current adolescence and budding adulthood. We have experienced at least some development in each chakra. We have learned how to survive as a species (first chakra), yet our expanding population is exhausting the environment, while much of the world still struggles daily for survival. We have begun to reclaim the body and its pleasures (second chakra), yet many see pleasure as their main pursuit. We have developed a massive infrastructure for power (third chakra), enabling heroic accomplishments, yet some who hold power abuse that privilege, with high cost to others. We have claimed rights for all kinds of minorities and issues (fourth chakra), yet we have not balanced the importance of rights with responsibilities. We have been steadily moving into the heart but are still organized by hierarchical power. Perhaps our partially arrested development in the heart chakra was simply waiting for science and technology to provide us the tools to connect as one planetary civilization in a global brain of higher consciousness. But now, we must consider the evolutionary *purpose* for which these tools—and our hard-won freedom, power, and awakening—have been developed.

Even with continual but incomplete opening of the heart chakra, we have created worldwide communication (fifth chakra), the ability to transfer images and moving pictures (sixth chakra), and a global organ of consciousness through the Internet, coupled with a spiritual revolution (seventh chakra). Though far from mastering it, we have at least pierced the upper end of the chakra spectrum on a cultural level. We are now ready to go back down and reclaim what has been repressed in the lower chakras: the earth and body (first chakra), the emotions and sexuality (second chakra), and our *personal* power and will (third chakra), for a grand integration in the heart chakra.

It is possible that our full evolution into the Age of the Heart could not complete until we had embraced the more transcendent qualities of the upper chakras and developed the technology to bring the communication of words, images, and information worldwide, thus having the means to unite ever more people in a common vision and higher wisdom. But that wisdom cannot deny the earth, our bodies, our need for joy and pleasure, and the rights and responsibilities of personal power. Now, at last, we can integrate the chakras above and below for a true awakening of the heart. We can reclaim what has been lost and integrate it with what we have gained, uniting higher and lower, heaven and earth, personal and collective, masculine and feminine in one holistic vision.

At the same time, we have experienced the social effects of the Static Feminine, Dynamic Masculine, Static Masculine, and, more recently, Dynamic Feminine valences or memes, appreciating the virtues and drawbacks of each. We can now integrate masculine and feminine values with deeper understanding, greater balance, and cocreative partnership, seeing the missing contribution of the feminine as essential to balancing the masculine dominance in our world today.

No matter where we are going in the future, we need a vehicle that can get us there. If our values, beliefs, structures, and institutions define the collective vehicle in which we move into the future, it is essential that we make that vehicle healthy, strong, and capable of the journey. Integrating the many elements we have discussed within both the self and society is the prime task of the heart chakra, which can bring us to wholeness. It is to this vision, and the journey forward, that we will turn next.

Part Three

WHERE ARE WE GOING?

14

WEAVING A NEW STORY

The Child of Our Future

The deepest crises experienced by any society are those moments of change when the story becomes inadequate for meeting the survival demands of a present situation.
—*Thomas Berry*

Before written history, we can only guess at the stories our ancestors told around the firelight. Projecting onto pregnant-bellied statues scattered across the land, we make an educated guess that their makers worshipped a goddess, a Great Mother, who was synonymous with nature. Nor do we know how our ancestors defined themselves, but from our present perspective, we could say that they were infants in the primal garden, mere babes in the woods, symbiotically immersed in nature. According to the primal thesis with which we began this story of humanity, the Mother was divine, a living goddess, who miraculously gave birth to all of life, seemingly without a male partner.

This original monotheism of the Mother Goddess gradually evolved into a polytheism of both Gods and Goddesses, who gave birth to many children. In the human realm, this corresponding expansion of population sent us into our teeming toddlerhood, spreading across the land and seas, farming and trading. Knowing little about how the world worked, we believed that our sacrifices appeased the gods and increased the chances that rain would fall, crops would grow, and we would birth many children. Time passed, and we did birth many children, who prospered and multiplied.

Later, in the early civilization of Babylonia, the story enacted each year was that of the God-king, Marduk, slaying the Great Mother, Tiamat, and then establishing a new order of men upon her dead body—a story that was celebrated for a thousand years as the rites of spring. At the end of this story, we are told that the gods created humans to take on the drudgery of work. Our identity was named: slaves to the gods, or at best servants—a safe, humble role. We paid tribute to the gods through human God-kings who acted as intermediaries between the worlds. Worship shifted from earth to sky, female to male, body to spirit. Now it was the Father who was divine, the Mother reduced to the background. This was the antithesis to our primal thesis.

The Christian myth tells us that humans had fallen to a lowly existence on earth as punishment for sin, whether from Eve's transgressions or our own. We no longer saw ourselves as slaves to the gods; now we were sinners. God no longer needed our labors but our obedience. We no longer sacrificed bulls or goats, for the sacrifice of the Savior served to redeem us all. Jesus's initiation into death and resurrection forgave us our sins and spared the rest of us the painful process of our own rite of passage. In this story, the son and the Divine Father become one; the life-giving Mother is replaced by a neutered "ghost."

Our sins may have been forgiven, but they were not corrected. Penance is not the same as amends. We were asked not to address those we had harmed but to address God instead. For Catholics, forgiveness occurred by mere confession, along with saying a few Hail Marys and *mea culpas*, but restitution wasn't part of it. For Protestants, redemption was passive, occurring not through our own will but only through God's grace—at least for the few chosen ones. After the Reformation, people were good, God-fearing folk who kept their heads bowed low, worked hard, and followed the Bible. Now God was without a female partner in a wholly masculine monotheism.

In the Scientific Revolution, humans gained power through observation of nature. We had a new and promising identity—as discoverers, creators, shapers of our surroundings. The world was our workshop and we were its artists. Nature's power was diminished, while our power was heightened. Nature was an "it" from which we could take what we wanted, no longer infused with divine consciousness, if any consciousness at all.

With industry and technology to aid us and oil as an adolescent growth hormone to grease the gears of progress, we grew exponentially, spreading across the globe. We were cogs in the machine, marching toward progress. We established global trade and international councils, such as the United Nations. Computers became small enough to fit in our shirt pocket and were distributed everywhere. We created a global network of consciousness, a *noosphere*, the beginnings of a global group mind. We developed a new identity, becoming points of consciousness weaving an intricate planetary web, intelligent cocreators of our reality.

Yet even as we extended ourselves into the farthest reaches of the Earth, the skies, and the seas, we spent increasingly more time indoors, within the walls of our homes, offices, and institutions. Now we spend ever more time looking at electronic screens, whether at a desk, on the couch, or on the phone. Our separation from nature in our everyday life is accepted as normal.

As we follow the course of history from our embeddedness in nature to our eventual triumph over nature and now to its possible destruction, we see that it is not the *fall* where we went wrong but perhaps the *rise*. By this, I mean our separation from the Earth as the ground of our being. In this separation, nature was first denigrated and is now degraded, to the point where our future survival is threatened.

If in the Christian myth a single man had to be crucified and resurrected for our redemption, now it is the collective of humanity that is undergoing its initiation of death and resurrection. This death will also be for our sins, but on a different scale. Not for the transgression of a sexual fantasy, but for the rape of the environment; not for the killing of a brother, but for the bombing of a nation; not for the corruption of the money changers, but for the rapacious greed of our economic system; not for the worship of the old gods, but for allowing the false idols of the dollar and the Hollywood image to be worshipped as gods. Our sins have become global, and we have no one else to clean them up. If there is to be a judgment day for our actions, it will be for our failure to care for the well-being of each other and our environment. These are the sins for which we must all make amends. Facing them is part of our collective initiation.

Let's summarize this dilemma another way: When we were children, our needs were taken care of by others. In our infancy it was the Great Mother who provided. In our toddlerhood it was the World Parents, pantheons of gods and goddesses who ensured the stability of the seasons, the crops, and animals. In our middle youth, it was a single Father, alternately wrathful and loving, who forged city-states into empires and empires into military-industrial complexes. As we grew in knowledge, we relied on science to provide the answers, and many still do, thinking that, given enough time, science and industry will find solutions to all our problems. But the brilliance of science has given rise to many of the problems that need solving—and the scientific data now tells us that time is running out.

We no longer have the luxury of remaining as children. The archetypal parents won't save us this time. Mother Nature is going bankrupt, and "bailouts" won't prop her up. The fish are disappearing from the oceans; the topsoil is being stripped from the land; urban air is filled with smog; the ice caps are melting; the sea level is rising. Mother Nature's cupboards of resources have not been replenished, and the masses are hungry and still multiplying. Children around the world are crying, with no mother to console them. Millions grow up with no parents at all.

And what has become of the Father? While he is ever more distant, his institutions are infected with corruption. There are priests who molest children and right-to-lifers who commit murder. Some Muslim fanatics explode themselves in crowds to glorify the name of Allah and vent their deeply held grievances. Heads of countries, heads of corporations, and financial oligarchies exploit our human and natural resources, while the mass media spin webs of illusion to cover up their actions. Like children, we are kept distracted from our pain with a constant supply of new toys and gadgets. Our identity is named by the media as "consumers." And like many affluent children who suffer a similar fate while Daddy works a 60-hour week, we find that toys are no substitute for love. The single Father just can't do it alone, and the children are left to fend for themselves. This makes for a pretty dysfunctional adolescence. Somewhere we lost sight of the power of love as the main ingredient of a healthy family: love between mother and father, between parents and children, and between each other, not to mention love for the beauty and majesty of our world.

Still, we continue to grow up. We are more educated, more sophisticated, more technologically powerful, and more connected than ever before. The world's entire knowledge base lies at our fingertips. The wisdom of all the world's religious traditions is now widely available. The tools of political power, formerly in the hands of the elite, are now in the hands of the common people—the tools to communicate, travel, publish, create, connect, and organize. Individuals have more power than they've had at any time in history. And now we have the capacity to join that power with others on a scale never before possible. Like the single-celled creatures that finally learned how to combine forces a billion years before us, we don't know what we are capable of when we overcome the isolation of separateness and use collaboration, with both human and divine resources, to solve our problems. These are the tools and powers with which we can face the initiation, the greatest of them being the power of love. For it is this great, divine power that hopefully will guide the way we use these sources of power to create our future.

In each of these mythic chapters in our evolutionary story, humans had an identity: as slaves, servants, sinners, cogs in the machine, and, most recently, consumers. But once again, our identity is changing. In the new story, humans are the *redeemers*. This is the resurrection side of the great initiation we are now entering.

We are the redeemers, and what needs to be redeemed is nearly every facet of our civilization: the environment, the economy, government, education, medicine, and religion. It's a big job, overwhelming to contemplate. Many find it easier to turn on the television and zone out than to feel so small in the face of such challenges. The bad news is that these challenges won't go away. The good news is that we don't have to do it alone. Working alone was part of the third-chakra Hero's Quest, where we had to face our challenges in solitude, one person against the world. To go it alone would be pure hubris today, a formula for certain failure. The very nature of our problems demands global cooperation. As we are "gods in training," our spiritual practices will help us to find guidance through connection with the divine. But what is our *purpose?*

The Mything Piece

A tribe's mythology is its living religion, whose loss is always and everywhere, even among the civilized, a moral catastrophe.
—C. G. Jung

Before rational thinking freed us from the antics of capricious gods, myths were the uniting stories of a people. Myths gave meaning and value to their lives and allowed them to be part of something larger.

For better or worse, people's actions were guided by their myths, as they aligned with ancient gods and goddesses who represented both outer world and inner psyche. Myths gave them something to reach for, something to identify with, to expand beyond their own meager lives. Knowing little about the world in the scientific sense, our ancestors would have been lost without their guiding myths. There would have been no temples to build, no art to create, nothing to inspire great deeds. Myths explained the questions that scientific knowledge had not yet answered. They defined who we were and where we were going.

Yet, because mythic thinking preceded rational thinking, these guiding myths of the past were incomplete, often filled with fear and superstition. As testaments of symbolic truth, they did not reflect actual truths. Roasting a baby in the fire to make him immortal, as the grain goddess, Demeter, did in the Homeric Hymns, is not something we should try at home. Jesus, no matter how advanced he may have been, did not walk on the surface of deep water. There is no literal place called the Underworld, but there is a metaphoric one.

When mythic and rational thinking first began to clash in the Golden Age of Greece, and increasingly through the dawn of modernity, rational thinking supplanted the mythical. Empirical proof put a sword through our irrational superstitions. Many harmful things, such as animal sacrifices and witch burnings, came to an end. As rationalism became the new creed, myths were regarded as artifacts of a primitive mind, something we had outgrown, like the childhood fantasies of Santa Claus and the Easter Bunny. Culturally, as we grew up through the Christian era, we were told to put those things away, often brutally punished for coveting idols, practicing rituals, or honoring the old gods. The word *myth* even came to mean a "lie," as in "That's just a myth."

Rationalism provided answers to the questions that myth could not explain. Knowledge from the scientific method was objective, logical, methodical, reproducible. We passed out of a dark age of naïve explanations. Myths became the dreams from which we had awakened, rubbing our eyes as we entered the rational world. We took a giant step forward into the future, paving the way for modernism.

But we lost something vital in the process.

Rational and mythic thinking are like two legs of an upright creature. Neither one alone can take us more than a single step. Myth gives us meaning but often ignores fact. Rational thinking, while factual, fails to give us meaning. By definition, it is impersonal. Being objective rather than subjective, it does not define values. It tells us how something works but doesn't tell us what it's for. And most of all, it fails to tell us what *we* are for—why we are here, where we're going, and what purpose this exquisite universe might have for us.

It's not that we have no myths today. We still have a distorted myth of the Hero's Quest to go forth and conquer. We have the myth of the dollar that says money will make you happy. We have the myths of modern fundamentalism, which often distort a religion's original message. We have many smaller myths that act as collective beliefs: that war is inevitable, that you can't fight city hall, that emotions are weakness, that women can't govern, that science will solve everything, and that myth has no value at all.

Rationalism and modern science may not provide us with ultimate meaning, but these disciplines have been brilliant providers of *information*. Industry and technology have been brilliant providers of *things*. We are now flooded with information and things—more than we know what to do with. We have streams of data, piles of books, shelves full of DVDs, hundreds of millions of websites full of information. This surplus has even been called *exformation*, meaning data no one will ever see. Everywhere we look, we have an abundance of "things": shopping malls, houses, trucks, and storage units, all full of things, most of which we don't need or seldom use.

What we're missing is a guiding myth for what to do with it all. We need a new story for our time, beause we fail to understand the greater meaning of what this information is describing as a whole.

Even the data on global warming, with its tables and statistics, has so far failed to grab the public with an urgent sense of its meaning: that we are burning ourselves alive, or that our masculine fires are too hot and too yang without the yin waters to balance them, or that we are facing the most significant threat to the planet that our species has ever encountered. However we frame the climate crisis, it is undeniable that it has dimensions of meaning that are mythic in scale.

When carpenters and plumbers show up at a building site, they find piles of raw material, such as lumber, glass, bricks, nails, and pipes. The architect's blueprint provides the *vision* that tells the builders what to do with these things. It gives purpose to their hammers and saws, describes how the boards are nailed together, and guides the workers' actions. In the same way, a higher vision of what we are creating together organizes humanity's efforts, as we each take on our particular duty, destiny, or *dharma* of living in these shifting times. To save ourselves and this glorious planet, we need an overarching vision for our time, a vision that inspires our hearts.

Our myths are the blueprints for our purpose. They give us something to live for; they provide meaning and direction. They need not deny rational thinking but should complement it. Science need not negate mystery but instead reveal just how intricate and intelligent our mysteries are. The new myth that is emerging is not counter to science but instead allows the whole of creation to have an evolutionary meaning, purpose, or entelechy that pulls us toward the future. That future is calling us toward an emerging Age of the Heart, collectively organized through the power of love.

Hieros Gamos: The Sacred Marriage

Myth is the secret opening through which the inexhaustible energies of the cosmos pour into human cultural manifestation.
—*Joseph Campbell*

The mythical stories of the gods and goddesses are not over. Instead, they are shifting from an external projection to an internal awakening. If evolution is the Gods' way of making more gods, then we, ourselves, are becoming gods. As Stewart Brand said in the *Whole Earth Catalog*, "We might as well get good at it." With enough power to create and destroy on a planetary scale, we have the power of gods but not yet the realization. How do we find our divinity and step into our roles as cocreators of the future? What is the process by which we mature into our divine selves?

We have discussed the Divine Mother and her son/consort who eventually grew into his own power. We have talked about the Divine Father, who brought unity and order, and his daughter/wife who served him. As the son overthrew the mother in the distant past and as the daughter overthrows the oppressive father in the modern feminist movement, both genders have been slowly maturing into their adolescence, meeting perhaps for the first time as equal players in the evolutionary journey. Over millennia they have been growing up and developing their power as children playing largely in their separate realms. Now they are ready to come back together and find their love. This ultimate union is referred to by mythologists as the Sacred Marriage, or the *hieros gamos*. But first the adolescent boy and girl must find their own personal divinity before they can arive at such a divine consummation.

A common theme in fairy tales worldwide reflects this process. It begins when the king and queen give birth to a child whom for some reason they feel compelled to reject. The baby is left under a bush, sent down the river, or exposed to the elements and left to an unknown fate. Moses was left in a basket by the side of the Nile. The child Dionysus arrived on Earth in a chest with his dead mother. Romulus and Remus, the founders of Rome, were orphans, nursed by a she-wolf. Exposing or abandoning babies was a very common practice in ancient times.

Jung described the mythic importance of this abandonment:

> Nothing in all the world welcomes this new birth, although it is the most precious fruit of Mother Nature herself, the most pregnant with the future, signifying a higher stage of self-realization. That is why Nature, the world of the instincts, takes the "child" under its wing: it is nourished or protected by animals. . . . This it cannot do without detaching itself from its origins: abandonment is therefore a necessary condition, not just a concomitant symptom.[1]

We know in these myths that the baby does not die but is found by a commoner and raised lovingly without knowledge of his royal status. He learns the ways of nature and simplicity, growing up in the woods, among slaves, or on the sea. Later, as the child matures into adolescence, a series of synchronicities takes him back to the original kingdom. Here he discovers who he really is: inheritor of the royal crown. Raised humbly, he does not forget his past. But entering the kingdom, he steps into a glory previously unimagined. He begins the process of accepting the rights and developing the responsibilities to rule the kingdom wisely, to eventually become a king (or if a girl child, a queen) in his or her own right. Jung continues:

> It is a striking paradox in all child myths that the "child" is on the one hand delivered helpless into the power of terrible enemies and in continual danger of extinction, while on the other he possesses powers far exceeding those of ordinary humanity . . . though unknown, he is also divine.[2]

We are all children of mundane parents, most of whom were disconnected from the Divine Mother and Divine Father, for so many had forgotten their ways. Our parents were well-meaning but often wounded men and women, doing the best they could to raise us in the world they knew. As we heal our childhood wounds, we move from identification with our mundane parents to realization of our heritage with the more universal Divine Mother and Divine Father. Acknowledging our lineage to both, we can finally recognize our own divine nature. This awakening prepares us for the final step: the *hieros gamos*.

We are the higher synthesis of the union of the archetypal Mother and Father. As we recognize the divinity within ourselves, we see it in each other and all around us. Through this realization, the world becomes sacred again, infused with intelligence, spirit, and a grand plan for evolutionary awakening.

The story I have told in this book suggests that we have grown up to adolescence, yet we are still largely unaware of our divine nature. We are arrested in the third chakra, but since development is not always linear, we have at least breached the heart and higher chakras. As slaves, sinners, obedient children, cogs in the wheel, or mindless consumers, we put the divine outside ourselves, losing touch with our true heart but gaining much else in the process. Of course there are notable exceptions to this in the teachers of the past who have seeded the spiritual landscape with advanced teachings. For example, the Sanskrit word *namaste* means "the divine within me salutes the divine within you." In the Bible, John 10:34 says, "Jesus answered them, 'Is it not written in your Law, "I have said you are gods"?'"

But let's take a step back and consider what we mean by divine. How is it understood from the standpoint of the Divine Father or the Divine Mother archetype?

When attributed to the Father archetype, the divine has been described as omniscient, omnipotent, and omnipresent—all knowing, all powerful, and everywhere present. This describes something infinite, limitless, like the nature of consciousness itself. In Sanskrit, the divine is *satchidananda:* truth, consciousness, and bliss. In Oriental religions, it is the ever-present Tao. In Christianity, it is the Eternal Father. In Jewish mysticism, it is the *Ein Sof.* To the Muslims, it is the divine will of Allah. In Buddhism, it is empty presence and awakened consciousness. If we find ourselves feeling lost and limited, not knowing where to turn or how to solve our problems, perhaps, then we have turned too far from the infinite creative intelligence of the Divine Father.

When the divine is attributed to Mother Nature, we find miraculous life-giving power, exquisite intelligence, and abundant beauty. We see a living Goddess, a colossally complex, self-regulating entity who is evolving like all other life forms. We see her in the intricate relationships within nature, personified in her many aspects through the Maiden, Mother, and Crone, the eternal cycle of nature: the spring renewal of the Maiden, the summer fertility of the Mother, and the withering plants in winter reflecting the elder archetype of the Crone. We encounter her universal love as a power that nourishes, heals, and holds everything together. We find mystery.

Discovering divine power is the ultimate purpose of initiation. By stripping away all that is ephemeral, we are left with the eternal, that which cannot be destroyed. As we partner with each other—in the workplace, in education, in politics, and in our personal relationships (of any sexual persuasion), we encounter gods and goddesses in their many forms, with the potential to actualize these divine attributes in our deeds and actions. We escape our mundane limitations through practices of transcendence that lift us up and out to the great beyond. But we *actualize* our divinity through the realization of immanence— that the divine is *within us* and moves through us into the world. It is with this balanced combination of transcendence and immanence that we can create heaven on earth.

As we encounter the divine within, and as we regard ourselves and each other as gods and goddesses, even if only in training, we set the stage for divine partnership. The archetype of Sacred Marriage, or *hieros gamos,* is a Jungian concept for the mystical union between polarities. The most obvious polarity is masculine and feminine, but since these archetypes are often equated with other qualities—such as yang and yin, light and dark, mind and body, or heaven and earth—the Sacred Marriage implies an integration of far more than just gender, indeed a synthesis of opposites in general. This is not to dissolve these opposites into a dull sameness but to create from them a dynamic, constantly fluctuating relationship.

Psychologically, the Sacred Marriage first occurs within the self, as we integrate mind and body, light and shadow, static and dynamic, and the subpersonalities of our inner feminine and masculine, or what Jung called the *anima* and *animus.* Through this process of integration, we become more balanced and whole. As we embrace that wholeness, we take another step toward our divinity, with a deeper understanding of who we are and what we are becoming.

Culturally, the Sacred Marriage symbolizes not only the integration of masculine and feminine value systems, but also the combining of matter and spirit through philosophies of science and religion, bringing heaven back down to earth, with the idea of finding union— or creating it—wherever we are. Through this balance and integration of polarities we move toward peace and stability.

The Divine Child

One of the essential features of the child motif is its futurity. The child is potential future . . . a symbol which unites opposites.
—*C. G. Jung*

The Sacred Marriage of God and Goddess produces the *Divine Child,* a new and higher synthesis of divine masculine and feminine. This Divine Child is more than the sum of its Mother and Father. It is something wholly new that has never before existed, an emergent entity with unexpected powers and capacities that reach far beyond its parents. As we embrace our divine heritage of both masculine and feminine, honoring their synthesis within ourselves and within our institutions, humanity can become something greater than we have ever been before.

We are that Divine Child, both individually and collectively. We have been growing up in our own lives, just as humanity has been evolving through history. But now the child within and without is maturing into adulthood—facing the initiation that will awaken new powers to innovate and collaborate, powers needed to turn the trajectory of destruction into a cascade of creation. The challenges ahead will burn away our childishness, but it is the act of becoming parents that will bring about our maturity. For parenting is a universal initiation into the heart.

Our next step in evolution, then, is to become adults and form sacred partnerships with each other for the process of cocreating the Divine Child. *This child is nothing less than the future itself.* Our next evolutionary step is to consciously birth and foster a new era. This will be formed from a humanity that is becoming spiritually sophisticated, technologically brilliant, hyperconnected, painfully aware, and facing a time of unprecedented challenges and opportunities. These capacities are coming together just in the nick of time to help us face the initiation and guide each other through humanity's rite of passage. Parenting the future is no small task, but just as it happens in pregnancy, this process is something that is emerging *through* us at this time.

And what does a child need most after it enters the world? *Love.*

If a child is to become a healthy, loving, and creative being, then it needs a constant supply of love in the form of nourishment, attention, guidance, and support—and let's not forget play! If we are to create a thriving future, then we must also do it with love—for ourselves, for each other, and for our world and its infinite possibilities. Our challenge is to take responsibility and to work together cooperatively, just as young parents must do when they bring a human child into the world.

When a child is first born, we have no idea who she will become. We willingly pour out our love, sacrifice time and sleep, spend our hard-earned money, and teach her the best of our values and beliefs. As any parent knows, this challenge develops a deeper *capacity* to love, and with it a budding maturity. Within this crucible of service, we learn the most fundamental aspect of love: *caring*. Not that this can't be learned without becoming parents of a living human child. But I would argue that it can't be learned without taking responsibility and caring for something beyond oneself, whether it be another person, an organization, your neighborhood, or the larger world.

In the new story, we are no longer dependent children or rebellious adolescents, but interdependent adults, creating a world together, raising the Divine Child of the future. We are not passive recipients or dominant controllers, but active participants. In the new story, we are in a cocreative relationship with each other and with the divine—not from the arrogance of thinking we are equal, but from the attitude of being gods in training, starting our new employment with the humility of someone in an entry-level position. That humility requires deep respect for what the gods have given us: the mystery and balance of nature and the infinite possibility of the great beyond. We are not in any way abandoning God, but we are rediscovering broader concepts of the divine: the simultaneity of immanence and transcendence, the passionate love between God and Goddess, the infinite realm of non-local mind, the awesome power and exquisite beauty of nature. To evolve from adolescence into maturity is to move from ignorance of our divine nature to a world infused with spirit—alive, intelligent, sentient—a world of which we are an integral part.

This is our emerging myth: We are here to first realize and then restore the divinity of ourselves, each other, and the world. We are evolving into gods and goddesses to work in partnership, with the task of cocreating a divine future—a future whose purpose is to create heaven on earth through the universal organizing principle of love.

I, Thou, and We

If the universe assumes a face and a heart, and so to speak personifies itself, then in the atmosphere created by the focus of the elemental attraction it will immediately blossom.[3]
—*Pierre Teilhard de Chardin*

Since the global heart is built on relationships, the real question is, *what kind?* Are they unconscious, fused relationships, or are they differentiated? Do we see the world as an inanimate object, an "it," or is it a sentient, responsive field of intelligence, a "thou"? Do we regard ourselves as the dominators of the world, or as part of a complex web? And, the biggest question of all—*what* are we in relationship with? Who is this person we refer to as *I*? Who or what is the larger *Thou*?

To awaken the global heart is to fall in love with the world once again—or perhaps for the very first time. To fall in love with the world is to realize that everything around us is a living, sacred essence, a Thou, not an It. Trees, people, animals, mountains, oceans, and other cultures—all have a mythic reality and a unique purpose. Each carries important information that feeds the whole. Each has stories to tell, notes to sing in the grand symphony of life. Each is an essential piece of the puzzle we must solve to see our world as whole again.

Systems theorist Erich Jantsch, in his book *Design for Evolution*,[4] outlines three levels of systems, or ways of relating to our world: the *rational*, the *mythic*, and the *evolutionary* (see Figure 5). The rational system is based, as we have said, on objective reasoning and logic. It observes, measures, records, and analyzes data. It is based on an

I–It relationship. The mythic system sees the world in terms of I–Thou, seeing the subject as having its own sentience and interiority. A relationship between two people or two nations is an I–Thou—each has its interiority. The evolutionary system is based on the concept of We—a cocreative joining of I and Thou.

If we are to pass through adolescence into a responsible realization of the evolutionary power that rests in our hands, we must create balance between the rational I–It and the mythic I–Thou relationships. Only then can we begin to entertain the notion of an evolutionary We. It's not that the rational is abolished, for it forms an essential ground of our reality. It tells us how to manipulate matter and exert our will, an aspect of maturity that allows us to overcome the helpless dependency of children. But if we are merely counting (or felling) trees and failing to save or even perceive the forest, then we are destroying the larger mythic reality before we even understand what it is—and ultimately what *We* are.

How do we shift this framework in our relationships?

The basis of I–Thou relationships is authenticity. Authentic relationships can occur only between two or more subjects, not objects—each recognizing its own and the other's interiority. This requires deep introspection into our own nature and truthful communication of that nature to another. Authentic communication is a practice in which one speaks truthfully from one's interior, listens empathetically and respectfully to the other, and brings one's full awareness into the present. Authentic communication is essential for forging meaningful relationships between the interior realities of two different beings. We could say that authentic communication is a vital aspect of the fifth or throat chakra, the next chakra above the heart. Communication, both personal and global, is a skill that we can consciously develop to help open, stabilize, and balance the heart.

It is important to remember that we do not lose the I in this process. Just as an onion in the soup works best when it retains its unique flavor, the individuated I adds more to the whole by retaining its distinct qualities. Martin Buber, who wrote extensively about the I–Thou relationship, disdained the mystic idea of completely losing the self, for it precluded genuine relationship. We cannot connect to a deep awareness of the other until we have an authentic connection to the self within. It is true enough that we are one—but our diversity is essential to keep that one from becoming an undifferentiated mush.

The shift from an I–It to an I–Thou relationship with our world is one that imbues a sacred intelligence or sentience to the Earth—the biosphere of life and the Earth as a whole. To see the Earth personified as a self-regulating living entity has for some implied that She has consciousness. It is so radical to consider that the field of nature has sentience that it could be considered a second enlightenment— the discovery of consciousness, not just in ourselves but in the self-regulating, evolving, complex body of Gaia, the living Earth.

This I–Thou realization is essential if we are to coevolve with our environment to become a sustainably designed We. It is part of the initiatory experience, an essential step in the process of becoming gods, cocreating with the field around us as divine source. For in this realization, we are no longer passive recipients of reality as we find it. Nor are we ego-driven dominators, driving ourselves to extinction. Nor do we have to solve our problems alone in isolation. We are interfacing with a divine intelligence that has coordinated our world for billions of years. We can see nature as our guide, science as our teacher, and our inner experience as a feedback mechanism to help steer the way.

Rational	Mythic	Evolutionary
I–It	I–Thou	We
Subject–object	Subject–subject	Intersubjective
How	What	Where
Physical	Social	Spiritual
Science	Humanities	Future design
Experiment	Analogy	Modeling
Logic	Experience	Creation
Quantities	Qualities	Effectiveness
Laws	Values	Purpose
Behavior	Individual ethics	Group ethics
Objectivity	Subjectivity	Creativity

Adapted from Erich Jantsch, *Design for Evolution: Self-Organization and Planning in the Life of Human Systems* (New York: George Braziller, 1975).

Figure 5. Three ways of relating.

15
INTEGRATION

A Higher Synthesis

The poetic and the veridical, the proven and
the unprovable, the heart and the brain—like
charged particles of opposing polarity—exert
their pulls in different directions. Where they are
brought together the result is incandescence.
—*Pierre Teilhard de Chardin*

Thesis, antithesis, synthesis. It's an old story, espoused by philosophers since the beginning of reflective thinking. From Socrates to
Jesus, from Goethe to Hegel, from Karl Marx to the integral world
of Ken Wilber, the song of synthesis has been sung again and again
as one of the basic expressions of cultural evolution. The pattern
is clear: we begin with a basic thesis; then split off from it to make
something different; then reintegrate with the former thesis again at
a higher, more complex level. The new synthesis can become its own
thesis, from which the pattern repeats. From the splitting of chro-
mosomes in cell division to the rebellion of children in their "terrible
twos" to the bifurcation of social systems and political movements,
evolution proceeds by differentiation and reunification, novelty and
confirmation.

We can reclaim the lost ground of our past and unite it with the
technologies of the present and future. We can create mythic stories

that are tempered by rational logic and critical thinking. We can claim our personal power and sovereignty as individuals, yet know we are part of something greater than our personal ego needs. Now, as masculine and feminine forces approach a mutual maturity, we are ready for a grand synthesis. Between our common ground of the Earth and Gaia's noosphere of collective consciousness, the global heart awakens!

The archetypal Mother and Father have played their roles in our development. We are their children, now moving into adulthood, which means that, quite simply, *We are the synthesis*. We are now ready to enter relationships as adult to adult rather than parent to child, maturing to the point where we take back the reins from the past and steer the course of evolution in a new direction. As Barbara Marx Hubbard has said, we are moving from "procreation to cocreation," from the primary emphasis on the parent–child relationship to one of mutual cooperation in the service of cocreating our future. That is our child. More than just a human child, it embraces all of life and its infinite possibilities.

If the dance of thesis, antithesis, and synthesis has happened repeatedly, what's different now? Today's synthesis is the process of throwing ourselves headlong into integration itself. At our current level of complexity, it's not only a *synthesis of dualities* that is occurring, but *a convergence of plurality*. Yes, there are many dualities to unite: the politics of left and right; the values of masculine and feminine; and the balance between progress and sustainability, order and freedom, civilization and nature, inner contemplation and outer activism, mind and body, heaven and earth, us and them.

But the grandest synthesis in our world today is to to find a common purpose for a plurality of beings, a common identity in a higher order. We don't lose our individuality, any more than bone cells and blood cells become the same thing in the unity of the body. Our diversity is a necessary contribution to the whole. Those who think we are all moving into an undifferentiated oneness are missing the point that our divinity is a unique spark within each one of us. But those who fail to see the unity in our diversity are missing the larger purpose we have together.

Just as single-celled organisms cooperated to make complex creatures, just as our ancestors worked together to create the mass irrigation projects in the cradle of civilization, just as the Marshall Plan helped rebuild Europe after World War II, our impending crises will call forth global cooperation and creative innovation like nothing ever has before. For the first time in history, the entire human population is confronted with the kinds of problems whose solutions can be found only through cooperation and collaboration. Our anxiety may be no less than the pressure of planetary convergence breaking down our isolated selves in the global cauldron that's cooking our collective soup for the next banquet of the gods.

What follows is a brief look at some of the various forms of synthesis that need to take place as we enter the archetypal Sacred Marriage, give birth to the Divine Child, and create a new myth for our time. It's by no means exhaustive, but it covers some of the basic polarities that are now integrating at a higher level as the global heart emerges.

Heaven and Earth

Our task at this time is to create heaven on earth—a world so exquisite that we describe it as heavenly—a world that works for all, honoring the beauty and abundance of the natural world, the ease and expansion that technology can bring, living by the wisdom of our best spiritual traditions, guided by the intelligence of an increased knowledge base, and connected by the love in our hearts. Obviously a utopian vision, but there is no intrinsic reason why this can't be our primary goal, even if it takes many generations to be realized.

"A map of the world that does not include Utopia is not worth even glancing at for it leaves out the one country at which humanity is always heading," wrote Oscar Wilde back in 1891.[5]

The suffering, scarcity, confusion, illness, and poverty that we have created are all human made—they can be corrected. There are always obstacles and limitations, severe problems to solve, powerful political wills that fight solutions, and an immense ignorance and apathy to overcome. But we are living at the time of the greatest promise that humans have ever experienced, a new era of possibility, with knowledge, tools, and technology never before available for the solving of global problems. Can we keep from destroying ourselves and our biosphere long enough to realize our early adulthood?

To bring heaven down to earth, we must turn our spiritual reverence toward the exquisite harmony, beauty, and perfection of nature. The Earth *is* divine. As believed in the era of the Great Mother, the Earth is infused with spirit, animate and living. It is intelligent, conscious, and evolving. Human intelligence and creative abilities can be an enhancement to the Earth's creative power and need not be a detriment. The long divorce between the realms of the Sky Father and the Earth Mother can come to an end. They don't need to split up the property and go their separate ways. The children of the future can know both Mother and Father in the divine realms and see them united.

Matter and Consciousness

Without consciousness, matter would remain inert, virtually unchanging. We would be unaware of its beauty, its usefulness, or its meaning. Without matter, consciousness would have nothing to focus upon, no edges to contemplate, and no challenges to solve. Duane Elgin states this relationship beautifully:

The goal of evolution is not to move from matter to consciousness; rather it is to integrate matter and consciousness into a coevolving spiral of mutual refinement that ultimately reveals the generative ground from which both continuously arise.[6]

Both matter and consciousness exist on a continuum as partners in a dynamic dance of mutual influence and cocreative evolution. Each informs the other; each is enhanced by the other. Together, they form an integration that reflects the essence of who we are.

Matter and consciousness represent the opposite poles of the chakra system: the first chakra represents matter, earth, and the body, while the seventh or crown chakra represents pure awareness. The full system of chakras represents the continuum between matter and consciousness, with each of the seven chakras reflecting a different aspect of their integration. Chakra six, for example, as the center of intuition, insight, and imagination, is more mental and symbolic in nature, yet a bit more defined than the abstract awareness of chakra seven. Chakra five, the realm of communication, brings the conceptual thinking of chakra seven and the imaginative process of chakra six into a more tangible form as we speak our ideas to others. Chakra two, in the sacrum, representing emotions and sexuality, is more weighted toward the physical experience of desire and pleasure, arising from the body. Chakra three, the power chakra, takes mental aspects of the upper chakras into the realm of action in the physical world. The heart chakra sits in the exact center of this system, as the prime point of balanced integration.

The symbol of the heart chakra, from the ancient Tantric texts, is a 12-petaled lotus surrounding a six-pointed star. (A typical representation of this symbol is shown below.) Its intersecting triangles represent the descent of spirit into matter and the rise of matter into spirit, perfectly balanced and integrated in the center of the heart. The six-pointed star in Hindu symbology also represents the union of the goddess Shakti—the innate power of creation, related to *prakriti*, causal matter—with her consort, Shiva, related to *purusha*, supreme consciousness. This symbol has also been used to represent the intersecting masculine and feminine in the Sacred Marriage. Neither triangle is dominating; both are balanced and interpenetrating. This is a key to our awakening in the heart.

Mind and Body

Within individuals, matter and consciousness come together through the integration of mind and body. While this is changing rapidly, the term *mental health* implies that the body has little to do with our mental state, and mental health professionals are often forbidden to even use touch in the healing process. Allopathic medicine, by contrast, treats the body but until recently has given little importance to the role of the mind in health and disease.

We are now learning that chronic emotional stress can cause physical symptoms, and that illness is strongly influenced by beliefs and attitudes. We are discovering that a healthy body contributes to a sharp mind and that physical practices can have a profound effect on consciousness. We know without a doubt that chemistry alters awareness, for better or worse, whether through antidepressants, food additives, coffee, or recreational drugs. As a long-time practitioner of somatic therapy, I have been witness to the profound changes that occur when awareness and beliefs are connected to our bodily experience, or, conversely, when body sensations are awakened into realization of important truths and insights.

Too often, we live disembodied lives—spending much of our working life typing on a computer, driving a vehicle, eating things that can barely be called food, harming ourselves and each other out of numbness and ignorance. By integrating mind and body, we heal the primary relationship within the self that precludes any other relationship.

Civilization and Nature

If you read the book of Nature, no scriptures are needed.
—*Meister Eckhart*

If mind and body form the primary relationship within the individual, then the love affair between civilization and nature is the primary relationship of our collective future. This love affair is not a duty or a sentence, but a passionate partnership of beauty, pleasure, joy, abundance, health, and creativity. Like any relationship, it will have its challenges, especially when we consider the harm we've already caused. But if we can master the challenges of this love affair so that it is mutually beneficial, sustainable, and long lasting, then we will indeed have survived the initiation to the heart chakra as a global civilization. We can see civilization as enhancing nature and the natural world enhancing every aspect of civilization.

My own love of nature took me backpacking in the wilderness so often that I finally decided to live there. I was only in my 20s at the time. The spiritual revolution of the '60s had morphed into the back-to-the-land movement of the '70s, marked by the first Earth Day in April 1970. Rachel Carson's literally groundbreaking book, *Silent Spring,* had sounded the alarm of chemical pollution, and it is credited with the banning of DDT and some say the start of the environmental movement. Slowly, the world was waking up to the nightmare of our ancient struggle to dominate nature.

Single and childless at the time, I gave up everything that didn't fit in my funky old Jeep and moved to a remote mountaintop in Northern California called Radical Ridge. Here I spent several months living in nothing but a tent. Much as I loved the beauty of my surroundings, my survival and personal comfort involved a constant battle to keep the rain off my head and the bugs out of my bed. Dirt became part of everything I ate, while ants were constant mealtime companions. When the temperature dropped, the only warmth I had was my campfire and sleeping bag. I often remarked that I didn't know how people had lived in the ancient past before the invention of plastic and flashlights. Even with the modern accouterments of tools and meager technology, life was a daily struggle. These difficulties did not diminish my love of the natural world around me.

The struggle between humans and nature is ancient. From the first walls around our cities to the skyscrapers of today, from cobble-stoned streets to six-lane freeways, from dirt huts to insulated houses to high-rise apartment buildings, from stone tablets to the Internet, the ability to hold our own against nature is as much a part of our survival as the need for her preservation. Considering how long this struggle against the weeds and the bugs has been going on, we can appreciate how difficult it is to turn it around. But turn it around we must, because our successful triumph over nature has equally become our peril.

In one of her moving speeches, Julia Butterfly Hill said, "We cannot have peace *on* the earth until we have peace *with* the earth." Our long struggles with the forces of nature have left their legacy in a mind-set of "eat or be eaten." Businesses fear that environmental regulations will curtail their profits. Efforts to curb carbon emissions threaten people's accustomed lifestyles. Once when I was giving a talk, a man who ran a cabinetmaking business described how he wanted to "go green" in his materials, but the extra cost meant he couldn't keep up with his competitors. He had payroll to meet and kids entering college. What should he do? If our economics is built upon enslaving nature, then nature and economics are set at odds with each other—a battle both will lose.

Though it harks back to an ancient struggle, the separation of nature and civilization is a false one. Nature has always been our provider, the foundation for our survival, and the divine teacher. It's not that nature *has* a plan, but that nature *is* a plan. Humans, as the fanciest model yet to appear at the evolutionary unfolding, are part of this plan. When we design *with* nature in mind, we not only ensure humanity's survival but also live in a way that is more pleasant, beautiful, and harmonic with the design of our bodies and minds.

Biomimicry is a new discipline of solving human problems by studying nature's best ideas. It regards plants, animals, and microbes as the senior designers with the best engineering. From nanoparticles to flying machines, biomimicry is providing innovative solutions to common problems. Self-healing plastics, based on the body's ability to heal wounds; better aeronautics, based on the flight of birds; energy-saving buildings, based on termite mounds; visual screen technology, modeled on iridescent butterfly wings; and the ubiquitous Velcro, inspired by the burrs that stick to our socks when hiking—are all examples of biomimetic design.

While *sustainability* is an accepted and necessary buzzword of the new era, it doesn't imply a love affair. It doesn't tell us what it would be like to wake up in the morning in the midst of beauty and birdsong; to breathe clean air as we walk or bicycle to work; to have whisper-quiet transportation that emits only water vapor; to have beautiful cities adorned with parks, trees, and rooftop gardens to offset carbon emissions. It doesn't reflect the pleasure of picking your dinner fresh from a community garden made by neighbors who took their fences down, all the while being able to work from home without adding to traffic, receive news without felling trees, and be connected to the rest of the world without leaving the comfort of your home. Living in harmony with nature is not a sentence but a ticket to the liberation of the human soul.

Science and Religion

As such memorable books as Fritjof Capra's *The Tao of Physics* or Ken Wilber's *The Marriage of Sense and Soul* have suggested, science and religion are beginning to converge. Many sciences grew out of mystical traditions: chemistry grew out of alchemy, astronomy from astrology, and physics from natural philosophy.[7] The deeper we look into the cosmos—be it micro or macro—the more science looks like mysticism. Essentially, science and religion are trying to do the same thing but from very different points of view and with different kinds of data: explain the mysteries of creation and give us guidelines for how best to live. About their separation, Wilber says this:

> So here is the utterly bizarre structure of today's world: a scientific framework that is global in its reach and omnipresent in its information and communication networks, forms a meaningless skeleton within which hundreds of sub-global, premodern religions create value and meaning for billions; and they each—science and religion each—tend to deny significance, even reality to the other. . . . This is exactly why many social analysts believe that if some sort of reconciliation between science and religion is not forthcoming, the future of humanity is, at best, precarious.[8]

In Wilber's analysis, science gives us truth without personal meaning, while religion gives us meaning without empirical truth. The commonality, says Wilber, resides in the fact that they both describe a "Great Nest of Being," a holarchy of self-organization, from subatomic particles to galaxies and from primitive to expanded states of consciousness.

Both science and religion are discovering the intimate relationship between spirit and matter. Quantum physics suggests that the observer influences the experiment. Lynne McTaggart has shown how the power of intention can affect reality.[9] Physician and author Larry Dossey has published statistical evidence showing that distant prayer can effect physical healing. He describes three eras in medicine—the first is "mechanical medicine," the second is "psychosomatic medicine," and the third is based on what he calls "non-local mind."[10]

Science provides our rationality, religion our sense of meaning. When they are no longer regarded as divergent but are seen as complementary disciplines, we can have a coherent framework for guiding our future.

Masculine and Feminine

The balance between masculine and feminine is one of the most basic and necessary social healings we can make at this time. Emerging from the last 5,000 years of our collective middle childhood, where "boys" and "girls" played in separate realms, we are now, in passing through adolescence to adulthood, just beginning to create equal, authentic relationships—in the home; in the workplace; in government, religion, and education.

Clearly, we have a long way to go to achieve this balance. Women still earn far less than men. We won the right to vote only as recently as 1920 in the United States and even later in many other countries.

We still make up a small percentage of the government in most nations; and in some places, women cannot even drive or show their faces in public. Most educational institutions are founded almost entirely on Static Masculine principles, developing intellectual rigor more than emotional intelligence or intuitive development, and teaching by linear logic or rote memorization more than by experience. Politically and financially, the elite class is still an "old boys' network," much as it was in ancient times. To succeed in such a world, women often become masculinized—becoming more like men in order to achieve power.

This divide is the most marked in the religious realm. Consider the number of active temples dedicated to a goddess compared with the number of churches, synagogues, and mosques where God is worshipped as male. In the Western world, few people could name a single public place of worship dedicated to a female deity. Meanwhile, Roman Catholics still forbid women to become priests, and the church hierarchy that sets moral standards argues against women's most intimate rights: birth control, abortion, and divorce. Islam seems furthest behind of all, with some sects inflicting heinous brutality on women, such as the Taliban, who throw acid in the faces of girls wanting to go to school.

We may still have a ways to go, but at least in the West we've already "come a long way, baby." In the early 19th century, only one woman could read for every two men. Now women make up nearly 60 percent of college graduates.[11] Women do hold positions of power, even as a minority. Women's faces are now among television announcers, CEOs, and political leaders. We can own property without the permission of a husband. We can divorce, remain single, or declare a relationship with another woman without becoming an outcast. Though our rights are tenuous, we do still have the ability to obtain birth control or an abortion should we need it.

Volumes have been written on this subject. What I have tried to show in these pages is that history has progressed as a developmental process through masculine and feminine valences. We can waste precious energy blaming men for the society they were indoctrinated into. We can blame women for not stepping up to the plate, forgetting the millennia of oppression that kept them down. Both genders have been oppressed. Both have essential contributions to make to the whole. And both males and females can abuse power.

It is not only rights for women that are important. It's the understanding of how *the oppression of women has robbed the world of the feminine contribution*. Not only women but also men have suffered as a result. Men have been robbed of the softness, the balance, the beauty, and the renewal that the feminine can bring. Their work lives are often hard and cold, inhumane and competitive. Urban environments so often lack beauty and harmony that we shut down our senses in order to live there. The tendency of women to be more relational, nurturing, and community oriented is exactly what is needed to balance the brilliant masculine accomplishments of modernism.

The archetypal Sacred Marriage requires that both genders be seen as carrying essential divine aspects. Both men and women have internal opposites to integrate; both are needed to parent the Divine Child of the future. This balance is not only about male-female intimate relationships, but also about the qualities brought to any relationship—gay or straight, brothers and sisters, coworkers and cocreators. Just as this integration occurs within the self as a part of maturation, I have pointed out that it also needs to occur within our organizations, families, communities, governments, and educational and financial institutions if we are to attain our social maturity.

A global era of the heart is one in which men and women work and play together in partnership, as equals, each enhancing the other. To retain the individuality that both masculine and feminine can bring, however, it is necessary for each gender to be strengthened by contact with their own kind. Both women's groups and men's groups can strengthen a person's remembrance of his or her intrinsic masculine or feminine nature. This is especially true for women, who are often subsumed into the masculine culture and easily forget their intrinsic feminine nature.

Static and Dynamic

Our collective history reveals four distinct social patterns that combine static and dynamic and masculine and feminine archetypal energies. To review once again, we began with the Static Feminine, back in the times of the Great Mother. The Dynamic Masculine overthrew the Static Feminine and established the beginnings of the power-over paradigm. The Dynamic Masculine then evolved into the Static Masculine rigidity of law and order. We finally looked at the newly emerging Dynamic Feminine, with its free-flowing creativity and its emphasis on relationship and community (see *Figure 6*).

None of these archetypal patterns ever rule by themselves. There are always elements of each quality in any given time period and stage of life. Each pattern has its positive aspects, and each has its shadow, as shown in *Figure 7*. What is important is to integrate all four aspects into our evolving social system. The Static Feminine provides nourishment and stability, with respect for nature and her limits. The Dynamic Masculine provides power and innovation—the ability to go in a new direction. The Static Masculine provides order, distinctions, and rationality, while rules and regulations provide stability. The Dynamic Feminine provides freedom and creativity, integration and wholeness. Indeed, these qualities all occur within us and fluctuate naturally. When allowed to do so, they become complementary principles for balancing stability and innovation, consistency and change.

	Static Feminine	Dynamic Masculine	Static Masculine	Dynamic Feminine
Central Archetypes	Mother-son	Warrior-king	Father-daughter	Partnership
Organizing Principle	Nature	Kingship	Written law	Love
Values	Birth, magic, nature, body, tribe, cycles	Conquest, trade, wealth, sacrifice, dominion	Obedience, control, rationality, industry, citizenship	Freedom, creativity, inclusiveness, community, ecology
Accomplishments	Cave art, sculpture, tools, farming, pottery, weaving	Writing, mathematics, militarization, trade, architecture, empires	Philosophy, literacy, capitalism, education, science, middle class	Global communication visual media, computing, human rights, gender equality
Challenges	Survival	War, slavery	Poverty, pollution	Maturity, complexity
Era	Paleolithic and Neolithic	Bronze and Iron Ages	Antiquity to Scientific Revolution	Era of Heart

Figure 6. Masculine and feminine valences.

Static Feminine	
Positive	**Negative**
Sustaining	Devouring
Stable	Restrictive
Cyclic	Boring
Wholeness	Infancy
Undifferentiated	Unconscious
Ground	Limitation
Good Mother	Bad Mother

Dynamic Masculine	
Positive	**Negative**
Assertive	Dominating
Commanding	Violent
Innovative	Reckless
Powerful	Tyrannical
Transformative	Destructive
Heroic	Egotistical
Innovative	Disrespectful
Differentiating	Destructive

Static Masculine	
Positive	**Negative**
Stable	Rigid
Ordering	Controlling
Systematic	Bureaucratic
Detached	Dissociated
Sets standards	Disempowers
Good Father	Patriarch
Intellectual	Heady
Makes distinctions	Fragments

Dynamic Feminine	
Positive	**Negative**
Transformative	Chaotic
Creative	Undisciplined
Erotic	Indulgent
Playful	Irresponsible
Egalitarian	Indiscriminate
Inclusive	Boundary-less
Holistic	Undifferentiated
Imaginative	Unrealistic
Free	Unfocused

Figure 7. Masculine and feminine valences through time.

East and West

The cultures of East and West are converging, each contributing to the other. Some say this began in Chicago, where in 1893 the World Parliament of Religions marked the first formal interface between Eastern and Western spiritual traditions. Master yogi Swami Vivekananda, a student of Ramakrishna, attended the gathering and later traveled throughout the United States to spread the yoga tradition. In the 19th and 20th centuries, many Eastern texts were translated, and even Jung explored the chakras in his book *The Psychology of Kundalini Yoga*.[12] The '60s revolution in consciousness produced renewed interest in yoga and meditation, Buddhism, Hinduism, and contemplative traditions in general. Yoga centers have sprouted up everywhere, and books on Eastern spiritual traditions are numerous enough to fill whole bookstores. Many in the West are now practitioners of various forms of Hinduism, Taoism, and Buddhism.

The East has a rich spiritual tradition but is marked in many places by material poverty. The West has a strong material base, but one could argue that it suffers from spiritual poverty. The Eastern traditions reflect the values of the upper chakras, while the Western lifestyle is more centered on the lower chakras. To combine the two is to echo all that we have been saying about the heart—as an integration of above and below, spirit and matter, echoed through the teachings of Eastern and Western thought.

Darkness and Light

Truly, it is in darkness that one finds the light, so when we are in sorrow, then this light is nearest of all to us.
—*Meister Eckhart*

Darkness and light are the oldest and most primal of archetypal divisions. They are the primary forces in our most ancient myths, ever present in the cycles of life: sleeping and waking, seasonal turnings, and periods of depression or elation. Out of this duality springs everything we know and see—the darkness defining and outlining while the light reveals, the shadow enhancing the color and form. Beautifully paired in every striking picture you see, darkness and light are eternal partners, neither existing without the other.

If you've ever lived off the grid or endured an extended power failure, you can appreciate the ancient struggle between light and darkness. It's easy to curse the dark when your lamp goes out, when you can't find what you need, or when you're lost in the woods without a flashlight. Navigating in the darkness makes everything more difficult. When we can't see, it's easy to be afraid, to make stories out of unfamiliar shadows. We can imagine then how it might have been for our ancestors, surviving the long nights of winter without much light to guide them. It is no wonder that we have demonized darkness and equated it with everything negative: evil, ignorance, repression, the unconscious, and realms that are cold and dead.

Meanwhile, we call states of advanced consciousness "enlightenment," and most spiritual traditions favor the light as the triumph over darkness. Our quest for the light mirrors the growth of nearly all living things. We gestate in the darkness and push outward and upward toward the light.

As the challenges of our global initiation intensify, we will have to face darkness on a global scale. Whether it's a power failure due to severe storms or flooding, the inability to find a job or keep your home, the devastation of a coastal city, or the hunger that will visit much of the population, darkness will activate our initiation process. For some, this will activate the "darker" parts of their personality, causing them to reach for guns to loot and plunder wherever they can. For others, it will awaken their noble virtues, to reach out and help others.

In our quest for light, we have not only negated the darkness but have tried to pretend it doesn't exist. Acknowledging our shadow is part of the maturation process. Doing our own inner work to reclaim this shadow helps prevent it from being projected onto larger figures of society. Collectively facing our shadows of violence and militarism, greed and domination, will help us to move more fully into the light.

Agency and Communion

Evolution progresses towards greater cooperation by discovering
ways to build cooperative organization out of components
that are self-interested. . . . The only way to transcend the
opposing forces of part and whole is to move beyond them
in a way that includes them both on their own terms.
—*John Stewart*

Agency and communion are two distinct tendencies in relating to group energy. Agency is characterized by focus on the individual: self-protection, self-assertion, self-enhancement. Communion refers to behaviors that tend toward the grourp: contact, connection, and service.

As agents in the process of evolution, we must become sustainable within ourselves. We need to fortify ourselves for the work. Unless we have a healthy amount of self-protection, we are not sustainable, and many well-meaning activists have discovered the burnout that can come from too much communion and not enough agency. As individuals, we need to be able to assert ourselves appropriately when needed, or we won't be effective enough to make any difference in the world. And in this day and age, unless you are out there promoting your brand, no one will listen to you, no matter how valuable your message.

The individual serves the group by becoming the most he or she can be: enhancing self-development and mastering skills while engaging in spiritual practices, such as meditation, that help bring maturity. Ideally the group does not negate the individual but celebrates his or her unique contribution. Much as each cell in the body needs to be exactly what it is—a bone cell, a blood cell, or a nerve cell—yet is part of a singular being, we are each needed as unique individuals in the creation of a larger whole.

Yet, individualism is a trap if we don't balance it with service to a larger community. As I look out on the expanse of individual houses in any suburban area, I know that each has its own appliances and lawnmowers and countless other devices. Many of the inhabitants don't even know their neighbors but live insulated lives pursuing their own agendas. If we only pursue our individual dreams, we will create a collective nightmare. The Age of the Heart is calling us into communities of all kinds, to serve and to save what we love. Only by working together can we solve the crises that face us in this initiation to the heart.

The Path to Wholeness and Divinity

The greater the tension, the greater is the potential. Great energy springs from a correspondingly great tension of opposites.
—C. G. Jung

In one of the ten incarnations of the Indian deity Vishnu, the gods and demons line up on either side of a great serpent. The serpent's middle is wrapped around Mount Mandara, the center of the world, and his two ends stick out on either side, like a churning rope. As the polarized gods and demons continue to fight, each team pulls the "serpent-rope" in its own direction. This spins the mountain back and forth, which churns the ocean of milk, from which new possibilities emerge. (Think of the agitator in a washing machine.) From this churning pours forth both poison and the nectar of immortal life, called Amrita. As the story is told, the god Shiva, pure consciousness, drinks and transforms the poison, giving him the nickname "blue-throated one." Vishnu then procures the nectar of immortality for the gods, and the crisis is solved.

I've always liked this myth because it suggests a higher synthesis that comes out of the wrestling of dualities. As our world becomes increasingly polarized, we are witnessing the struggle to reconcile opposites, churning the ocean of milk into new possibilities. Carl Jung suggested that maturity is marked by the ability to hold the tension between polarities. He said, "The opposites always balance each other—a sign of high culture. One-sidedness, though it lends momentum, is a mark of barbarism."[13]

Jung called this integration the *transcendent function*—a place where creativity and power arise. He deplored the fact that the world had no cohesive myth, without which internal and external chaos would reign. He described the new myth emerging from a creative synthesis of mortal and immortal, shadow and light, masculine and feminine, heaven and earth. He suggested that the successful union of these opposites leads to an incarnation of the divine, or the realization of godliness.

Jung was speaking mostly about the internal aspects of the psyche but saw that this same principle of integration applied to the collective consciousness as well. *The ability to embrace and integrate polarity is essential to our maturity.* This integrative vision is exactly what we are talking about in awakening the heart: finding our wholeness and divinity through the union of opposites representing the Sacred Marriage.

In Tantric philosophy, from which the chakra system emerged, the weaving of polarities is said to create the fabric of life. When these polarities are given unequal value, with one pole exalted at the cost of the other, the fabric of life is strained. Today we see the web of life fraying everywhere. An essential step in mending that web is to rebalance polarities and weave them together once again. From the primal thesis of the Great Mother to its antithesis in our 5,000-year period of patriarchy, we are at last moving to an emerging synthesis as a ground for the future. (Some of these qualities are shown in *Figure 8*.)

The tension between opposites that Jung refers to is primarily due to the fact that these polarities are not integrated. Even worse, these archetypal polarities are often seen as "dueling dualities," where one part is pitted against another for domination and control, such as mind dominating the body or civilization dominating the biosphere. We often witness such dualistic struggles between nations and ideologies, between political parties, and within our personal relationships. More deeply, it occurs within the psyche, between our internal masculine and feminine, between our light and shadow, between our indoctrinated beliefs and our more organic emotions—internal conflicts that are then in turn projected onto the world around us. Such battles keep us in a third-chakra stage of competition and domination rather than the wholeness and integration of the fourth chakra. Ultimately, if we are to become Gods and Goddesses parenting the Divine Child of the future, we need to come from a place of wholeness within and without.

Thesis	Antithesis	Synthesis
In nature	Against nature	With nature
Prerational	Rational	Integral
Body	Mind	Heart
Feminine	Masculine	Partnership
Polytheistic	Monotheistic	Syncretic
Immanent	Transcendent	Holistic
Organic	Industrial	Ecological
Mythos	Logos	Ethos
Mythic	Rational	Evolutionary

Figure 8. From thesis to antithesis to synthesis.

16

THE PERSONAL HEART

Opening the Inner Chambers

 Life is crazily in love with us—wildly and innocently in love with us. The universe always gives us exactly what we need, exactly when we need it.
—*Rob Brezny*

We are the first beings with the intelligence to grasp how much we are loved. The eternal Thou has been courting our love with incredible gifts of abundance and beauty since time began: a planet with the perfect balance of temperature, gases, and gravity for our form of life, a food supply of unending variety, and the immeasurable beauty of mountains and flowers, trees and birds, even in remote places we might never see. The heavens provide clouds to shade the sun and make glorious sunsets by evening, followed by a canopy of stars to remind us of eternity, with a gleaming moon to light our way in the dark. Our bodies are exquisitely designed for the journey. Our brains surpass anything we've encountered in other species. Not only can we perceive the many colors and sounds, smells, textures, and tastes of the world around us—we can penetrate their mysteries.

The World Parents have been kind. The Gods have been good to us. The greatest gift we can give in return is to mature into glorious beings, worthy of our inheritance. It is time to walk into an I–Thou relationship and allow ourselves to experience profound love.

How do we embrace the eternal Thou in a relationship of sacred reciprocity? How do we open our own hearts? How do we serve the global heart? What are its realms and its requirements? What can we do to help birth the emerging Age of the Heart?

Everywhere I go to lecture on these topics, the question always remains: What can we *do*? While theory is fine, ultimately we must begin with ourselves, by opening our own hearts. This chapter explores the virtues that lift our own consciousness into an awakening heart, the first step in waking the global heart. The chapter that follows will then look at the collective areas of our world that are moving toward an era of the heart.

Waking the global heart begins with you. It is a place to begin, a daily practice to develop. For each of our hearts is a cell in the global heart, giving and receiving love. Each time we create an act of love, we inspire others to do the same. This love radiates outward from your daily thoughts and actions. It begins with increasing your capacity to really love, with the joy of giving service, and with the dedication to a higher purpose. It begins with your daily offering, your way of making something—anything—a little better than you found it. It is there, with arms open, at any moment you stop and witness the amazing miracle of creation swirling around you. Each time you remember, the trees will whisper to each other that it is beginning. The wind will carry the word. Somewhere, someone will breathe a little deeper.

Begin in Emptiness

If one is able to stay perfectly in the Emptiness, there is a quality that begins to manifest right above the surface. It has something to do with the source of all life, with Love, and with an evolutionary impulse.
—*Andrew Cohen*

Initiation usually begins with loss or separation from what we know. Such loss redirects our attention and stimulates the search for new answers. As we look squarely at the devastating effects of global warming, it is clear that loss will be rampant, whether it's loss of jobs, homes, habitats, or human life. As we have seen in disasters like Hurricane Sandy in 2012 and Hurricane Katrina in 2005, these losses are traumatic. It is important to keep in mind the bigger picture—that these traumas are a part of the collective initiation process, begging a new way of being. The loss of people's homes in the mortgage crisis highlights financial corruption. The loss of life from shootings in schools raises the question of gun control.

One of the hallmarks of loss is that it creates room for something new. Our material abundance has filled every inch of space with objects, activities, and information, along with the billboards to sell them and the oil and packaging necessary to deliver them. We are drowning in excess, and its garbage is overflowing into the oceans and rivers and landfills faster than we can remove it. We need less, not more.

Most people I know are busier than they've ever been. They can't find the time to read the books they have, watch the DVDs they own, or listen to the teleseminars they've bought. They can barely answer their e-mails or return their phone calls, let alone spend enough time with their family and friends or alone in contemplation. We have light pollution in our cities and can no longer see the stars. It is hard to find silence anywhere, even in remote wilderness areas as planes fly overhead.

We can see our losses as an invitation to emptiness. Having less, we appreciate more. Spending some time each day in silence allows us to listen to the voice of spirit urging us on to something new. There is guidance available, but we must let go of what we know, empty our vessels, and turn toward the deeper mystery of life to find it. The insights we receive may not come in the form we expect. They may not look the way we want. But just as we disengage the clutch and let up on the gas in order to shift to a new gear, we must *stop* for a moment to shift to the next level. It requires letting go of what is to make room for something wholly new to emerge.

Reach for the Divine

Human beings must be known to be loved;
but Divine beings must be loved to be known.
—*Blaise Pascal*

If initiation is for us to become more fully realized in our potential—to become as young Gods in training—then we must find a way to interface with the divine, however we perceive it. For me it is the beauty of nature and the light in the sky, but for another it may be found in a church or accessed through deep meditation, making love with a partner, or caring for children. It may be found in visiting a temple or holy place or planting a garden in your backyard. The sacred can become the ground of the new world. This means that a chosen moment anywhere—alone, with others, at work, or in the wilderness—can become a sacred moment of presence and remembering.

As we enter a state of surrender, we make room for grace to enter. Find time each day to make room for the sacred, however you define it. Whether it's your meditation cushion or your church, your desk or your dinner table, every moment when you pause to remember who you are and what an incredible privilege it is to be here at this time—you take a step into the heart.

Consecrate the ground of your home, yard, neighborhood, or workplace as sacred. When you forget, go outside and take in the light of the sun, the expanse of open air, the infinite vastness of the stars sparkling in the night sky. If you don't love the Earth, perhaps you haven't seen enough of her lately in her natural state. Consider getting reconnected with your lost and forgotten Mother Nature by visiting the wilderness.

Learn How to Care

Nobody cares how much you know until
they know how much you care.
—*Theodore Roosevelt*

When Jeffrey Betcher, a gay white man in San Francisco, relocated to a largely black neighborhood on Quesada Avenue in 2002, he discovered that he'd moved into an area riddled with violent crime, drug addiction, and homelessness. Coming home from work one day, he was deeply touched to find that his neighbor Annette had planted flowers in the corner of his yard. He was so inspired by her caring that he organized the neighborhood to plant a garden in the median strip of the street. Today the Quesada Gardens Initiative[14] has transformed a danger zone of guns and needles into a hub of community life, sporting brightly colored gardens of flowers and edible plants. Children in the neighborhood protect their garden proudly, and others are following suit in nearby neighborhoods. His actions gave the residents something to care for and took them from a path of destruction to cocreation.

In a goal-oriented society, where the ends are given greater importance than the means, there is tacit permission to avoid caring. Men on the battlefield have to deny caring for the enemy and suppress their longing for loved ones at home. Indeed, when one is fighting for survival, caring about anything except staying alive is a luxury. When we are bombarded daily with statistics of war casualties, environmental degradation, violence, and tragedies, our ability to care is eroded. Some call it "compassion fatigue"— there is just too much to address, so we numb out and push it all away. So many times when I try to talk about current events to those around me, people tell me that they gave up caring about that. The world will go as it will, they say, so why worry about it? Unless we learn to care, the world *will* go as it will—in a direction devastating for all.

Caring is an essential facet of heart-chakra consciousness. It's how the heart pays attention. If I care for you, it means I give you attention from my heart, from a place that combines both feeling and intellect, empathy and compassion. It means your experience is important to me, that I consider it in my decisions and actions. Caring says that the well-being of something or someone matters.

Caring is contagious. If I care for my children, that teaches them to care for themselves. If they see me care for my home or for the well-being of others, it teaches them to do the same. I remember working in the garden with my son, Alex, who was about seven years old at the time. I kept pulling snails off the plants and squishing them with my feet. My son burst into tears, saying, "How can you do that? You taught me not to be mean to things!" There I was, caught in my own hypocrisy. Together, we put the snails into a bucket and carried them to a nearby creek. We took the time to care.

In a world where people don't feel cared about, they have little incentive to care for their surroundings. Broken windows in run-down neighborhoods invite more vandalism. When there's garbage on the streets, more people litter. Traveling in India, when my taxi driver threw garbage out the window, I had the kind of fit my seven-year-old son had had over the snails. "How can you do that?" I shrieked. The driver wagged the top of his head and said in his Indian accent, "What does it matter, madame? There is already so much garbage on the ground."

Disempowerment diminishes our ability to care. Mistreated factory workers are not going to care about the quality of their work. David C. Korten's book *The Great Turning: From Empire to Earth Community* begins with a story about farmworkers in Central America. When the story begins, they were living in filthy conditions, sleeping on floors with no beds. As you might imagine, the *peones*, as they were called, cared little for their own appearance, their health, or the quality of their work. They would stand frozen to the spot while cows escaped through a hole in the fence unless they were given direct orders to do something different. They had little capacity to care for themselves or their surroundings. Under new management, they were treated differently: better food to eat, clean clothing, something to sleep on, medical care. As they were given more responsibility, the peones took better care of themselves, and the horses and cattle also began to thrive. During a two-year period under new management, the herd increased from 700 to 1,300 with no increase in staff, and the calving rate nearly doubled.

Caring is easiest when we have direct contact. If you feel connected to your cat, you can't imagine eating her for dinner—but you might have less qualms about the meat in the grocery store. As we become more connected in our world, our capacity for caring increases. Publicizing the plight of factory workers making iPhones in China produced pressure on Apple to improve working conditions. Violence, torture, and cruelty of all kinds has been in steady decline, largely because of humans' increased capacity to care about these things—to empathize with the interior experience of another.

What is more difficult to maintain is an attitude of caring for what is beyond our immediate range of contact. To care about climate change, for example, is to care about something in the future, the worst of which you might not live long enough to witness. It is to care about the millions who live in coastal cities, to care about the countless species that will go extinct, to care about subsequent generations. To care whether your shoes were made in a sweatshop, your food was packaged in a factory, the animals you eat were raised in captivity, or your actions affect someone on the other side of the world requires a capacity of caring that is a new evolutionary skill.

Extending one's care into the larger world begins by caring for yourself. Far from being a narcissistic indulgence, self-care is a way of being fully present. I interrupted my writing this afternoon to go to a yoga class because my body needed to stretch and my attention on my work was wandering. I wrestled with the dilemma of caring for my deadline and caring for my body. I looked at what would be most sustainable, even optimal, and now I'm back, calm and clear to continue my work. I suggest that deep self-care actually *replaces* narcissism. When we care for ourselves, we free others from having to do it for us.

Coming through the individualistic third chakra is a necessary precursor to learning to care for others. The psychotherapy movement that caused baby boomers to be dubbed the "me generation" taught us that there really was someone inside, someone with wounds and feelings, desires and destiny. By getting in touch with our own vulnerability, we develop the ability to sense the interior of another. Indeed, you can see in the history that preceded this discussion that humans have operated without regard for the interiority of another for most of our collective childhood. Caring is a hallmark of maturity and evidence that we have entered the global heart.

Unfortunately, it's not so simple to just say we need to care more. The world is hugely complex, and the problems are extensive. Do we have the capacity to care for everything? What if we care about two or more things that are mutually exclusive, such as caring about our children's need to have us home and also about our work and service to the world? What happens when caring for ourselves is in seeming contradiction to caring about another—such as when we need to leave a relationship, hurting someone we love? What happens when so much is ailing that we become overwhelmed with caring? Can we care about the wars and the financial crisis and climate change and human trafficking and GMO foods and economic corruption and orphaned children and not get fatigued?

Sheva Carr, from the HeartMath Institute, told a story during a Shift Network teleseminar in 2012 about an experience she had had several years before. She had been thinking about the dire conditions of women in Afghanistan living under the Taliban. She wondered what she could do but felt powerless, as she held a regular job working in a store in America at the time. She decided to do a daily meditation of imagining Afghani women and bringing them into her heart. After she had done this practice for some weeks, three women in burkas coincidentally walked into where she was working at the time. She told them about her practice and got their names and addresses, asking if she could write to them. She began a correspondence, telling them how much she cared about their horrible conditions. Later the women wrote back to her and said what a difference her letters made back in Afghanistan. They said that women on the verge of suicide were choosing to stay alive because they knew someone cared about them.

The first step is to care for what you can directly influence: your home, your family, your neighborhood, and your work. If caring is contagious, the act of caring sparks that consciousness in others, as well as improving your surroundings. We also have choice over what we buy—where the products come from and how they are made. While we can't take direct responsibility for every ill in the world, what we buy is a statement about what we support. Is it worth a few extra dollars to make a statement about clothing made in sweatshops, wood that destroys the rainforest, or practices that cause harm? Even the commitment to stay informed is an act of caring.

As we develop a culture of the heart, we make it fashionable to care. Mother Teresa was lauded for her extreme generosity and service to others. The Caring Institute, founded in 1985 and inspired by Mother Teresa, has the distinct goal of promoting the values of caring, integrity, and public service, nominating people annually for caring awards.[15] Many organizations reward philanthropy and are too numerous to list. Volunteerism is higher than it's ever been: Gen X'ers (born between 1965 and 1981) more than doubled their volunteer rate between 1989 and 2010, from 12.3 to 29.2 percent. In 2010, 8.1 billion hours were volunteered, at an estimated value of $173 billion.[16]

Finally, caring is its own reward. Senior citizens who live alone have better health when they have a pet to care about. People heal more quickly from cancer and other illnesses when they have a support system of people who care. Giving youth something to care about makes them less likely to get into trouble. Caring about our world not only revitalizes our surroundings but boosts our health and well-being.

Grow Your Gratitude

If the only prayer you say in your life is "thank you," that would suffice.
—Meister Eckhart

Imagine that you are giving a gift to each of two children. One claps delightedly, thanking you, and runs off to play, appreciating her gift. The other plays with the gift briefly and then tosses it aside or complains, "This isn't what I wanted!" Which child opens your heart? To which child do you want to give more?

The heart opens when we truly appreciate the many gifts in our lives. The food we eat each day that someone else grew, harvested, trucked, and sold; entertainment at the flick of a switch; instant access to the world's information; clothing that's just our size; a climate-controlled shelter to sleep in—all these are here to support us in making a contribution. They take away the struggles of survival so that we can give more of our gifts. Can you receive these blessings and say "Thank you!" with all your heart?

Now for the harder part: can you be just as grateful for your challenges? Think back on the difficulties you've faced in the past. How much did you grow? What did you learn? Where did they lead you? To curse the world is to separate from it. To thank your fate is to embrace the lessons. When tragedies occur, simple things that we take for granted become as precious as life itself: water, food, shelter, clothing, legs that can walk, hands that can reach, eyes that can see, friends or strangers that help us out. To those who have lost these things, their return is a rich blessing, each one met with immense gratitude.

What we appreciate appreciates. Gratitude is a remembrance of all that we have received, which increases the experience of value. We don't need more "stuff." We need more appreciation of what we already have. Gratitude opens the heart.

Practice Generosity

Real generosity toward the future lies in giving all to the present.
—*Albert Camus*

A question often asked at parties is "What do you do for a living?" We might better ask, "What is your giveaway?" For some people, their work and their offering are one and the same. For others, work is just an exchange in order to receive a paycheck that allows them to *get* what they want.

If gratitude opens the heart, then generosity gives it wings. The real test of character—that which lasts beyond our few decades of life—is what did we leave behind? What did we improve? There is freedom and lightness when an act is done without the purpose of reward. We work hard to *get* the things we want. What if that effort went equally into giving?

Success occurs when you leave something better than you found it. If you have a relationship and your partner is better off because of your influence, that relationship has been a success, whether or not it lasts forever. If you work at a business, and each day you leave it in better shape because of what you've offered, your work has been successful. If you visit someone's house and leave it cleaner than you found it, you have left behind a gift of grace.

Our talents are the gift that the Divine gave to each of our lives. What we make out of those talents is the gift that we give back. You have an opportunity to give at every moment. Whatever you can create as an offering, whatever help you can give, whatever compassion and empathy you can extend beyond yourself, do it now. Contribute to the future. Make it a priority. Ask what you can give rather than what you can take. Even if it is just a daily prayer or a small act like picking garbage off the street or helping an elderly neighbor, do something *daily* to improve the world around you.

If you have money, contribute to struggling organizations that are working hard to save this world. Help someone go to school, get out of debt, start a business. If you have time, volunteer at a nonprofit you believe in. If you have influence, use it to create change, inspiring others to work from the heart. If you have artistic talent, make an offering where it is most needed—singing in a retirement home, beautifying your street, or reading poetry to prisoners. If you have more than enough of something, give some away. Even if you think you could sell them, see what it feels like to just give some of your possessions away.

Think of something wild and crazy to do as a surprise for someone. Create a special present: clean her house, babysit for her children, mow her lawn, leave cookies on her front porch. If you really want to challenge yourself, do this for someone you scarcely know—or even someone you dislike!

If we create a culture of generosity, there is more for everyone. Competition, if it is a function of human nature, then becomes a competition for how much we can give rather than what we can get. The poet Rabindranath Tagore wrote: "I slept and dreamt that life was joy. I awoke and saw that life was service. I acted and behold, service was joy!"

Cultivate Compassion

If you want others to be happy, practice compassion.
If you want to be happy, practice compassion.
—Dalai Lama XIV

Empathy is the connective tissue of an I–Thou relationship. If generosity gives the heart wings, then empathy gives the heart its ground. It occurs whenever we can see and feel another's experience. It is the glue of relationships, the sacred connection with another person's interior, the key to I and thou.

Jeremy Rifkin, in *The Empathic Civilization*, says, "Empathy becomes the thread that weaves an increasingly differentiated and individualized population into an integrated social tapestry, allowing the social organism to function as a whole. Each new stage of consciousness represents an enlarged central nervous sustem encompasing broader and deeper realms of reality."[17]

Empathy is the building block of compassion. It begins when we learn to listen with the heart. Here we drop all judgment and preoccupation with our own dramas. We simply extend our awareness to see and appreciate another's experience. Much of this happens on a feeling level, for feelings are the texture of experience. When we feel *with* another, we open to compassion, which literally means to be *with another's passion*. The opposite of compassion is judgment, which comprehends only the outer behavior, not the inner experience. Compassion is the warp and woof of the heart's tapestry. The Dalai Lama tells us,

As long as you have compassion, you will be free of the deepest anxiety. The capacity to devote yourself to the welfare of others yields otherwise unobtainable power and potential for good. Generate great compassion, and you become a friend to all sentient beings, a companion to all other altruistic beings and a cherished child of the enlightened.[18]

We had to go through the third-chakra stage of discovering the personal interior in order to be able to relate to another's interior. Compassion begins by being in touch with your own wounds and longings. It expands by being in touch with the suffering of others. It is expressed in the dedication to relieve that suffering as much as you can. As natural disasters and tragedies are blasted through the media, and as the Internet connects more people from disparate parts of the world, we have ample opportunity to practice compassion.

It is now believed that there is a neurobiology of compassion. We have discovered that human learning occurs, in part, through cells of the brain regarded as "mirror neurons." Neuroscientists, using functional magnetic resonance imaging (MRI), have discovered that when one person is watching another do a particular task, such as a child watching a parent peel a banana, identical parts of the brain light up in the child, mirroring the parent's activity. Mirror neurons have been suggested to be the basis for how we learn language and tasks and the means for emphathy.

Further MRI studies have confirmed that the more sensitive among us actually "feel" the pain of others, with activity in the pain centers lighting up, for example, while watching others get an injection.[19] Jeremy Rifkin, in his book *The Empathic Civilization,* states, "In virtually all of the studies of mirror neuron activation, researchers find that participants who score high on empathic profile tests show more active and elevated mirror neuron responses."[20] There is truth to the statement "I feel your pain."

It is the nature of the heart to resonate—heart cells on a petri dish beat in unison—and a healthy heart enters a kind of vibrational coherence whose field envelops the body and surrounding areas. The Institute of HeartMath has shown how the heart generates a measurable field, as much as eight to ten feet out from the body. When we are in the presence of another person or group, our electromagnetic fields overlap. If we are suffering or in pain, or if another in close proximity is hurting, it follows that the coherence of the shared field is affected. Dr. Daniel J. Siegel, who uses the term *interpersonal neurobiology*, suggests that the mirror neuron system forms a kind of *resonance circuitry* that has been shown to be fundamentally involved in human empathy and emotional resonance.[21]

Offer Forgiveness

Forgiveness is the fragrance that the violet
sheds on the heel that has crushed it.
—*Mark Twain*

In my former role as a therapist, I often told my clients, "Resentment is like drinking poison and hoping the other person will die." Resentment anchors us in negativity without changing our reality. Forgiveness, by contrast, frees the heart to love again.

Forgiveness is not the same as condoning. It doesn't mean that what someone did to you was OK. It just means that you are releasing yourself from the stance of victim and letting go of blaming your more difficult teachers. It doesn't mean that you have to go back into relationship with the person who harmed you, but it does create more freedom to love when you let go of that relationship and move on. Forgiveness gives us the opportunity to practice compassion and acceptance.

Often, forgiveness can happen only when the emotional work

of healing the wounds has been done. For those wounds need to be felt and grieved. Anger may need to be appropriately expressed, then released. Tears of grief and loss may need to be shed. Another person may need to witness the pain you have endured. Once the emotional clearing has taken place, forgiveness completes the healing process.

When we, ourselves, have been the wrongdoers, forgiveness is courted through genuine apology. This can come only from taking the time to see the harm we caused—not as a criticism we must defend against but from a place of empathy and compassion, seeing the other's reality from an I–Thou perspective. Without comprehending the depth of another's wounds, apologies can feel empty.

Embody Spirituality

Your task is not to seek for love, but to find all the barriers within yourself that you have built against it.
—A Course in Miracles

If evolution is the Gods' way of making more gods, then we have a long way to go. We don't look like gods, we certainly don't act like gods, and we don't treat each other *or* ourselves as gods. We are instead wounded, out of shape, unhealthy, insecure, and largely unconscious far too much of the time. *It thus becomes each person's responsibility to work on himself or herself.* Far from being a purely narcissistic impulse of the boomer generation, self-improvement is an imperative to realize our untapped potential as potential gods. The qualifying difference is whether we engage in this self-improvement from a place of ego—endlessly preening ourselves for a socially sanctioned beauty rating—or as an offering to the whole, creating ourselves as works of art, honing mind, body, and spirit into an expression of our glorious humanity.

It is no surprise that in the age of the couch potato, we have bodybuilders. In the overwhelming glut of information, we empty our minds in meditation. In the massive wounding that seems to leave some piece of emotional shrapnel in every man, woman, and child, we have psychotherapy and self-help books. In a drug-addicted culture, there are 12-step groups and treatment facilities in every major city. In an educational system that focuses almost exclusively on intellectual knowledge, we have exponential growth in workshops, yoga centers, and dance movements like Gabrielle Roth's 5Rhythms.

We improve ourselves because there is *so much more we can be.* We can do this as an offering, not a taking, a way of bringing beauty into the world, a contribution of intelligence, artistry, or strength— not just for ourselves, but as a contribution to the marvelous reality we are creating together.

A profound spiritual revolution is going on all around us. People are waking up to the underlying spiritual reality hidden in the miracle of life. They are leaving their churches to create spontaneous ceremonies in their backyards. They are leaving corporate boardrooms to take yoga retreats. They are voluntarily meditating, fasting, and reading books on spirituality—not to please God or avoid damnation but to regain a sense of the sacred. Sales of books on spirituality are growing faster than any other category of the book industry, with billions in sales annually. Spirituality has even become an industry, as more stores and catalogs feature spiritual accouterments, such as candles, incense, meditation cushions, yoga props, Tibetan bells, prayer flags, and statues of deities. Today's spirituality is not so much an act of worship, sacrifice, or petition as it is a means of elevating one's consciousness to a place where an overarching spiritual reality becomes apparent. Through these practices we enter the ultimate I–Thou relationship. As Martin Buber said, this is how we become fully human.

The spiritual revolution going on today is not made from dogmatic beliefs. It cannot be contained by a church. It does not have a dictatorial moral code. It is not even a social movement, as was Christianity, but a movement that is more often intensely personal. It takes place deep in the interior of one's being. Its focus is not on gaining access to a faraway heaven but on transformation and awakening right here, right now. As a do-it-yourself road to higher consciousness, it's a direct interface with the divine, through meditation, prayer, chanting, hiking, gardening, circling, dancing, drumming, lovemaking, singing, study, contemplation, and psychoactive substances. When practiced in groups, it is cocreative, egalitarian, and spontaneous.

Spirituality of the new era is not born of the mind alone, for it recognizes that we are glorious beings in phenomenal bodies, living on an exquisite, material planet. This is not an either-or value system that pits one part against another, but an integrative spirituality, integrating heaven and earth, mind and body, and bringing them into the sacred center of the heart.

As we expand our own consciousness and enter the reflexive self-awareness of internal questioning, we become more and more aligned with the truth of our own nature. Indeed, one of the necessary requirements in today's busy world is to learn how to remain centered.

In the chakra system, the heart is the very center of a system of seven centers, with three chakras above and three below. Indeed, I have often seen the chakra system as a spiral or set of concentric circles, rather than a linear system. This puts the heart at the very center indeed, perhaps the ultimate goal, the inner mystery. *The heart, then, is not the source of consciousness but is the prime integrator of consciousness.* The more we come into our deep core center, the more we integrate all levels of our being. The more deeply we honor the I–Thou relationship with the *anima mundi* (the soul of the world), the closer we get to the realization of a single unity, a very large and wonderful We.

The spirituality of the emerging era is both immanent and transcendent. The transcendent aspect allows us to step away from our petty concerns, to detach and see things from a distance. If you were holding this book against your eyes, you couldn't read (and the older we get, the farther away we have to hold it!). We all know that distance gives perspective. Archimedes said that if he had a lever long enough and a place to stand, he could move the world. Ken Wilber points out that we need to be able to differentiate from something before we can operate on it. When we identify an awareness distinct from the urges of our bodies, we have the capacity to override those instincts. By separating from matter, we can inspect and dissect the material world, solving many mysteries. While this separation has the danger of leading to fragmentation and dissociation, it is a necessary part of the evolutionary pattern—to separate, differentiate, and reintegrate at a higher level.

The separation that is needed now is to *take a step back from the culture itself*. As long as we are unable to detach from the incessant cries of advertising, sensationalist media, and political spin, we are hypnotized into the cultural trance that is consuming the biosphere. From that hypnotic state we can do little to change the world. We need to be able to disengage from its more insidious qualities in order to imagine something new. That means turning off the TV and breaking the hypnotic commands that tell us to consume. We need to listen to the birds and the wind at least as often as the evening news. We need to read poetry as often as the newspaper. We need to go online and get news stories from other sources, conducting our own investigations into truth. We need to separate from our culture in order to transform it.

As a vehicle for transcendence, meditation is by far the most ancient, tried-and-true, simple, effective, inexpensive, go-anywhere, do-anytime kind of practice there is. It is a vehicle for transcending the mental matrices that keep us behaving in unproductive patterns, beliefs, and habits. Meditation allows us to disengage the clutch of life long enough to shift to another gear, a shifting that is desperately needed at this time. Meditation allows us, in the words of Willis Harman, to shift from seeing external authority as the *source* to discovering internal authority as a *resource*.[22]

Meditation is not, however, something that affects the individual alone. In studies conducted by the Transcendental Meditation Society in 24 cities where 1 percent of the population meditated regularly, meditation was shown to be statiscally linked to drastically reduced crime, when compared with control cities of similar geographic region, population, and education (http://www.t-m.org.uk/research/46.shtml). Can the global brain meditate itself into a new world?

Practice Acceptance

Gratitude, compassion, and forgiveness all lead to acceptance. The heart gives a sigh of relief when you settle into acceptance of how you are right now, so that you can truly be here fully, in this moment. The heart purrs approvingly when you apply that acceptance to others and appreciate their beauty in spite of their flaws. Each person you see struggles against gravity each morning; each one has faced troubles and loss, obstacles and lessons. They are all doing the best they can with the tools they have. If you find yourself criticizing others, ask instead how you can help. For each of us truly wants to live the best way we can—we just need a little help in doing so.

The heart's sweetest blessing—and one that brings waves of gratitude—is the realization that what is here is enough, that we don't need more. It is amplified by reflecting the light we see in another back and forth until it is bright enough to light the world and herald a new dawn.

Celebrate

Let what you love occupy the center of your life. Make the fulfillment of your longing your highest priority. When your longing is answered, you will have cause to celebrate. The realm of the heart is filled with what you love and the things that make you happy. Our joy is made from the willingness not only to protect what you love but to enhance it—polish it until it shines, feed it your lavish attention, and bring it into the center of your life. If you love the wilderness, spend as much time there as possible. If you love music, play it often; listen to it even more. If you love children, find ways to spend more time with them.

The heart is nourished by celebration and play, pleasure and beauty, creativity and laughter. These are the seeds of love. They are the ground from which it grows, and they are present in every new relationship. It is not a loving act to wish suffering on anyone. Why would the *anima mundi* wish suffering upon humankind? Joy is a sign that the heart is open. Contentment is a result. Foster the Age of the Heart with glorious celebration, creative collaboration, and passionate production of continuous delight.

Be an Imaginal Cell

As the imaginal cells in the emerging butterfly that we discussed in Part One, we each need to awaken our own heart and then find each other through the calling of our hearts. Whatever calls to you, find like-hearted others with similar interests and understanding. Notice what you resonate with, what brings you to your highest. Organize among yourselves, and then join your groups with others. This doesn't mean that we avoid groups with different ideas—far from it— but that we nourish ourselves with what resonates within our hearts.

When I wrote the first version of this book over seven years ago, I felt that we were still largely at the stage of individual imaginal cells looking for their kindred others. As I traveled, I saw people isolated, being the only one in their geographic communities who understood their particular field of interest—whether they were engaged in a particular spirituality, worked as an alternative healer, researched new ideas in science or politics, or found new forms of relationships, such as being gay, bisexual, or polyamorous. I saw people coming together in conferences, yoga classes, coffee shops, events, and meetings, trying not to feel so alone in their views.

I see how we have increasingly coalesced into communities and organizations—but now we need to take the next step: bringing those organizations together. Organizations that collaborate will generate greater efficiency, more abundant economics, and more coherent power. When organizations combine instead of compete, we don't have to reinvent the wheel. We can have more powerful and coherent messages, making bigger impacts. We can compile data, share mailing lists, combine publications, and use fewer resources.

There is an organic process to becoming a butterfly, but the term *imaginal cells* implies that we have to keep imagining it—every day. Seeing is an active process of the imagination. We can look at a child and "see" what he or she is becoming. We can balance our media news stories of violence and gloom with images of healing, peace, and the greening of everything: the environment, technology, and the economy.

THE GLOBAL HEART

Opening the Outer Chambers

> Someday, after mastering the winds, the tides, and gravity, we shall harness for God the energies of love, and then, for a second time in the history of the world, man will have discovered fire.
> —*Pierre Teilhard de Chardin*

By living the values of the heart—in all our choices, large and small—we move from the love of power to the power of love. These values reflect the wholeness of relationships as much as their constituent parts, focus on cooperation over competition, networks more than markets, sustainability more than infinite growth, and compel us to be active cocreators of a world that works for all rather than passive victims of social and environmental collapse. The infrastructure of our society has been built—the buildings, houses, and roads are there, the tools and gadgets have been created, the channels of distribution established. Now the question is, *what do we do with it?*

In the last chapter, we looked at the personal attributes of living a heart-focused life. This chapter examines our collective social systems and the heart-based trends that are already under way—or need to be—to point us toward an Age of the Heart. While the first seeds go as far back as the Buddha's preaching of compassion, the first democracies of ancient Greece, and Jesus's preaching of forgiveness and love, then more recently the influence of Mahatma Gandhi's nonviolent actions for peace and Martin Luther King's demands for social justice, we are only now capable of implementing these principles globally instead of just locally or nationally. With the wonders of communication technologies to increase connectivity and spread information across the globe, and the rights and responsibilities of personal power moving ever more into the hands of individuals, we can now begin to realize the possibilities of this new operating system of the global heart.

We still have a long way to go before we are solidly in this era. Realization of such things as world peace and a sustainable global economic system will not take place quickly or without a struggle. Most of us alive today will not live long enough to see this accomplished. Much as we long for and even need quick fixes, the initiation of humanity into its next era is a long, slow process of dismantling what doesn't work and building new systems in their place. The changes are indeed under way. Many people are devoting their intelligence, creativity, finances, and time toward building this new world.

Adolescents live for the moment. Becoming parents of the future and cocreating the Divine Child of our new myth requires that we take the long view. Our challenge is to think beyond immediacy, to hold a vision of the big picture, and to roll up our sleeves and open our hearts to help make it happen.

The following categories describe some of the outer realms of the global heart. These trends show progress in the direction of the values we have discussed: freedom, justice, peace, sustainability, compassion, and joy. May the various factions and organizations within these trends recognize each other as imaginal cells in the emerging butterfly and join forces cooperatively. May you, dear reader, find resonance with these trends and help them come into being. And may the myth of cocreating heaven on earth become a reality.

From War to Peace

*Peace has the capacity to blow like a great wind of change
that transforms the entire social order, but it begins with a
breeze that must stir in the center of our own being.*
—James O'Dea

World peace, if we can attain it, could be the most essential social realization of our time. As great as the invention of writing or mathematics, airplanes or computers—greater than the discovery of subatomic particles or the creation of the great cathedrals—the accomplishment of world peace will produce blessings we can barely imagine. By harvesting the resources tragically wasted in defense, violence, and destruction, we can redirect our intelligence, capital, creativity, and collaborative efforts toward not only solving our many problems but creating exciting innovations. The military, when mobilized, as it was at the start of World War II, can accomplish amazing feats. Some of our best innovations, such as the Internet, began in the military as a way to protect information exchange during times of crisis. Can we use that same mobilization in the service of solving our problems rather than finding new enemies to kill?

The Sanskrit name of the heart chakra, *anahata* (meaning "unstruck"), implies nonviolence. We cannot evolve fully into the Age of the Heart without outgrowing war. This requires a sophistication that transcends third-chakra aggression and domination as a way to solve problems and moves toward the higher chakra attributes of communication and cooperation. Aggression becomes a developmental stage we can blessedly grow out of, rather than an inevitable facet of human nature.

The peace of *anahata* comes from preventing harm at all levels possible, from domestic violence to racial discrimination, from worker intimidation to poverty and violent ideologies. Peace is not merely the absence of warfare, any more than true health is simply the absence of disease. Nor is peace simply a quiet state of equilibrium—impossible to achieve in an evolving system. Though refraining from harm is an essential first step, lasting peace is created by actively redressing harm already done, through empathetic dialogue, values clarification, conflict resolution, apologies, and restitution. Peace is a creative process of uniting divorced polarities, settling the wars within ourselves, elevating consciousness to more mature and educated perspectives, using effective communication, and actively joining I and Thou into a cocreative We. It requires authentic communication and wildly creative solutions. It asks us to heal the traumas that perpetuate violence through the generations with skill and compassion.

Communication and creativity—which are related to the fifth chakra in the throat—offer ways of lifting us out of power struggles and into cooperation, ways of fostering empathy, compassion, and forgiveness. As the physical technology of communication gets ever more sophisticated, we need to simultaneously increase our skills in *how* we communicate. Universities now offer programs in conflict resolution, peace negotiation, and mediation. Marshall Rosenberg's Nonviolent Communication model is a brilliant and accessible form for evolving our interpersonal communication and reaping the benefits of true, empathetic understanding. James O'Dea, the author of *Cultivating Peace*, shows how we can all become "peace ambassadors." The absence of peace has in part been because of the lack of effective communication skills. Other aspects that need development are the hard work of building democratic institutions that ensure that the rule of law is aimed at guaranteeing human rights and social justice.

The process of peace building begs us to reduce the violence in our media. At the movies recently, I was bombarded for nearly 30 minutes with violence in the previews of coming attractions. I thought about how the average child growing up will have viewed *200,000 acts of violence* on television by the time he is 18.[23] How much are we all assaulted by images of violence every day, against our choosing? When the news continually directs our attention to stories of violence and gore, when we incessantly focus on what's wrong in each other (or ourselves), when we pit one side against another in all our debates, we are only affirming the old story. This framework permeates not only our language but our thoughts, our games, and our entertainment. We are reinforcing a culture of violence.

Michael Nagler, author of *The Search for a Nonviolent Future,* advises us to overcome the habit of using violent language in our communication, much as we sensitized ourselves to sexist language in the past few decades. To speak of the war on poverty, the drug war, the battle of the sexes, combatting racisim, even the fight for freedom, is to continue a way of thinking that is based on conflict. While these issues are all important, we need to focus on solutions rather than using a battle vocabulary. Instead we can speak of healing poverty, rehabilitating drug users, integrating the sexes, building bridges to minorities, and claiming our freedom.

The movement toward peace has been in process for a long time. That there is such a thing as the International Criminal Court to prosecute war crimes is progress. That the invasion of Iraq was debated as long and widely as it was is progress. That issues of torture have been brought into the public light is progress. That fewer died in the first *year* of the Iraq war than in the first *few days* of World War I is actually progress. It may not be fast enough to stave off the insane perpetuation of suffering that occurs daily, but clearly there's a worldwide trend away from war and toward peace. This is part of our maturation as a species.

Despite media that lead us to think otherwise, in truth our age is not nearly as violent as the 5,000 years of sibling rivalry that led us to this point. We simply are more aware of the violence and find it ever more intolerable. Harvard psychologist Steven Pinker, in his book *The Better Angels of Our Nature,* shows throughout 700 pages of pain-lessening detail how violence has declined in every known area of human life: warfare, genocide, homicide, torture, racial violence, domestic violence, child abuse, and public views about violence in general. At the time of this writing, Americans are now turning their attention toward gun control, something that was so accepted 240 years ago that it was written into the Constitution.

According to Pinker, the number of people killed in wars has declined a thousandfold over the centuries,[24] while the number of conflicts, as well as their scale, has also decreased. Prior to the establishment of countries, battles took the lives of more than 500 people per 100,000. Even in the 20th century, with two world wars, it was only 60. Now battlefield deaths are down to .3 per 100,000. In the United States, rape is down 80 percent since 1973.[25] Likewise, discrimination against blacks and gays is diminished, as is child abuse and capital punishment. When we consider that people in the Middle Ages used to brutally murder and torture each other for crimes as minor as criticizing the wrong person, the fact that we have moved from witch burnings to hangings to lethal injection and now toward the abolishment of capital punishment in general is remarkable progress.

The reasons, Pinker cites, are the increased powers of the state to enforce laws; the increased value of life, now that we live longer and have more quality of life; the realization that there is more benefit from cooperation, such as trade being more profitable than plundering; and an expanding circle of empathy, from clan to tribe to nation to the world through connection to ever larger groups of people. He also writes that the strengthening of human rights and the status of women is directly proportional to the decline in violence, and that IQ tests show that people are getting smarter with each generation, and simultaneously more peaceful.

On February 15, 2003, 10 million people around the world marched for peace. Not just in Washington, San Francisco, New York, and Boston, but in Paris, London, Madrid, Rome, Berlin, Copenhagen, Tokyo, and Mexico City—and several other cities around the world. Many of the nations represented were not going to war, but their people turned out in record numbers to plead with the United States to avoid the debacle that killed over 100,000 Iraqi civilians, took hundreds of billions of dollars out of our economy, and turned out to be based on lies. There is only one way to end terrorism, and that is to create a world in which it has no purpose.

No one escapes being hurt somewhere along the way. Wounding and betrayal, abuse or trauma, disappointment and loss—these painful demons come to us all and leave their marks upon the heart. In response, we tend to wall off our hearts. We create a separation inside, a kind of war within ourselves, which, like all wars, creates suffering and numbing and wastes precious energy. War against nature, war within our own nature, war against others, and war against nations—it's all been around for so long that we have accepted it as a fact of life. When forces that have been locked in struggle and aggression find their way into peace, there is a vibration of harmony that can be felt by all. So many times in my past therapy practice, when patients integrated warring parts of themselves or resolved a deep conflict with another, there were cries of relief and tears of joy—the sound of a soul coming back home to its natural state of wholeness. This results in a deep peace that comes not from self-control, laws, or regimentation but from deep, inner healing. When old battles are resolved and wounds are healed, the heart has more room to truly open and love.

When we make elements of peace into something triumphant, when good deeds are celebrated in front-page headlines, when the wars within us find resolution, we create peace day by day. We direct attention to the fact that it *is* possible, that it *is* occurring, and by this act we help it to increase. We can make peace a central value in our emerging myth of raising the Divine Child of the future and cocreating heaven on earth.

What would be the "unstruck" sound heard round the world when at last arms were laid to rest, nuclear weapons were dismantled, and the newspapers no longer featured violence on the front page? What would be the sound on the radio that announced that humanity had, at last, put an end to war as a means of solving differences? What kinds of programs could be supported by our tax dollars if we weren't spending the bulk of them supporting our military? What kind of news might we talk about instead?

The achievement of global peace is a survival imperative. For the escalation of armaments will surely make war obsolete—either by eliminating the species that persists in using them or because we'll no longer be able to afford them. In the larger world, the unstruck sound is the chorus of harmony rising from the masses, the great unfurling of evolution, set once again on its course of synthesis after thousands of years of divergence. For when society is ordered around violence and militarism, enormous energies and funds are squandered that could otherwise be used creatively. As global crises escalate and financial markets tumble, we will reach a stage where we simply can't afford to squander so much of our money on the military. Our greater "enemies" will not be other nations or people but environmental problems to solve, such as climate change, water shortages, and food shortages. In the past, a common enemy has united a people. Perhaps our common problems will unite us at last.

In the words of Michael Nagler, professor of nonviolence at the University of California, Berkeley, "Nonviolence is a creative force that contains within itself the principle of creative order." When we are no longer engaged in the duality of win/lose, we must instead invent creative solutions. When whole populations are no longer oppressed, then their creativity can be unleashed. The song that is waiting to arise is a harmonic, multisymphonic masterpiece of creation singing the morning song that signals the dawn of a new era.

In the words of Mahatma Gandhi, "There is no way to peace. Peace is the way." To this I add: The way of the heart leads to peace. Peace, in turn, opens the heart.

From Egosystem to Ecosystem: Embracing Deep Ecology

Environmentalism has been seen as a separate strand.
In fact it is the fiber that all strands are made from.
—Hazel Henderson

Ecology is literally the study of our home and the maintenance of its balance. How do we maintain our homes in daily life as we mature? Kids need to be told to clean up their rooms, whereas adults do it as part of their daily routine. If we are to mature as a species, humanity needs to be taught the lessons every teenager needs to learn: clean up after yourself, don't use the last of something without replacing it, conserve energy, recycle your garbage, think of others besides yourself, and treasure what's been given to you. Simple enough. Can we learn this as a species?

In living ecosystems, an immature species is by nature competitive, aggressive, and territorial, taking advantage of whatever niche or conditions bring it benefit. In a mature forest, the dynamic interplay of species has reached a balance with other life forms, using maximum employment and recycling everything. A mature ecosystem is not controlled by a single species. It is a dynamic balance in which each part serves the whole.

The biologist Elisabet Sahtouris states, "Young species are found to have highly competitive characteristics: They take all the resources they can, they hog territory, they multiply wildly. Sound familiar? But a lot of species have managed to grow up, to share territory, to cooperate. It's what keeps them alive."[26] Can we learn this simple principle of cooperation? If so, we can save energy, heighten creativity, and ensure the continuance of our place in evolution. Can we see our rapacious behavior, our refusal to limit population, and all our greed and denial as an act of immaturity and accept the responsibility that brings the privileges of adulthood?

Growing up is learning to cooperate not only with each other but also with the limits and laws of nature. Creating appreciation for the natural world would be a fundamental part of every child's education. When we mature as a species, we will pride ourselves on having a beautiful and healthy collective home. Pristine forests, undammed rivers, clean air and water, systems of clean energy and maximum recycling, would all be values considered *before* the dollar, not after.

We are too far removed and far too numerous to return to nature in the way we once lived so long ago. We cannot go back to our infancy and breastfeed, and we can't support the present world population by hunting and gathering in the wild. But we can employ a relationship with nature in all that we do. Schools can have beautiful gardens in addition to paved playgrounds. Children can take field trips to wilderness areas as often as to museums and factories. Urban homes can be built with rooftop gardens, and more suburban areas can have community gardens. We can imagine every newspaper carrying a section on the environment that is equally as detailed as the sports or finance section. For which item is more important to our survival—the winner of the latest football game or how to live sustainably with our environment?

History has come a long way since the natural world was so abundant that our ancestors could not imagine its diminishment. The train of evolution has been accelerating in a single direction—toward replicating ourselves and taking what we need to survive. As we then came into the power era, that train gained incredible momentum, multiplied exponentially by population and technology.

Living green goes beyond survival, however, revealing unexpected treasures. In areas of greater greenery there is a noticeable reduction in crime. In one Chicago study, buildings with high levels of greenery had 48 percent fewer property crimes and 56 percent fewer violent crimes than identical apartment buildings with less greenery.[27] In another study, there was less graffiti, vandalism, and littering.

Richard Louv, in his book *The Nature Principle*, has described how nature areas promote kindness and caring, mental performance and vitality, and faster healing from illness or surgery. What could we become if we lived healthier lives in the green cities of the future?

From Occupy to the New Economy

The human community and the natural world will go into the future as a single integral community, or we will both experience disaster on the way. However differentiated in its modes of expression, there is only one Earth community—one economic order, one health system, one moral order, one world of the sacred.
—*Thomas Berry*

Since the first ziggurats rose from the plains of the Tigris-Euphrates valley, all the way up to the struggle between Wall Street and Main Street in America today, the gap between rich and poor has always been a chasm of separation. From God-kings and emperors to their slaves, from feudal lords to the serfs who worked the land, and from the 1 percent of the population that owns a third of America's net worth to the 99 percent of the rest of us, the unequal distribution of wealth is fed by the love of power.

While the gap between rich and poor has always existed, the Occupy movement, which began in September 2011, brought public attention to our increasing inequalities. Even as one out of seven Americans worries about having enough to eat, sales of luxury goods, such as fancy cars, furs, and airplanes, are up. In 1962, the top 1 percent of Americans had a net worth that was 125 times that of the median household. By 2010, that difference had shot up to 288 times the median, according to the Economic Policy Institute.[28] Meanwhile, America's median income suffered a decline from $73,000 in 1983 to $57,000 in 2010, with 46 million Americans living below the poverty line. In the same period, the top 1 percent saw their average wealth grow from $9.6 million to $16.4 million.[29] The average pay of CEOs in the financial sector is $4.9 million, while the average annual salary across the United States is $26,000[30] (as of June 2012).

This is the state of affairs in one of the wealthiest countries in the world.

Outside of America, approximately two billion people live in abject poverty, with little or no access to safe drinking water, while 2.6 *billion* do not even have access to sanitation.[31] Eighty percent of the world's population lives on less than $10 a day, and thousands of children die each day from starvation, dirty water, and other preventable causes, many while you read this chapter. These statistics do not impart, however, the deplorable conditions of hopeless lives suffering miserable conditions, struggling for mere survival. Even on our own modern streets, most turn away from the panhandler on the corner. Yet I argue that from someone's perspective, we are all part of the 1 percent. The cost of my soy latte might supply someone with the only food he has that day. If I can't consider giving that up to offer a few dollars to the beggar on the street, how are the elite 1 percent going to contemplate parting with their millions? We are all part of this system of haves and have-nots at some level.

The increasing prosperity gap over the last 30 years shows that money is *not* trickling down from the rich to the middle class and below. If anything, the lower ranks keep trying to climb up the ladder of success to whatever degree is possible—not out of love for what they are doing but out of an urgent need to overcome powerlessness, seeing wealth as the only way to do so. If our economy is anything like the circulation system of an organism, in which each cell needs a constant supply of blood, then today's economic system resembles a blood clot, concentrating wealth among the few. It cannot survive this way much longer.

A good deal of the blame for our environmental degradation may lie with the economic system itself, thoroughly mired in the third chakra, power-over paradigm. In the words of Charles Eisenstein, author of *Sacred Economics*,

> The true culprit, the true puppet-master that manipulates our elites from behind the scenes, is the money system itself: a credit-based, interest-driven system that arises from the ancient, rising tide of separation; that generates competition, polarization, and greed; that compels endless exponential growth; and most importantly that is coming to an end in our time as the fuel for that growth—social, natural, cultural, and spiritual capital—runs out.[32]

Increasing debt due to interest on loans seems to be at the heart of it. If you lend me $100 at 10 percent interest, I must pay you back $110 (or more if it is compounded). At the risk of oversimplifying, a system based on credit requires unequal exchange—always paying back more than is given.

Ultimately, our goods are based on natural resources—many nonrenewable, such as oil, or slow to renew, such as forests. We continually draw down from this natural warehouse to pay for profit or to pay our increasing debt, unable to replace the raw materials at the rate we are taking them. When these resources are gone, they cannot be fixed with a bailout. Stimulating growth to buffer a failing economy only hastens this inevitable crash of our resources.

To keep the insatiable hunger of a profit-driven system going, we continue to do meaningless work, buy unnecessary goods, and contribute to pollution. Getting people to their jobs and getting goods to households uses oil and contributes to greenhouse gases. Extra costs for advertising to make people buy goods they don't need hikes up the prices, and the whole system keeps everybody too busy making a living to deal with the issues that are really important. Meanwhile, the ultrarich continue to buy our democracy, turning it into a corporatocracy—rule by the corporate interests.

Such a system is clearly unsustainable and will inevitably collapse. While a full discussion of economic theory is beyond the scope of this book, there are encouraging trends pointing to the gradual evolution of a new economy. Our economic crisis is creating alternative models more reflective of the heart's organizing principles: circulation, collaboration, peering, openness, sharing, gifting, and networking. Eisenstein foresaw this, saying,

> The next stage of human economy will parallel what we are beginning to understand about nature. It will call forth the gifts of each of us; it will emphasize cooperation over competition; it will encourage circulation over hoarding; and it will be cyclical, not linear.[33]

Underneath the doom and gloom of failed banks and epidemic foreclosures, a new economics is already happening. More cooperative practices are arising in communities everywhere: lending libraries for tools or cars so that we don't have to own things we rarely use; gifting and barter economies, where money doesn't even change hands; free-cycling networks where goods are given away for free; introduction of local currencies to keep wealth in communities; microcredit lending to help the poor get a leg up; and moving from high- to low- or even negative-interest loans. As the old system creates more scarcity, we are forced to innovate new ways, and many discover hidden abundance in the process.

Marjorie Kelly, author of *Owning Our Future*,[34] describes the difference between an extractive economy and a generative economy. The former has the sole purpose of increasing wealth by extracting resources and turning them into products. A generative economy is more focused on serving human needs, on what it can generate for others. We are shifting from a nonrenewable goods-based economy to a renewable service- and information-based economy. She encourages us to think like cathedral builders, whose labors would be realized by future generations.

Don Tapscott and Anthony D. Williams, in one of the most hopeful books I've read on the subject, *Wikinomics: How Mass Collaboration Changes Everything*, describe in case after case how established companies that are utilizing collaboration, peering, and networking are experiencing unparalleled success. They state,

> The real revolution is just getting started. Except this time the competition is no longer their arch industry rivals; it's the uberconnected, amorphous mass of self-organized individuals that is gripping their economic needs firmly in one hand and their economic destinies in the other.[35]

It's been a long-held belief that without the lure of money to get us motivated, no one would do any work. We would simply lie in bed all morning, watch TV, and eat bonbons. Yet enormous value is being created outside the realm of economic reward, with more examples every day. Who hasn't used Wikipedia, the people's encyclopedia, where entries are written and peer-reviewed by panels of experts, most of whom offer their expertise for free? What about Linux, an open-source operating system collectively created by various programmers in their spare time, working without pay, benefiting over a billion users directly or indirectly through Google, Yahoo!, home appliances, and cable boxes? Even IBM estimates that it saves nearly a billion dollars a year over what it would have to pay to develop an operating system as effective as Linux.[36] Open-source collaboration operates according to three basic rules that fly in the face of old economic platforms: (1) nobody owns it, (2) anyone can improve it, and (3) anybody can use it. What is the benefit to all of us when we emphasize what we can offer rather than what we can get? For the 50,000 people who attend the desert festival of Burning Man, which operates on a gift economy, the result is a world of unbridled creativity beyond belief or description.

Other examples abound: consider the vast array of YouTube videos, many quite good, created for free access. In his book *Blessed Unrest*, Paul Hawken observes that the largest movement on earth today is a people's movement into nongovernmental organizations (NGOs) that address issues of sustainability, social justice, peace, democracy, and consciousness. This movement is not inspired by monetary reward, dictated by power, enforced by regulation, or commanded by an authority. It is a self-organizing movement arising out of people's free will to serve and to save what they love.

> This is the largest social movement in all of human history
> . . . coherent, organic, self-organized congregations
> involving tens of millions of people dedicated to change.
> . . . If you look at the science that describes what is
> happening on earth today and aren't pessimistic, you
> don't have the correct data. If you meet the people in
> this unnamed movement and aren't optimistic, you
> haven't got a heart.[37]

When you look at the work we put into raising our children, maintaining our homes, or learning a skill, you can see that it is equally part of human nature to make a contribution, regardless of pay. By contrast, people doing a job "just for the money" are less likely to put their best creative effort into it. Most people I know would give even more to their communities if they didn't have to spend the bulk of their time making a living.

Just as the polis in ancient Greece created a town-square forum in which people could share ideas, the Internet today provides our new polis, which the authors of *Wikinomics* call an "ideagora"—a place where problems and solutions can be matched up, a kind of eBay or Craigslist for innovation.

The Human Genome Project is an amazing scientific advancement that resulted when pharmaceutical companies rose above their private interests to back open collaborations. InnoCentive, a privately held firm founded in 1998, connects over a quarter-million individuals from nearly 200 countries for the purpose of solving problems in business, science, technology, engineering, agriculture, statistics, and more.[38] Through their network, an obscure genius in China who may have discovered a new chemical agent can be connected with a researcher in any other country who might be looking for just that information. The search for the solution to problems can draw from a wider variety of researchers than any company could afford to employ. We are now witnessing the emergence of global networks that enable greater creativity, faster problem solving, and efficient money savings in ways that never before existed.

Centralized power and distribution worked well when we lived in small kingdoms. It works well in corporations, even in small to mid-size countries. When that system expands to global proportions, its reach becomes too extensive to be an efficient system. Banks "too big to fail" crash, with the taxpayers or depositors footing the bill. One proposed solution to decentralize banking and money supply is for states to have their own banks. The only state in the country that has done so thus far is North Dakota, and it's the only state with a budget surplus. Seventeen more states are considering following this model. In Germany, about half of the total assets of the banking system are in the public sector.[39] This enables workers in small firms to have as much access to capital as workers in larger firms, resulting in higher salaries for all—often 50 percent higher than U.S. average salaries for similar work.[40]

Hazel Henderson, author of *Ethical Markets: Growing the Green Economy*, reports on her website, EthicalMarkets.com, that in the third quarter of 2011, her Green Transition Scoreboard® showed private "green" investments worldwide at $2.4 trillion since 2007, with a prediction of $10 trillion by 2020.[41]

As we make the transition from a goods-based economy to a service and information economy, we make exchanges that cost less energy to produce, move, and maintain. More people in affluent countries today are divesting themselves of excess possessions and responsibilities, downsizing their homes and businesses to move into a lighter way of being. What is flexible is more resilient in times of rapid change. Adaptability in products is occurring through the phenomenon of *prosumers*: a combination of producers and consumers, where the customer contributes to the creation and upgrade of products.

The broad goal of the new-economy movement is participatory, ecological ownership—working in smaller, localized units ruled more by stakeholders who have a personal stake in a situation than by stockholders whose stake may be distant and merely financial. More than 130 million Americans belong to some kind of cooperative or employee-owned company. Twenty-five percent of American utilities are publicly owned. Credit unions are swelling with over 10 million accounts moved out of big banks into local credit unions as a result of the Move Your Money campaign that arose from the Occupy movement.[42] Microlending helps people in poverty worldwide, offering very small loans to the poor with a high success rate in responsible repayment.

Ultimately, economics should be tied to real value built upon preservation of the sacred ground that supports us all. When there is catastrophe, neighbors willingly roll up their sleeves to do what is necessary. If the economic system had a complete collapse, and not one dollar had intrinsic value, communities would engage in barter and generosity—neighbors pitching in together to grow food, take care of children, educate, and prosper as best they could. As the current economic system continues its decline, barter, gift systems, and local currencies will necessarily arise.

Economics today has reached a peak of abundance for an elite few yet extreme scarcity for others. Obvious to most, a new economic system is needed, and is indeed evolving under the radar of stock market ratings and corporate manipulation. Exactly what the new order will look like is not yet known, as this is yet another element in the process of our initiation. What we do know is that we will not survive unless we have an economic system that is more equitable, is less rapacious to the environment, and creates a circulation of currency that supports our highest values of sustainability and abundance.

Abundance allows for—and often requires—a new organizing principle. Such abundance not only frees up energy to move in a new direction but also can present unexpected challenges and negative consequences. In the broad sweep of history (shown in *Figures 9* and *10*), you can see how new eras began to form around the time when a previous era reached its peak. Following is a brief summary of the rise and fall of the various eras discussed in these pages.

In the first-chakra era, farming would have begun when our successful survival skills produced enough population that a tribal, nomadic lifestyle was no longer suitable. It is logical that our ancestors at the time would have settled in areas with abundant plants and animals, eventually learning how to farm for themselves. Here began the rise of agriculture as an organizing principle.

In the second-chakra era, as farming allowed settled villages to stabilize and prosper, hunting and gathering gradually declined. At the peak of this era, when large-scale irrigation projects, such as those in Egypt and Mesopotamia, allowed us to supply even bigger populations, we built the great cities of early civilizations. Thus began the third-chakra era, often organized by hierarchical power structures and military aggression, giving rise to the first dynasties and empires.

In the third-chakra era, as people slowly migrated from farms to cities over the ensuing millennia, the pastoral lifestyle of agriculture gradually declined, and the industrial lifestyle became the norm. Industry produced enough material abundance that some people had the freedom to separate from the status quo and begin a new inquiry. Starting with the Romantic writers of the early 19th century, who revived the values of nature and the feminine, the fourth-chakra

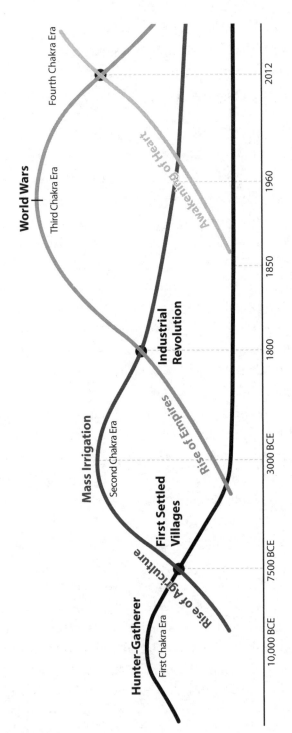

Figure 9. The rise and fall of chakra-based eras.

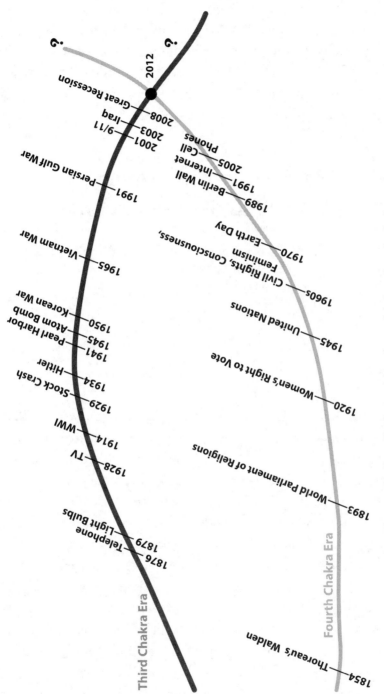

Figure 10. Detail of transition from third to fourth chakra era.

era then gained ascendency as industrial pollution and the atrocities of two world wars revealed the flaws in the imperial system. This movement toward the heart picked up momentum in the '60s and crossed paths with the gradual descent of the third-chakra paradigm only recently, with 2012 as a suggested date. *Figure 10* shows this part of our recent history in more detail.

From a Chain of Command to a Web of Connection

The history of the world is none other than the progress of the consciousness of freedom.
—*G. W. F. Hegel*

Man's capacity for justice makes democracy possible; but man's inclination to injustice makes democracy necessary.
—*Reinhold Niebuhr*

Mohamed Bouazizi was an educated man unable to find work. Whether through courage or lunacy, he set himself on fire in the streets of Tunisia to protest what for him was the last straw of police corruption—the tumbling of his vegetable cart over the lack of a permit.

It was December 2010. The desert world in which his body burned was a tinderbox of smoldering resentment, easily flaring into rage. Decades of rule by totalitarian regimes, vast gaps in wealth and privilege, and organizing made possible by electronic communication devices all led to a fiery revolt that spread across the Middle East and became known as the Arab Spring. Bouazizi's flame sparked a movement that at the time of this writing has overthrown rulers in four countries—Tunisia, Egypt, Libya, and Yemen—with civil uprisings in Bahrain and Syria, and major or minor protests in at least a dozen additional countries. Some say these revolts were the spark for Occupy Wall Street, which has spread all over the world. It is a movement from a top-down authoritarian rule toward a more democratic one, a clear shift from third-chakra organization to a fourth-chakra system of networks and collaboration.

It hasn't been easy. Tens of thousands have died horrendous deaths or been imprisoned or tortured in this ongoing fight for freedom in the Arab world. Nor are the current victories in Egypt, Tunisia, and elsewhere the end of the story. The Arab Spring movement exemplifies the difficulty of overthrowing the old order and the struggle of the new order to create any order at all. Religious fundamentalism, tribal fighting, and other entrenched beliefs still block the successful transition to good democratic leadership. The power paradigm that maintains strict authoritarian rule at all costs disempowers its citizens and thereby keeps them immature. When they finally rise up to take their power, there is no certainty that they have the knowledge or ability to govern themselves well. Establishing a new government in the midst of tumult is not easy. When it happens in organizations (let alone countries) where a father figure has some kind of failure—such as a fallen guru, corrupt CEO, or hypocritical religious leader, the result is a long and messy road to a new organizing principle. Many organizations don't survive this transition, but the ones that do come out stronger and more resilient than ever before. It's no wonder that in times of turmoil, joblessness, and uncertainty, people vote more conservatively, and we often witness a rise in religious fundamentalim.

From the progressive side, it's easy to shake one's fist at controlling regimes with old-world perspectives and play the victim. Whether it's a teenager to his parents, a worker to her boss, or a country to its dictator, criticizing the oppressive side of power is the easy part. Creating a better system is by far the bigger challenge. For this reason, old and new systems need ways of sharing power, utilizing the best of both.

The land-based community of my youth was countercultural to the core. Our activities were many: we produced events, built houses and barns, maintained a garden, published a magazine, taught workshops, led expeditions, and raised children. After several years of struggles and success, we set aside a day to examine what was and wasn't working, and why. Much to our surprise, we discovered that the projects that were headed up by a single person who took charge of the matter were more successful than those done by committee. This flew in the face of our philosophy, yet we had to admit it was true.

The top-down model of leadership has its place as an effective model for coordinating human effort—but the issue is most often one of scale. When the reach becomes global, such as corporations that exploit lands on the other side of the world, harming communities they will never see, there's a big gap between decisions made and people affected. When top-down models are dictatorial, they disempower participation and creativity. When the rulers of top-down systems are corrupt, the whole system is affected. In smaller organizations where people have more contact with each other, the gaps between power and its effects is smaller.

Growing up is messy business. It takes time. New regimes can seem as dysfunctional as the old. Committees can take longer to make decisions and implement policy than individuals or small boards. Yet, just because something is immature doesn't mean it's a failure. There is a new principle budding, and it continues to unravel the chain of command and reorganize itself into a web of connection. It is not an either-or process but a gradual reweaving of the way in which humanity governs in a complex and changing world.

The third-chakra power-over paradigm has held a growing humanity in some semblance of order for nearly 5,000 of its formative years. Static Masculine forces have held the job of maintaining ironclad rigidity—first forged in the Iron Age, then marshaled through the Dark Ages and smelted into the machinery of the Industrial Revolution. When humanity was younger and groups were smaller and more localized, top-down control worked appropriately. Ruling through a chain of command was the most direct way to combat the chaos that might have otherwise ensued in an illiterate pre-tech world of exploding population.

But now, humanity has grown to seven billion citizens, with increasing numbers who are educated and technically savvy, many armed with computers and smartphones, awakening to an uberconnected global civilization with a massive convergence of planetary crises. As moneyed interests continue to deny the realities of climate change and rip the financial guts out of social institutions designed to provide justice and equality and help people to survive, we see that the old order is now pushing us *toward* chaos, not away from it. But it is simultaneously stimulating the creativity that will lead to a new order by producing such disequilibrium, as systems theory suggests.

Like the butterfly coming out of the chrysalis, the new organizing principle can't take place before it's ready. Those who have power and wealth seldom want to let go of it. A parent holds the power until she deems her teenager mature enough to handle it—even if that parent is an abusive alcoholic. If you forcibly take the butterfly out before its time, it will die.

From an archetypal perspective, the old paradigm *can't* let go until there is enough maturity and organization in the new paradigm to keep society from descending into chaos. Like a new tooth pushing the old one out, this process is taking place beneath the mainstream view.

The wobbling of the powers that be is showing the strain. Extremism, lies, spin, and manipulation have gone to greater lengths than most of us could have imagined this far into the 21st century. There are those who say the American political system is broken, yet it's not much better in the rest of the world. Some countries have it far worse, with totalitarian regimes or excruciating tribal warfare. The majority of Americans (85 percent)[43] feel that the government is focusing on the wrong priorities. Less than half of the U.S. population shows up to vote, and our highly computerized voting system is easily subject to fraud. Politicians, forced to spend more than half of their time fund-raising and campaigning to stay in office, can't possibly stay ahead of the multiple issues they must address—each of which takes a lifetime of study in order to rule wisely. Our system of Congress, based on geographic representation, created when the United States comprised 13 colonies of land-based people, hasn't been updated for the highly nuanced complexities of an eco-techno-global operating system. No matter whom we elect, nor by what process, no single president, prime minister, king, or queen will solve our problems for us: it is part of the initiation that citizens roll up their sleeves and take part in the process.

What's the alternative?

As I have shown in this book, it's already happening. Mass movements of people into nongovernmental organizations (NGOs) are taking power into their own hands by creating vast webs of connection to replace old chains of command from the top. They are addressing topics that centralized governments are failing to solve, such as social justice, environmental sustainabilty, green technologies, the peace process, democracy, and the study of consciousness. NGOs are largely funded and supported outside government. Green technologies are funded more by private-sector investment than by government subsidies, which tend to favor oil interests and military contractors. Neighborhood coalitions, volunteer organizations, are creating self-governing entities to address the problems that matter to our future survival. Transition towns—communities that are working at the grassroots level toward becoming self-sufficient in response to peak oil, climate change, and economic instability—are popping up everywhere. The Transition Network lists over 1,000 registered transition initiatives worldwide.[44]

Our disillusionment with the current system is an evolutionary driver toward a new operating system. The second Bush administration's denial of climate change, for example, inspired 300 mayors to get together and see what they could do to address the issue at a municipal level, resulting in the U.S. Conference of Mayors Climate Protection Agreement in 2005. After the financial collapse in Iceland, more than 20,000 people gathered in conversation cafés to discuss the situation and redefine their values, which resulted in the election of a different kind of leader.[45] The Bush administration actually did wonders to indirectly further the evolution of such progressive organizations as MoveOn.org.

Systems theorist Meg Wheatley says, "In Nature, change doesn't happen from a top-down, strategic approach. There is never a boss in a living system. Change happens from within, from many local actions occurring simultaneously."[46] This is what we are now witnessing worldwide in local movements of reform and democratization.

Top-down representative democracy, paid for by special interests, is no longer representative. As long as a few make decisions for the many, we have a representative democracy that is subject to purchase and influence by corporations and special interests. "Participatory democracy" depends quite literally on how much we are willing to participate. David Korten, in *The Great Turning*, says,

> The practice of real democracy involves a continuing and vibrant citizen engagement in meaningful deliberations in a wide variety of public forums. These can range from a modest neighborhood gathering in someone's living room; to events organized by local churches, colleges, and community services organizations; and to complex networks organized by national citizen groups using electronic communications media and pulling technology to involve thousands, even millions, of people.[47]

America Speaks (AmericaSpeaks.org) is one such organization. Its mission is "to reinvigorate American Democracy by engaging citizens in the public decision-making that most impacts their lives." Through its 21st Century Town Meeting technology, more than 160,000 people from around the world have had an impact on their communities. Along this same line, the Kettering Foundation (Kettering.org) exists for the purpose of researching the question "What does it take to make democracy work as it should?" Its research is conducted from the perspective of citizens and focuses on people's collective power to address problems in their communities and nation. The National Issues Forum (Nifi.org) conducts forums on various issues of concern. In concert with Public Agenda (PublicAgenda.org), it produces informational pamphlets on these issues for distribution. These are just a few of the thousands of organizations forming to address deeper issues of democracy, ever more possible now that we have attained global communication, greater networking, and both local and global perspectives.

In the new world, it is not so much who has the answer but how to harvest collective intelligence for solutions far wiser than any one person can provide. Tom Atlee, founder of the Co-Intelligence Institute and author of *The Tao of Democracy*, has spent his life focusing on the kinds of processes that make public deliberation possible and effective. He states,

> "Power-with" involves cooperation and synergy. It is the power that arises when we use our collaborative intelligence to work with others or to work with nature. The "power-of-wholeness," or holistic power, is the power at work when we bring together all those involved in a situation, organization, or community for real dialogue that includes all relevant persepctives. It is the power of self-organization present in each person or system as a whole.[48]

A democracy is supposed to be a government "of the people, by the people, and for the people." It is only now, with our advanced technology, that this kind of participation, deliberation, and collaboration makes such a dream possible.

As our next level of cooperation moves from nation to planet, there will likely evolve some kind of limited, constitutional, democratic world government. This will not replace local or national governments, because its role will be to deal exclusively with global problems—such as war and pollution—that transcend national borders. To make it work, many checks and balances will need to be put in place to ensure against corruption. Yet if we can evolve a truly democratic world society where the benefit of the future and the well-being of the whole take top priority, this mode of governance will provide a platform for harvesting the expertise of the world's greatest minds to solve our most urgent global problems.

In the words of Plato, "The greatest price of refusing to participate in politics is being governed by your inferiors."

From Isolation to Connection

Driven by the forces of love, the fragments of the world seek each other so that the world may come into being.
—*Pierre Teilhard de Chardin*

We have only just begun to have a network of information that can act as a global feedback mechanism to help us know who we are and what we are becoming as a collective entity. A common vision to save what we love can impel us to cooperate and innovate. Our rational, scientific systems can tell us how to do that. Our webs of connection can show us how to collaborate to make it work. Our mythic framework can paint the vision. The crises of our time will impel us to innovate and mature.

As civilization grows more complex, it is simultaneously becoming increasingly interrelated. Throughout cultural evolution, the trend has been toward uniting larger areas of land, populations, and cultures under a single system of government, language, or customs.

Modern technology has made possible a global network of consciousness. Information travels through this network at the speed of light. News of any major event reaches broadcasters in a matter of minutes, makes its way to a majority of listeners and readers within hours, and seeps into even outlying areas within days. If intelligence is measured by the speed at which information is absorbed, the global brain is getting pretty darned smart. If intelligence is defined by memory capacity, the Internet is the most colossal storehouse of information next to the biosphere itself, and both have their library doors open around the clock. If intelligence is defined by the ability to learn and evolve, the global brain—at least in geological time—is organizing itself and evolving at lightning speed. Higher states of consciousness have been defined as ones in which consciousness is omnipresent—everywhere at once. When I can access the Internet from an airplane six miles high or check e-mail on my smartphone while riding a chairlift up a ski slope, I have entered a neural net whose consciousness is simultaneously everywhere.

There are basically three levels in the human brain, responsible for different levels of consciousness; this is called the *triune* brain by neuroscientist Paul D. MacLean. The reptilian brain is oriented to survival instincts, such as eating, sleep, and sex. It is the source of the kill-or-be-killed mentality. The mammalian brain, or the limbic system, is largely oriented to emotion and bonding. It rules over our feelings, the emotions of rage and joy, envy and loneliness. The neocortex is what makes us distinctly human. It is this latest development of the triune brain that has evolved the intellect of the rational mind, the reasoner and the thinker. The neocortex gave us the mother of invention and the father of abstraction. The frontal lobe of the brain, in particular, is said to be responsible for the ability to plan for the future and the capacity for compassion, empathy, and moral behavior. As authors Lewis, Amini, and Lannon of *A General Theory of Love* point out, "Emotions reach back 100 million years, while cognition is a few hundred thousand at best."[49]

If the Internet is analogous to a growing neocortex for the Earth, or Gaia, as an evolving entity, then perhaps the global brain is at last evolving to a state where *collective* intelligence becomes capable of future planning, moral behavior, and acts of empathy and compassion. This noosphere of consciousness is still so new in evolutionary terms that we have yet to see what will result.

Pierre Teilhard de Chardin described the noosphere as moving steadily toward a coalescence of consciouness, which he named the Omega Point, a supreme center of a higher order. He describes Omega as a "distinct center radiating at the core of a system of centers."[50] Within this system, each element of consciousness is at least partly centered upon itself. Even when looking outside, our waking consciousness is fundamentally self-referential. He believes that by centering within our own core, we automatically come into association with a greater center that encompasses us all.

The heart is the center of the chakra system, which in turn is aligned vertically along the center core of our being. This makes the heart the center of centers, the core of the core, the unifying chakra of an evolving collective organism. It is the integrator of polarities, the coordinator of synchronous beating, the distributor of circulation, the center of that which brings things into relationship through the universal power of love.

18 WHAT'S LOVE GOT TO DO WITH IT?

The Heart Has Its Reasons

 The heart has its reasons of which reason knows nothing.
—*Blaise Pascal*

Mike Herr is not your typical postal worker. For 38 years he has made it his mission to cheer up the customers in the long lines at his post office. He jokes with them or offers a compliment, even if it's simply writing "Nice Sneakers!" on an envelope. His motto: "If you can't say something nice about someone, you're just not looking hard enough." As a result, his community has made him the grand marshal of the homecoming parade. The kids took to the streets when his boss told him to take down the decorations he had put up in his office. People line up to buy stamps from him just because he's so much fun to talk to. They walk away uplifted with a better attitude for the day. Even schoolteachers have said that Mike inspired them to be more positive with their students, showing how simple acts can have ripple effects.[51]

I used to drive my kids to school in Berkeley, California. Every morning, rain or shine, a beaming elderly man would be standing on the corner with a big smile, waving and saying "Have a nice day" to each car that passed by. He was always greeted with honks of appreciation, and it seemed that he exuded positivity into the otherwise dreary commute. He became a much-loved fixture for many years with this simple act.

In a Canadian drive-through coffee establishment, the generosity of one customer who paid for the customer behind him set up a "pay-it-forward" momentum that lasted for three hours and 228 customers. A seven-year-old boy, Dylan Siegel, raised $30,000 for research for his best friend, who had a rare disease.[52] At five years old, Haley Whatley set up a yearly donation of stuffed animals for her local children's hospital. By the time she entered college, she had donated nearly 30,000 stuffed animals to sick children.[53] A homeless man returned a diamond ring mistakenly dropped into his begging cup and received $100,000 in donations from the community. In Dallas, sisters Isabelle and Katherine Adams, ages six and nine, improved lives in distant Ethiopia and India by raising $120,000 through selling origami ornaments and collecting matching funds for their cause.[54]

These are small acts of kindness and generosity that ripple into the collective field in unexpected ways. They can be enacted by anyone, rich or poor, young or old. They are not done with hope of reward, but from an open heart. They do not solve all the world's problems, but each one helps to bring a little more heaven down to earth. Even small acts make a difference. We can all be part of this awakening, inspiring others to do the same.

Our Neural Network of the Heart

Heart-based living is about including your heart's intuition as you navigate through life's relationships and events. This brings balance to your mind and emotions and unfolds your authentic self.
—Doc Childre, founder of HeartMath

The human heart has its own kind of intelligence. It operates like a neural network, exhibiting such sophistication that it's even been called a "little brain" or a "heart brain." With over 40,000 neurons, this intricate network is capable of memory, cognition, intuition, and even decision making.[55] Those who receive heart transplants, for instance, often report that they experience memories, feelings, or preferences of their heart's donor.[56] In addition, the heart produces oxytocin, the hormone that promotes bonding, and emanates an extensive electromagnetic field that surrounds the body.

Neural networks process information through interconnected links and hubs, much as the Internet does today. In their book *A General Theory of Love*, authors Lewis, Amini, and Lannon write, "Understand how a neural network functions, and you will know the innermost secrets of the intuitions that guide us in love."[57]

We know from studies in neuroscience that "neurons that fire together wire together." This means that nerve pathways are strengthened through repetition, which is why we find it so hard to break bad habits and change our strongly held associations. But we can also use this principle to develop good habits, through consciously repeating the patterns we want to create.

The authors also discovered that children's brains possess far more neurons than they can ultimately keep. These neurons die off by the billions, which may explain why we lose so much memory of our childhood. At adolescence, there is a huge purging—greater than at any other time in life—with an enormous "synaptic reorganization" as a result. This occurs especially in the frontal lobe: *the part of the brain responsible for empathy and future planning.*

Since so many neurons are lost in the process of maturation, the authors ask why some neurons survive and others don't—an interesting question that may have important parallels to our social situation. They realized that *connectedness* makes all the difference. "Neurons that establish strong interconnections with their fellows . . . make it through the winnowing phase. Those that do not join in stable bonds wither and drop from the consolidating template."[58]

We have seen how our global initiation from adolescence to adulthood is resulting in changes in infrastructure, power distribution, and values. Through this "winnowing" of established social channels, we are entering a period of grand reorganization. Our increased connectivity through global media and the Internet seems to be generating empathy and future planning, even for children as young as those in the stories above. Online chat rooms and social media are quickly becoming the new polis where people connect up, discuss ideas, proffer news, submit petitions, and generate activism and mutual aid. Perhaps the noosphere of the planet's global brain is at last evolving its "frontal lobe," generating a greater maturity with increased compassion and a newfound ability, if not imperative, to plan for the future.

Could this imply that—much like our brains' and hearts' neural networks—what will make or break our ability to survive our collective initiation is precisely our capacity for cooperation, collaboration, networking, and community? The very pressures of our initiatory ordeals will force us to reach out to others—especially where we can make direct contact, with localized networks acting in alignment with global thinking. A popular bumper sticker comes to mind: "Think globally, act locally." That is exactly what we are being asked to do: identify our purpose in terms of the larger whole, and serve from our unique gifts wherever we are.

In our earlier analogy of the imaginal cells becoming the butterfly, the new cells eventually overwhelm the caterpillar's immune system that attacks them—but only when they start to clump together and organize. If we are the imaginal cells in the emerging global heart, it is our ability to organize with strong bonds of love and connection that will sustain us through the metamorphosis. In both our personal brains and hearts and our larger social systems, the convergence of ideas—neurons firing and wiring together—grows stronger with time, attracting even more like minds and hearts into their net. In the same way, the larger and more cooperative the group, the more influence it has on others, just as the more we practice something, the better we get at it.

Steven Pinker, in *The Better Angels of Our Nature*, suggests that bonding and empathy emerge from shared identity. It's long been apparent that people will rally for those in their own identity group, be it a tribe, an ethnic group, or a nation. Looking over our long history, we can see that the scale of our identity expands as evolution proceeds. From identifying with only one's family or tribe to identifying with a city-state and then a nation, we are now evolving a shared identity as members of an emerging planetary civilization, cells in the awakening global heart, parents of the future. In previous writings, I have called such members of a heart-based consciousness "co-hearts." [59]

The Institute of HeartMath has conducted an enormous amount of research into the nature of the heart and its optimal functioning. As mentioned earlier, the heart generates a measurable field that extends beyond the self, a field much stronger than the brain—in fact, the strongest field in the body. When this field's vibrations are coherent, meaning that its oscillating frequencies are in resonance, there is a corresponding state of mental clarity, physical vitality, and general well-being. They have found that simple exercises that involve focusing on positive feelings of love can increase the coherence of the heart's field and bring the body into greater harmony. HeartMath refers to this measurable coherence as "the physiological signature of love at the core of the human system."[60]

Their research has also discovered that signals from the field of one person's heart can be detected in the nervous systems of other people and animals. In other words, the state of our being influences more than just ourselves; it affects others in subtle but profound ways through this field of the heart—either positively or negatively.

According to HeartMath, the vibrations within that field can be coherent or incoherent, generating either harmony or stress—both in our own bodies and in the social field around us. As a result, HeartMath has been looking at how this principle affects us collectively. Their Global Coherence Initiative is designed as a "science-based, co-creative project to unite people in heart-focused care and intention, to facilitate the shift in global consciousness from instability and discord to balance, cooperation, and enduring peace."[61] Their intention is to get as many people as possible to practice their techniques of "heart-coherence" as a way of ultimately influencing the larger field of our social synergy and global trends.

The basic HeartMath practice is easy and can be done anywhere and anytime. It requires focusing on your heart, breathing into your heart area, and remembering positive feelings of love, appreciation, genuine care, or compassion. This simple practice produces measurable results in increased heart-rate coherence and well-being. The HeartMath Institute's theory is that if enough people practice this technique to enhance their own coherence, it will eventually result in greater global coherence. You can learn more about how to join this Global Coherence Initiative at http://www.glcoherence.org.

In our global network of consciousness, each of us is a point of light within the web. What we focus on, what we say, and what we do influences every other point of the web to some degree. As evolutionary agents, we are all part of influencing this profound evolutionary shift by understanding who we are, how we got here, and where we're going. But even more, by the simple practice of focusing on love, gratitude, appreciation, and joy, we create more harmony in the world. Each of us can take responsibility for what we project into the collective. In times of strife, it becomes especially important to balance stress with the coherence of love.

The mythic story of becoming divine parents of the future, with the capacity to choose between promise and peril, harmony and discord, gives us a potent role in the drama of initiation that will play itself out in this century. A vision of where we're going, with the possibility of what we can create, will inspire hope and generate creativity. While we navigate the difficult initiation, it will be crucially important to remember its larger purpose, as an evolutionary driver toward a higher organizing principle. To those with eyes to see, such a vision can create a field of heart resonance that over generations will become global.

Our Emerging Global Heart

It has become fashionable today to mock or treat with suspicion anything which looks like faith in the future. If we are not careful, this skepticism will be fatal, for its direct result is to destroy both the love of living and the momentum of humankind.
—*Pierre Teilhard de Chardin*

Can you hear it now? Can you feel it? Can you see the patterns emerging? The grand evolutionary journey is urging us toward the global heart's awakening. It is calling humanity back together again, bringing us home. It is reminding us to wiggle our toes in the earth below, gaze up at the sky above, and witness the great expanse of love that has always joined heaven and earth in perpetual reciprocity. If home is where the heart is, then it may be that the last leg of the Hero's journey—the return home—is the 18 inches between our head and our heart.

Thus for love's sake is the universe divided. The journey of separation that split everything apart is changing direction—reuniting divorced archetypes in a new synthesis with love as the integrating principle: men and women in partnership as equals, mind and body holistically integrated, matter and spirit mutually interwoven. We are the unification of the Divine Mother and Divine Father, becoming the parents of the Divine Child, embarking on the adventure of redeeming past harms and creating a magnificent future. It is now time to embrace the divine gift of creation and return the gift by cocreating heaven on earth. There is no holier or more important task than to help mend the ills that threaten us and help create this world that we are birthing together.

For between our able bodies and infinite minds, and between our shared ground and the vast expanse of space, lie innumerable relationships. The intricacy, balance, and longevity of these relationships demonstrate a profound universal love, a force that is calling to be recognized in both our scientific and spiritual understanding. Through science, we discover that these relationships are not a haphazard mix, nor are they controlled by a top-down hierarchy of command and obedience. Rather, they operate by self-organizing principles that have their own hierarchy of holism, or holarchy. We find intricately woven patterns, repeated at all levels of scale, continually organizing at ever more elegant levels.

We see give-and-take cooperation everywhere, with symbiosis as essential to evolution as competition, if not more so. We find the miracle of love in the mother's care for her newborn and the oxytocin that floods her system to foster bonding with her infant. We find this miracle in the heart's ability to forgive grievances, in the joy of a child's laughter, and in the entwined fibers of lasting relationship. We witness love multiplying through cooperation and collaboration, the infectious process of caring making a new meme of an empathic civilization. We find that caring enhances the value of what we care for, that what we appreciate appreciates, and that gratitude is an attitude of recognizing love in all of its many forms.

Once again, we acknowledge that the heart is the center of the chakra system. For a long time, this system has been interpreted as a linear journey moving from bottom to top, reflective of our linear mentality in general. A common assumption in this upwardly mobile view is that we deny or transcend the lower chakras in order to reach the crown or highest chakra. Higher consciousness is certainly the aim of Axial Age religions and most spiritual practices. It is the ticket to our maturity, with the tools of our spiritual practices handed down to us through the millennia to help us evolve, especially at this crucial time. Indeed, higher consciousness is necessary to move from our overidentification with the love of power to the higher center of the heart. Since we began with the basic thesis of our fused embeddedness in nature, moving to the other pole of pure consciousness has been portrayed as the ultimate destination. But now we realize that this is only a step.

Having worked with the chakra system for nearly 40 years and traversed this vertical axis both upward and downward countless times, I have finally come to see that this map for our journey may be more like a spiral or even concentric circles, whose sacred center is the heart. The heart may have been the destination all along, the center that integrates above and below in the chakra system. As we enter the Sacred Marriage that integrates the polarities we have discussed, we find that the heart is the integrating center of both higher and lower consciousness, each of them equally important. In this way, moving from the third chakra's love of power to the heart's power of love is not only a step *toward* higher consciousness but also a result of bringing higher consciousness *down* into our daily actions, into the principles by which we organize our society and the way we treat the Earth, our bodies, and each other. In this way, the evolutionary trajectory not only moves upward but is a constant weaving of both transcendence and immanence, upward and downward flow.

We stand on the shoulders of giants. The blessings we have today are the result of countless generations of discoveries. Our ancestors fought and died for the freedoms we take for granted today. It is up to the generations now living to make this transformation a reality. We will not live long enough to see its full results, but the least we can do in return for all we've been given is to leave this glorious world intact for future generations.

We now stand ready to walk down the aisle of our reunion, with pledges to treat our world and each other with respect, to honor and cherish, for richer and poorer, in sickness and in health. We continue the work of learning to love ourselves. We take that work into our relationships, learning to speak authentically and forge new partnerships in which each is honored. Now it is time to take this love global and embody the heart in all our interactions—united with power and purpose. The future is calling us forward, guided by what we love, calling us through the crucible of the awakening global heart.

Part 1 Notes

[1] Joseph Campbell in conversation with Bill Moyers, in *The Power of Myth* (New York: Doubleday, 1988), 32.

[2] Michael Dowd, *Thank God for Evolution: How the Marriage of Science and Religion Will Transform Your Life and Our World* (New York: Penguin, 2009), 54.

[3] Duane Elgin, *Promise Ahead: A Vision of Hope and Action for Humanity's Future* (New York: HarperCollins, 2000), 1.

[4] For an up-to-date number, see the World Population Clock at http://www.census.gov/main/www/popclock.html.

[5] Thomas Malthus, *An Essay on the Principle of Population, as It Affects the Future Improvement of Society, with Remarks on the Speculations of Mr. Godwin, M. Condorcet, and Other Writers* (London: Johnston, 1798).

[6] Jean Houston, *Jump Time: Shaping Your Future in a World of Radical Change* (New York: Tarcher/Putnam, 2000), 1.

[7] Carl Jung, *Two Essays on Analytical Psychology*, 2nd ed., trans. R. F. C. Hull (Princeton, NJ: Princeton University Press, 1966), 53.

[8] Martin Luther King Jr., remarks at Southern Christian Leadership Conference, August 16, 1967, quoted on Wikiquote, http://en.wikiquote.org/wiki/Martin_Luther_King,_Jr.#Where_Do_We_Go_From_Here.3F_.281967.29.

[9] Elisabet Sahtouris, author's website, http://www.sahtouris.com.

[10] Wikipedia, "Imaginal disc," http://en.wikipedia.org/wiki/Imaginal_disc.

[11] Rainer Maria Rilke, *Letters to a Young Poet* (New York: Norton, 2004).

[12] Joseph Campbell, *The Hero with a Thousand Faces* (Princeton, NJ: Princeton University Press, 1968), 51.

[13] National Oceanic and Atmospheric Administration, "NOAA: Carbon dioxide levels reach milestone at Arctic sites," U.S. Department of Commerce, May 31, 2012, http://researchmatters.noaa.gov/news/Pages/arcticCO2.aspx.

[14] Lester Brown, *Plan B 3.0: Mobilizing to Save Civilization* (New York: W. W. Norton, 2008), 52.

[15] Ibid., 49.

[16] Peter Senge et al., *The Necessary Revolution: How Individuals and Organizations Are Working Together to Create a Sustainable World* (New York: Broadway Books, 2010), 18.

[17] Lester Brown, *Plan B 4.0: Mobilizing to Save Civilization* (New York: W. W. Norton, 2009), 33ff.

[18] World Health Organization, Fact sheet no. 313, "Air Quality and Health," September 2011, http://www.who.int/mediacentre/factsheets/fs313/en/.

[19] Rebecca Solnit, *A Paradise Built in Hell: The Extraordinary Communities That Arise in Disaster* (New York: Penguin Books, 2009), 3, 7.

[20] Ibid., 8.

[21] Ibid., 208.

[22] Water.org, "The Crisis: Water Facts," http://water.org/water-crisis/water-facts/water/.

[23] Solnit, *A Paradise Built in Hell*, 145ff.

[24] As quoted by Solnit, *A Paradise Built in Hell*, 143.

[25] As quoted by John R. Van Eenwyk, *Archetypes & Strange Attractors: The Chaotic World of Symbols* (Toronto: Inner City Books, 1997), 139.

[26] Samuel Noah Kramer, *Inanna, Queen of Heaven and Earth: Her Stories from Sumer* (New York: Harper & Row, 1983), 127.

[27] One could argue that these roughly correspond to the chakras, from top to bottom.

[28] R. J. Stewart, *The Underworld Initiation: A Journey Towards Psychic Transformation* (Guildford, UK: Aquarian Press, 1985), 67.

[29] Steven Pinker, *The Better Angels of Our Nature: Why Violence Has Declined* (New York: Penguin Books, 2011).

Part 2 Notes

[1] Joseph Campbell, *The Hero with a Thousand Faces* (Princeton, NJ: Princeton University Press, 1968), 61.

[2] Barbara Marx Hubbard, *Birth 2012 and Beyond: Humanity's Great Shift to the Age of Conscious Evolution* (San Rafael, CA: Shift Books, 2012), 43.

[3] Anodea Judith, *Eastern Body, Western Mind: Psychology and the Chakra System as a Path to the Self* (Berkeley: Celestial Arts, 2004), 58–59.

[4] Richard Leakey, *Origins* (New York: Dutton, 1977), 61.

[5] Marija Gimbutas, *The Civilization of the Goddess: The World of Old Europe* (San Francisco: HarperSanFrancisco, 1991), 364.

[6] Erich Neumann, *The Origins and History of Consciousness* (Princeton, NJ: Princeton University Press, 1973).

[7] Gareth Hill, *Masculine and Feminine: The Natural Flow of Opposites in the Psyche* (Boston: Shambhala, 1992).

[8] Sam Keen, *Collective Myths We Live and Die By*, audiotape (Mystic Fire Audio, 1994).

[9] Richard Louv, *The Nature Principle: Reconnecting with Life in a Virtual Age* (Chapel Hill, NC: Algonquin Books, 2012), 3.

[10] Michael Meade, *Men and the Water of Life: Initiation and the Tempering of Men* (San Francisco: HarperSanFrancisco, 1993), 12.

[11] Hesiod's *Theogony*, trans. Norman O. Brown (Indianapolis: Bobbs-Merrill, 1953), 15.

[12] Alain Danielou, *The Gods of India* (New York: Inner Traditions, 1985), 312.

[13] Erich Jantsch, *The Self-Organizing Universe* (Oxford: Pergamon Press, 1980), 137.

[14] Riane Eisler, *The Chalice and the Blade: Our History, Our Future* (San Francisco: Harper & Row), chap. 2.

[15] Mircea Eliade, *A History of Religious Ideas*, vol. 1 (Chicago: University of Chicago Press, 1978), 40.

[16] Ibid.

[17] Anne Baring and Jules Cashford, *The Myth of the Goddess: Evolution of an Image* (London: Penguin Arkana, 1993), 75.

[18] Estimates of the time period during which Stonehenge was built vary greatly, spanning anywhere from 600 to 2,000 years, depending on the source.

[19] Larry E. Sullivan, *The SAGE Glossary of the Social and Behavioral Sciences* (Thousand Oaks, CA: SAGE Publications, 2009), 73.

[20] Alfred North Whitehead, *Process and Reality: An Essay in Cosmology,* ed. D. R. Griffin and D. W. Sherburne (New York: Free Press, 1978), 340.

[21] Joseph Campbell, *Creative Mythology* (New York: Penguin Books, 1962), 420.

[22] The first wave of Kurgans occurred from 4400 to 4300 BCE, the second at 3500 BCE, and the third after 3000 BCE. Gimbutas, *Civilization of the Goddess,* 352ff.

[23] As quoted by Baring and Cashford in *Myth of the Goddess,* 152.

[24] Hari Meyers, from a lecture given in Sebastopol, California, 2004.

[25] Andrew Bard Schmookler, *The Parable of the Tribes: The Problem of Power in Social Evolution* (Boston: Houghton Mifflin, 1984).

[26] Andrew Bard Schmookler, *Out of Weakness: Healing the Wounds That Drive Us to War* (New York: Bantam, 1988), 5.

[27] John Keegan, *A History of Warfare* (London: Random House, 1993), 304.

[28] Ken Wilber, *Up from Eden: A Transpersonal View of Human Evolution* (Wheaton, IL: Quest Books, 1981), 179.

[29] Time-Life Books, *The Age of God-Kings* (Alexandria, VA: Time-Life Books, 1987), 63.

[30] Joseph Campbell, *The Hero with a Thousand Faces,* 40ff.

[31] Ibid., 15.

[32] Ibid., 44.

[33] Richard Tarnas, *The Passion of the Western Mind: Understanding the Ideas That Have Shaped Our World View* (New York: Ballantine, 1991), 69.

[34] Jacob Burckhardt, *History of Greek Culture,* trans. Palmer Hilty (London: Constable Publishers, 1963), 289.

[35] BrainyQuote, http://www.brainyquote.com/quotes/authors/s/socrates.html.

[36] "The Grandeur of Imperial Rome," in *Empires Ascendant: TimeFrame 400 BC–AD 200* (Alexandria, VA: Time-Life Books, 1987), 45.

[37] For a list of these countries, see http://www.roman-empire.net/maps/empire/extent/rome-modern-day-nations.html.

[38] "The Grandeur of Imperial Rome," 47.

[39] Seventy-three percent of those polled in 2012. See Wikipedia, "Christianity in the United States," http://en.wikipedia.org/wiki/Christianity_in_the_United_States.

[40] According to Timothy Freke and Peter Gandy, in *Jesus and the Lost Goddess,* there is no record of a place called Nazareth. Instead, they suggest that "Jesus the Nazarene," as he was called, meant "Jesus the Initiate." Freke and Gandy, *Jesus and the Lost Goddess: The Secret Teachings of the Original Christians* (New York: Three Rivers Press, 2001), 102.

[41] "Is it not written in your law, 'I said, You are Gods'?" John 10:34.

[42] Freke and Gandy, *Jesus and the Lost Goddess*, 119.

[43] The story of Jesus restoring eyesight to the blind can be interpreted as Jesus opening the eyes of the initiate, as noninitiates were called by the Greeks *mystae*, meaning "eyes closed," and initiates were called *epopteia*, meaning "those who could see."

[44] Elaine Pagels, *Adam, Eve, and the Serpent: Sex and Politics in Early Christianity* (New York: Vintage Books, 1989), 4.

[45] See Burton L. Mack, *Who Wrote the New Testament? The Making of the Christian Myth* (San Francisco: HarperSanFrancisco, 1995), 124ff.

[46] Joseph Campbell, in conversation with Bill Moyers, *The Power of Myth* (New York: Doubleday, 1988), 199.

[47] Pagels, *Adam, Eve, and the Serpent*, 82–83.

[48] An interesting footnote to Theodosius's reign was that he was originally protective of Pagan cults and shrines. His own crime, however, was to massacre 7,000 civilians in response to a tumult, for which he served eight months' penance. It was apparently after this that he changed his attitude about non-Christian religions and set out the decrees that led to their destruction. See the online Catholic Encyclopedia, "Theodosius I," http://www.newadvent.org/cathen/14577d.htm.

[49] In December 1945, an Arab peasant discovered a jar containing ancient Gnostic texts near the town of Nag Hammadi. These texts, known as the Gnostic Gospels, had been buried to keep them from being destroyed. They reveal a view of the Christian story that is very different from the orthodox view that has prevailed. See Elaine Pagels, *The Gnostic Gospels* (New York: Vintage Books, 1989).

[50] Sandra Lee Dixon, *Augustine: The Scattered and Gathered Self* (St. Louis: Chalice Press, 1999), 109–11.

[51] Pagels, *Adam, Eve, and the Serpent*, 107–20.

[52] Ibid., 112.

[53] Ibid., 134.

[54] Ibid., 126.

[55] Elaine Pagels, *The Gnostic Gospels*, 34.

[56] Jeffrey Burton Russell, *A History of Medieval Christianity: Prophecy and Order* (New York: Thomas Y. Cromwell, 1968), 92.

[57] James A. Haught, *Holy Horrors: An Illustrated History of Religious Murder and Madness* (Buffalo, NY: Prometheus, 1990), 25–26.

[58] Steven Pinker, *The Better Angels of Our Nature: Why Violence Has Declined* (New York: Penguin, 2011), 132.

[59] Helen Ellerbe, *The Dark Side of Christian History* (San Rafael, CA: Morningstar, 1995), 42.

[60] Serenity Young, ed., *An Anthology of Sacred Texts By and About Women* (New York: Crossroad, 1993), 46, as quoted by Leonard Shlain, *The Alphabet Versus the Goddess: The Conflict Between Word and Image* (New York: Viking, 1998), 244.

[61] Karen Armstrong, *The Gospel According to Woman: Christianity's Creation of the Sex War in the West* (New York: Doubleday, 1986), 71.

[62] St. Thomas Aquinas, *Summa Theologica* (London: Blackfriars), Questions 92, 35.

[63] Armstrong, *The Gospel According to Woman*, 69.

[64] Jacques Maritain, *Three Reformers: Luther, Descartes, Rousseau*, as quoted by Shlain, *The Alphabet Versus the Goddess*, 329.

[65] Ellerbe, *The Dark Side of Christian History*, 95.

[66] Jean Delumeau, *Catholicism Between Luther and Voltaire: A New View of the Counter-Reformation* (London: Burns & Oats, 1977), 438–39.

[67] William Edward Hartpole Lecky, *History of Rationalism in Europe* (London: Longmans, 1904), 1:387, as quoted by Shlain, *The Alphabet Versus the Goddess*, 328.

[68] Charles Beard, *The Reformation of the Sixteenth Century in Its Relation to Modern Thought and Knowledge* (London: Williams & Norgate, 1907), 250.

[69] Ellerbe, *The Dark Side of Christian History*, 88.

[70] Brian Levack, *The Witch-Hunt in Early Modern Europe*, 3rd ed. (London: Longman, 1987), 49, as quoted in Ellerbe, *The Dark Side of Christian History*, 121. Also see the entry for *Summis desiderantes affectibus,* the papal bull in question, on Wikipedia, http://en.wikipedia.org/wiki/Summis_desiderantes.

[71] Tarnas, *The Passion of the Western Mind*, 251.

[72] James Burke, *The Day the Universe Changed* (Boston: Little, Brown, 1985), 149.

[73] Fritjof Capra, *The Turning Point: Science, Society, and the Rising Culture* (New York: Simon & Schuster, 1982), 56.

[74] Rupert Sheldrake, *The Rebirth of Nature: The Greening of Science and God* (New York: Bantam, 1991), 43–44.

[75] Ibid.

[76] In *New Atlantis* (1624).

[77] It could be argued that the Gnostic Christians were aware of the powers of consciousness, but they were heavily repressed by the rise of orthodoxy.

[78] "Dualism in Descartes: The Logical Ground," in Michael K. Hooker, ed., *Descartes* (Baltimore: Johns Hopkins University Press, 1978), as quoted Capra, *The Turning Point*, 59.

[79] See Pinker, *The Better Angels of Our Nature*, throughout, but especially chap. 3.

[80] Burke, *The Day the Universe Changed*, 266.

[81] David Loye, *Darwin's Lost Theory of Love: A Healing Vision for the New Century* (Lincoln, NE: toExcel, 2000), 5.

82 Burke, *The Day the Universe Changed*, 261.

83 As quoted by Burke, 266.

84 As quoted by Burke, 272.

85 Ken Wilber, *The Marriage of Sense and Soul: Integrating Science and Religion* (New York: Random House, 1998), 44.

86 Jeremy Rifkin, *Biosphere Politics: A New Consciousness for a New Century* (New York: Crown Publishers, 1991), 158.

87 Thanks to Leonard Shlain for this insight, in *The Alphabet Versus the Goddess*, 390.

88 From John Stuart Mill, *The Subjection of Women*, as quoted by Shlain, *The Alphabet Versus the Goddess*, 389.

89 Bryan H. Bunch and Alexander Hellemans, eds., *The Timetables of Technology: A Chronology of the Most Important People and Events in the History of Technology* (New York: Simon & Schuster, 1993), 283.

90 See Wikipedia, "Abolition of Slavery timeline," http://en.wikipedia.org/wiki/Abolition_of_slavery_timeline.

91 Wilber, *Marriage of Sense and Soul*, 41ff.

92 Mark Morford, "What's on your iGod?" SFGate, August 26, 2005, http://www.sfgate.com/entertainment/morford/article/What-s-On-Your-iGod-Your-answer-to-the-2614773.php.

93 Hill, *Masculine and Feminine*, 17.

94 Tribe.net, http://www.tribe.net/welcome.

95 Paul H. Ray and Sherry Ruth Anderson, *The Cultural Creatives: How 50 Million People Are Changing the World* (New York: Harmony Books, 2000).

96 Wikipedia, "Tim Berners-Lee," http://en.wikipedia.org/wiki/Tim_Berners-Lee.

97 Emily Elert, "How the Internet Has Spread Around the World," *Popular Science*, December 11, 2012, http://www.popsci.com/science/article/2012-12/widening-world-web-internet-infographic.

98 Ibid. For a great infographic, see the interactive map of the spread of the Internet worldwide, at BBC News, "SuperPower: Visualising the Internet," http://news.bbc.co.uk/2/hi/technology/8552410.stm.

Part 3 Notes

[1] Carl G. Jung and Carl Kerenyi, *Essays on a Science of Mythology: The Myth of the Divine Child and the Mysteries of Eleusis* (Princeton: Princeton University Press, 1951), 87.

[2] Ibid., 89.

[3] Pierre Teilhard de Chardin, *The Phenomenon of Man* (New York: HarperCollins, 1955), 293.

[4] Erich Jantsch, *Design for Evolution: Self-Organization and Planning in the Life of Human Systems* (New York: George Braziller, 1975).

[5] As quoted by Rebecca Solnit, *A Paradise Built in Hell: The Extraordinary Communities That Arise in Disaster* (New York: Penguin, 2009), 18.

[6] Duane Elgin, *Awakening Earth: Exploring the Evolution of Human Culture and Consciousness* (New York: Morrow, 1993), 295.

[7] Thanks to Richard Ely for these insights, published in the article "Science and Mysticism: Siblings Under the Skin," *Pan Gaia*, no. 16 (Summer 1998).

[8] Ken Wilber, *The Marriage of Sense and Soul: Integrating Science and Religion* (New York: Random House, 1998), 4.

[9] Lynne McTaggart, *The Intention Experiment: Using Your Thoughts to Change Your Life and the World* (New York: Free Press, 2007).

[10] For more on this, see Larry Dossey, *Healing Words: The Power of Prayer and the Practice of Medicine* (San Francisco: HarperSanFrancisco, 1993).

[11] Ashley Hennigan, "Missing Men: Addressing the College Gender Gap," Higher Ed Live, http://higheredlive.com/missing-men/.

[12] Carl Jung, *The Psychology of Kundalini Yoga*, ed. Sonu Shamdasani (Princeton, NJ: Princeton University Press, 1996).

[13] C. G. Jung, as quoted by David Rosen, *The Tao of Jung: The Way of Integrity* (New York: Penguin, 1996), 92.

[14] Quesada Gardens Initiative, http://www.quesadagardens.org/.

[15] Caring Institute, http://www.caring.org.

[16] Corporation for National & Community Service, "Volunteering and Civic Life in America 2012: Research Highlights," http://www.volunteeringinamerica.gov/assets/resources/FactSheetFinal.pdf.

[17] Jeremy Rifkin, *The Empathic Civilization: The Race to Global Consciousness in a World in Crisis* (New York: Tarcher/Penguin, 2009), 37.

[18] Dalai Lama, *How to Expand Love: Widening the Circle of Loving Relationships*, trans. and ed. Jeffrey Hopkins (New York: Atria, 2005), 134.

[19] J. Osborn, S. W. Derbyshire, "Pain sensation evoked by observing injury in others," *Pain* 148, no. 2 (February 2010): 268–74, as quoted by Robin Kelly in *The Human Hologram: Living Your Life in Harmony with the Unified Field* (Santa Rosa, CA: Energy Psychology Press, 2011), 151.

[20] Rifkin, *The Empathic Civilization*, 85.

[21] Daniel J. Siegel, *The Mindful Brain: Reflection and Attunement in the Cultivation of Well-Being* (New York: W. W. Norton, 2007), 165.

[22] Willis Harman, "The Shifting Worldview: Toward a More Holistic Science," *Holistic Education Review* (September 1992).

[23] National Center for Children Exposed to Violence, citing A. C. Huston et al., *Big World, Small Screen: The Role of Television in American Society* (Lincoln, NE: University of Nebraska Press, 1992), http://www.nccev.org/violence/statistics/statistics-media.html.

[24] Steven Pinker, *The Better Angels of Our Nature: Why Violence Has Declined* (New York: Penguin, 2011), statistics throughout, but see especially pages 49 and 53.

[25] Ibid., 402.

[26] Elisabet Sahtouris, "Understanding Globalization as an Evolutionary Leap," presented to the Institute of Noetic Sciences, July 2001.

[27] Frances E. Kuo and William C. Sullivan, "Environment and Crime in the Inner City: Does Vegetation Reduce Crime?" *Environment and Behavior* 33, no. 3 (2001): 343–67.

[28] Tami Luhby, "The wealthy are 288 times richer than you," CNNMoney, September 11, 2012, http://money.cnn.com/2012/09/11/news/economy/wealth-net-worth/index.html.

[29] Ibid.

[30] Triple A Learning, "Visualizing Statistics: 99% and the Occupy Movement—November 26, 2011," video blog on http://blogs.triplealearning.com/2011/11/diploma/dp_tokglobal/visualizing-statistics-99-and-the-occupy-movement/. Also see Quora, "Is there any statistical data behind the 99% claim from Occupy Wall Street?" http://www.quora.com/Is-there-any-statistical-data-behind-the-99-claim-from-Occupy-Wall-Street-OWS.

[31] Poverty Program, Poverty Statistics, http://www.povertyprogram.com/statistics.php.

[32] Charles Eisenstein, *Sacred Economics: Money, Gift, and Society in the Age of Transition* (Berkeley: North Atlantic Books/Evolver Editions, 2011), chap. 1, "The Gift World."

[33] Ibid.

[34] Marjorie Kelly, *Owning Our Future: The Emerging Ownership Revolution* (San Francisco: Berrett-Koehler Publishers, 2012).

[35] Donald Tapscott and Anthony D. Williams. *Wikinomics: How Mass Collaboration Changes Everything* (New York: Portfolio/Penguin Group, 2006), 14.

[36] Ibid., 78.

[37] Paul Hawken, *Blessed Unrest: How the Largest Movement in the World Came into Being and Why No One Saw It Coming* (New York: Viking Penguin, 2007), 4.

[38] InnoCentive, "Frequently Asked Questions," https://www.innocentive.com/faq/Solver#26n1253.

[39] Ellen Brown, "Cooperative Banking, the Exciting Wave of the Future," May 24, 2012, *AlterNet Report*, http://truth-out.org/news/item/9352-cooperative-banking-the-exciting-wave-of-the-future?

[40] Ibid.

[41] Hazel Henderson, "Overview from Green Transition Scoreboard® 2012," EthicalMarkets.com, http://www.ethicalmarkets.com/2012/03/07/overview-from-green-transition-scoreboard-2012/.

[42] Brown, "Cooperative Banking."

[43] "American Values Survey: Initial Report," October 25, 2006, conducted by People for the American Way Foundation, http://media.pfaw.org/pdf/cav/AVSReport.pdf.

[44] "Transition Initiatives Directory," Transition Network, http://www.transitionnetwork.org/initiatives.

[45] James O'Dea, *Cultivating Peace: Becoming a 21st-Century Peace Ambassador* (San Rafael, CA: Shift Books, 2012), 40.

[46] Margaret J. Wheatley, "Restoring Hope to the Future through Critical Education of Leaders," *Vimukt Shiksha*, March 2001, as quoted by David Korten, *The Great Turning: From Empire to Earth Community* (San Francisco: Berrett-Koehler Publishers, 2006), 315.

[47] Korten, *The Great Turning*, 346.

[48] Tom Atlee, *The Tao of Democracy: Using Co-Intelligence to Create a World That Works for All* (Cranston, RI: Writer's Collective, 2003), 111.

[49] Thomas Lewis, Fari Amini, and Richard Lannon, *A General Theory of Love* (New York: Vintage, 2000), 228.

[50] Teilhard de Chardin, *The Phenomenon of Man*, 288.

[51] Steve Hartman, "Penn State postman delivers lesson in happiness," CBS News, February 6, 2013, http://www.cbsnews.com/8301-18563_162-57568495/penn-state-postman-delivers-lesson-in-happiness/.

[52] Karen Keller, "Boy, 7, Raises More Than $30,000 for Sick Friend," ABC News, February 28, 2013, http://abcnews.go.com/blogs/health/2013/02/26/boy-7-raises-more-than-30000-for-sick-friend/.

[53] Good News Network, "Girl Delivering Thousands of Toys to Sick Kids Makes Final Tally After 13 Years," March 13, 2013, http://www.goodnewsnetwork.org/most-popular/girl-delivering-toys-to-sick-kids-final-tally-after-13-years.html.

[54] Good News Network, "Little Sisters with Big Hearts Use Origami to Fund Water for Africa," February 13, 2013, http://www.goodnewsnetwork.org/most-popular/little-sisters-with-big-hearts-use-origami-to-fund-water-for-africa.html.

[55] Institute of HeartMath, "emWave® Self-Regulation Technology—The Theoretical Basis," http://www.heartmath.org/education/education-research/emwave-self-regulation-technology-theoretical-basis.html.

[56] See Paul Pearsall, *The Heart's Code: Tapping the Wisdom and Power of Our Heart Energy* (New York: Broadway Books, 1999).

[57] Lewis et al., *A General Theory of Love*, 123.

[58] Ibid., 149.

[59] I introduced this term in the first edition of this book, *Waking the Global Heart* (Santa Rosa, CA: Elite Books, 2006), 318–19.

[60] As quoted by Claudia Welss in Barbara Marx Hubbard, *Birth 2012 and Beyond: Humanity's Great Shift to the Age of Conscious Evolution* (San Rafael, CA: Shift Books, 2012), 235.

[61] Global Coherence Initiative, http://www.glcoherence.org.

BIBLIOGRAPHY

American Museum of Natural History. *The First Humans: Human Origins and History to 10,000 B.C.* San Francisco: HarperCollins, 1993.

Armstrong, Karen. *The Gospel According to Woman: Christianity's Creation of the Sex War in the West.* New York: Anchor Books, 1986.

Atlee, Tom, with Rosa Zubizarreta. *The Tao of Democracy: Using Co-intelligence to Create a World That Works for All.* Cranston, RI: The Writer's Collective, 2003.

Baring, Anne, and Jules Cashford. *The Myth of the Goddess: Evolution of an Image.* London: Penguin Arkana, 1993.

Barraclough, Geoffrey, and Richard Overy, eds. *Hammond Atlas of World History.* New Jersey: Hammond, 1999.

Bateson, Gregory. *Mind and Nature: A Necessary Unity.* New York: Dutton, 1979.

Bourne, Edmund J. *Global Shift: How a New Worldview Is Transforming Humanity.* Oakland, CA: New Harbinger, 2008.

Briskin, Alan, Sheryl Erickson, John Ott, and Tom Callanan. *The Power of Collective Wisdom and the Trap of Collective Folly.* San Francisco: Berrett-Koehler Publishers, 2009.

Brown, Lester R. *Plan B 3.0: Mobilizing to Save Civilization.* New York: W. W. Norton & Co., 2008.

———. *Plan B 4.0: Mobilizing to Save Civilization.* New York: W. W. Norton & Company, 2009.

Brown, Norman O., trans. *Hesiod: Theogony.* Indianapolis: Bobbs-Merrill, 1953.

Buber, Martin. *I and Thou.* Trans. Walter Kaufmann. New York: Simon & Schuster, 1970.

Bunch, Bryan H., and Alexander Hellemans, eds. *The Timetables of Technology: A Chronology of the Most Important People and Events in the History of Technology.* New York: Simon & Schuster, 1993.

Burckhardt, Jacob. *History of Greek Culture.* London: Constable Publishers, 1963.

Burenhult, Goran. *People of the Stone Age: Hunter-Gatherers and Early Farmers.* New York: HarperCollins, 1993.

Burke, James. *The Day the Universe Changed.* Boston: Little, Brown, 1985.

Campbell, Joseph. *Creative Mythology (The Masks of God).* New York: Penguin Books, 1962.

———. *Hero with a Thousand Faces.* Princeton, NJ: Princeton University Press, 1968.

———. *The Masks of God: Primitive Mythology.* New York: Viking Press, 1959.

———. *The Mythic Image.* Princeton, NJ: Princeton University Press, 1974.

———. *The Way of the Animal Powers.* San Francisco: Harper & Row, 1983.

Campbell, Joseph, with Bill Moyers. *The Power of Myth.* New York: Doubleday, 1988.

Capra, Fritjof. *The Tao of Physics: An Exploration of the Parallels between Modern Physics and Eastern Mysticism.* Berkeley: Shambhala, 1975.

———. *The Turning Point: Science, Society, and the Rising Culture.* New York: Simon & Schuster, 1982.

Chopra, Deepak. *Peace Is the Way: Bringing War and Violence to an End.* New York: Harmony, 2005.

Dalai Lama. *How to Expand Love: Widening the Circle of Loving Relationships.* New York: Atria, 2005.

Danielou, Alain. *The Gods of India: Hindu Polytheism.* New York: Inner Traditions, 1985.

Delumeau, Jean. *Catholicism Between Luther and Voltaire: A New View of the Counter-Reformation.* London: Burns & Oats, 1977.

Dossey, Larry. *Recovering the Soul: A Scientific and Spiritual Search.* New York: Bantam, 1989.

Dowd, Michael. *Thank God for Evolution: How the Marriage of Science and Religion Will Transform Your Life and Our World.* New York: Plume/Penguin, 2009.

Duhm, Dieter. *Eros Unredeemed: The World Power of Sexuality.* Belzig, Germany: Verlag Meiga, 2010.

Earley, Jay. *Transforming Human Culture: Social Evolution and the Planetary Crisis.* New York: State University of New York Press, 1997.

Easterbrook, Gregg. *The Progress Paradox: How Life Gets Better While People Feel Worse.* New York: Random House, 2003.

Eisler, Riane. *The Chalice and the Blade: Our History, Our Future.* San Francisco: Harper & Row, 1987.

———. *The Power of Partnership: Seven Relationships That Will Change Your Life.* Novato: New World Library, 2002.

———. *Sacred Pleasure: Sex, Myth, and the Politics of the Body—New Paths to Power and Love.* San Francisco: HarperSanFrancisco, 1985.

Eisler, Riane, with David Loye. *The Partnership Way: New Tools for Living and Learning, Healing Our Families, Our Communities and Our World.* New York: Holistic, 1998.

Elgin, Duane. *Awakening Earth: Exploring the Evolution of Human Culture and Consciousness.* New York: Morrow, 1993.

———. *The Living Universe: Where Are We? Who Are We? Where Are We Going?* San Francisco: Berrett-Koehler, 2009.

———. *Promise Ahead: A Vision of Hope and Action for Humanity's Future.* New York: Morrow, 2000.

Eliade, Mircea. *A History of Religious Ideas.* 3 vols. Chicago: University of Chicago Press, 1978.

———. *The Myth of the Eternal Return.* New York: Pantheon Books, 1954.

———. *Rites and Symbols of Initiation: The Mysteries of Birth and Rebirth.* New York: Putnam, 2005.

Ellerbe, Helen. *The Dark Side of Christian History.* San Rafael, CA: Morningstar Books, 1995.

Freeman, Charles. *The Closing of the Western Mind: The Rise of Faith and the Fall of Reason.* New York: Knopf, 2003.

Freke, Timothy, and Peter Gandy. *Jesus and the Lost Goddess: The Secret Teachings of the Original Christians.* New York: Three Rivers, 2001.

Friedman, Thomas L. *The World Is Flat: A Brief History of the Twenty-first Century.* New York: Farrar, Straus & Giroux, 2005.

Gadon, Elinor. *The Once and Future Goddess: A Sweeping Visual Chronicle of the Sacred Female and Her Reemergence in the Cultural Mythology of Our Time.* San Francisco: Harper & Row, 1989.

Gimbutas, Marija. *The Civilization of the Goddess: The World of Old Europe.* San Francisco: HarperSanFrancisco, 1991.

———. *The Goddesses and Gods of Old Europe: Myths and Cult Images.* Berkeley: University of California, 1982.

———. *The Language of the Goddess.* San Francisco: Harper & Row, 1989.

Goodman, Lion. "A Shot in the Light." In *I Thought My Father Was God*, ed. Paul Auster. New York: Holt, 2001.

Hammond, Debora. *The Science of Synthesis: Exploring the Social Implications of General Systems Theory.* Boulder, CO: University Press of Colorado, 2003.

Harman, Willis. "The Shifting Worldview: Toward a More Holistic Science." *Holistic Education Review.* September 1992.

Haught, James A. *Holy Horrors: An Illustrated History of Religious Murder and Madness.* Buffalo, NY: Prometheus, 1990.

Hawken, Paul, Amory Lovins, and L. Hunter Lovins. *Natural Capitalism: Creating the Next Industrial Revolution.* New York: Back Bay Books/Little, Brown, 1999.

Heinberg, Richard. *Power Down: Options and Actions for a Post-Carbon World.* Gabriola Island, British Columbia: New Society Publishers, 2004.

Henderson, Hazel. *Paradigms in Progress: Life Beyond Economics.* Indianapolis: Knowledge Systems, 1991.

Hill, Gareth S. *Masculine and Feminine: The Natural Flow of Opposites in the Pysche.* Boston: Shambhala, 1992.

Hillman, James. *The Terrible Love of War.* New York: Penguin, 2004.

Houston, Jean. *The Hero and the Goddess: The Odyssey as Mystery and Initiation.* New York: Ballantine, 1992.

———. *Jump Time: Shaping Your Future in a World of Radical Change.* New York: Tarcher/Putnam, 2000.

Hubbard, Barbara Marx. *Birth 2012 and Beyond: Humanity's Great Shift to the Age of Conscious Evolution.* San Rafael, CA: Shift Books, 2012.

———. *Emergence: The Shift from Ego to Essence.* Charlottesville, VA: Hampton Roads, 2001.

Jantsch, Erich. *Design for Evolution: Self-Organization and Planning in the Life of Human Systems.* New York: George Braziller, 1975.

———. *The Self-Organizing Universe: Scientific and Human Implications of the Emerging Paradigm of Evolution.* Oxford: Pergamon, 1980.

Jantsch, Erich, and Conrad Waddington. *Evolution and Consciousness: Human Systems in Transition.* Reading, CA: Addison-Wesley, 1976.

Judith, Anodea. *Eastern Body, Western Mind: Psychology and the Chakra System as a Path to the Self.* Berkeley: Celestial Arts, 2004.

Jung, Carl. *Man and His Symbols.* New York: Doubleday, 1964.

———. *The Psychology of Kundalini Yoga.* Ed. Sonu Shamdasani. Princeton, NJ: Princeton University Press, 1996.

Jung, C. G., and C. Kerenyi. *Essays on a Science of Mythology: The Myth of the Divine Child and the Myseries of Eleusis.* Princeton, NJ: Princeton University Press, 1993.

Keegan, John. *A History of Warfare.* London: Random House, 1993.

Kegan, Robert. *The Evolving Self: Problem and Process in Human Development.* Cambridge, MA: Harvard University Press, 1982.

Keller, Catherine. *From a Broken Web: Separation, Sexism and Self.* Boston: Beacon Press, 1986.

Kelly, Robin. *The Human Hologram: Living Your Life in Harmony with the Unified Field.* Santa Rosa, CA: Energy Psychology Press, 2011.

Koestler, Arthur. *The Ghost in the Machine.* New York: Hutchinson, 1967.

Korten, David C. *The Great Turning: From Empire to Earth Community.* San Francisco: Berrett-Koehler Publishers, 2006.

Kramer, Kenneth Paul. *Martin Buber's I and Thou: Practicing Living Dialog.* Mahwah, NJ: Paulist, 2004.

Laszlo, Ervin. *The Chaos Point: The World at the Crossroads.* Charlottesville, VA: Hampton Roads, 2006.

Leakey, Richard. *Origins.* New York: Dutton, 1977.

Lerner, Gerda. *The Creation of Patriarchy.* New York: Oxford University Press, 1986.

Lewis, Thomas, Fari Amini, and Richard Lannon. *A General Theory of Love.* New York: Vintage, 2000.

Louv, Richard. *The Nature Principle: Reconnecting with Life in a Virtual Age.* Chapel Hill, NC: Algonquin Books, 2012.

Loye, David. *Darwin's Lost Theory of Love: A Healing Vision for the New Century.* Lincoln, NE: toExcel/iUniverse, 2000.

Mack, Burton L. *Who Wrote the New Testament? The Making of the Christian Myth.* San Francisco: HarperSanFrancisco: 1995.

Macy, Joanna, and Molly Young Brown. *Coming Back to Life: Practices to Reconnect Our Lives, Our World.* Gabriola Island, British Columbia: New Society Publishers, 1998.

Mahdi, Louise Carus, Steven Foster, and Meredith Little. *Betwixt and Between: Patterns of Masculine and Feminine Initiation.* Chicago: Open Court, 1987.

Malthus, Thomas Robert. *An Essay on the Principle of Population.* London: Johnston, 1798.

McIntosh, Steve. *Evolution's Purpose: An Integral Interpretation of the Scientific Story of Our Origins.* New York: Select Books, 2012.

———. *Integral Consciousness and the Future of Evolution.* St. Paul, MN: Paragon House, 2007.

Meade, Michael. *Men and the Water of Life: Initiation and the Tempering of Men.* San Francisco: HarperSanFrancisco, 1993.

Meadows, Donella H. *Thinking in Systems: A Primer.* White River Junction,VT: Chelsea Green, 2008.

Merchant, Carolyn. *The Death of Nature: Women, Ecology, and the Scientific Revolution.* San Francisco: HarperSanFrancisco, 1983.

———. *Reinventing Eden: The Fate of Nature in Western Culture.* New York: Routledge, 2003.

Nagler, Michael N. *The Search for a Nonviolent Future: A Promise of Peace for Ourselves, Our Families, and Our World.* Maui, HI: Inner Ocean, 2004.

Neumann, Erich. *The Origins and History of Consciousness.* Princeton, NJ: Princeton University Press, 1973.

Nolan, Albert. *Jesus Before Christianity.* New York: Orbis Books, 1980.

O'Dea, James. *Cultivating Peace: Becoming a 21st-Century Peace Ambassador.* San Rafael, CA: Shift Books, 2012.

Pagels, Elaine. *Adam, Eve, and the Serpent: Sex and Politics in Early Christianity.* New York: Vintage, 1989.

———. *The Gnostic Gospels.* New York: Vintage, 1989.

Pfeiffer, John E. *The Creative Explosion: An Inquiry into the Origins of Art and Religion.* New York: Harper & Row, 1982.

Phipps, Carter. *Evolutionaries: Unlocking the Spiritual and Cultural Potential of Science's Greatest Idea.* New York: HarperCollins, 2012.

Pinker, Steven. *The Better Angels of Our Nature: Why Violence Has Declined.* New York: Penguin, 2011.

Prideaux, Tom. *Cro-Magnon Man.* New York: Time-Life Books, 1973.

Ray, Paul, and Sherry Ruth Anderson. *The Cultural Creatives: How 50 Million People Are Changing the World.* New York: Harmony, 2000.

Reich, Wilhelm. *Children of the Future.* New York: Farrar, Straus & Giroux, 1983.

Rifkin, Jeremy. *Biosphere Politics: A New Consciousness for a New Century.* New York: Crown, 1991.

———. *The Empathic Civilization: The Race to Global Consciousness in a World in Crisis.* New York: Tarcher/Penguin, 2009.

———. *The European Dream: How Europe's Vision of the Future Is Quietly Eclipsing the American Dream.* New York: Tarcher/Penguin, 2004.

Rosen, David. *The Tao of Jung: The Way of Integrity.* New York: Penguin, 1996.

Sahtouris, Elisabet. *EarthDance: Living Systems in Evolution.* New York: iUniversity Press, 2000.

Sandars, N. K., trans. *Epic of Gilgamesh.* New York: Penguin, 1964.

Schmookler, Andrew Bard. *Out of Weakness: Healing the Wounds That Drive Us to War.* New York: Bantam, 1988.

———. *The Parable of the Tribes: The Problem of Power in Social Evolution.* Boston: Houghton-Mifflin, 1984.

Senge, Peter, et al. *The Necessary Revolution: How Individuals and Organizations Are Working Together to Create a Sustainable World.* New York: Broadway Books, 2010.

Sheldrake, Rupert. *The Rebirth of Nature: The Greening of Science and God.* New York: Bantam, 1991.

Shlain, Leonard. *The Alphabet Versus the Goddess: The Conflict Between Word and Image.* New York: Viking Penguin, 1998.

Siegel, Daniel J. *The Mindful Brain: Reflection and Attunement in the Cultivation of Well-Being.* New York: W. W. Norton & Co., 2007.

Singer, June. *The Power of Love to Transform Our Lives and Our World.* York Beach, ME: Nicolas-Hays, 2000.

Singer, Thomas. *The Vision Thing: Myth, Politics, and Psyche in the World.* New York: Routledge, 200.

Solnit, Rebecca. *A Paradise Built in Hell: The Extraordinary Communities That Arise in Disaster.* New York: Penguin, 2009.

Stewart, John. *Evolution's Arrow: The Direction of Evolution and the Future of Humanity.* Canberra, Australia: Chapman Press, 2000.

Stewart, R. J. *The Underworld Initiation: A Journey Towards Psychic Transformation.* Guildford, UK: Aquarian, 1985.

Stone, Merlin. *When God Was a Woman*. San Diego, CA: Harcourt Brace Jovanovich, 1976.

Tannen, Deborah. *The Argument Culture: Moving From Debate to Dialog*. New York: Random House, 1988.

Tapscott, Don, and Anthony D. Williams. *Wikinomics: How Mass Collaboration Changes Everything*. New York: Portfolio/Penguin, 2006.

Tarnas, Richard. *The Passion of the Western Mind: Understanding the Ideas That Have Shaped Our World View*. New York: Ballantine, 1991.

Taylor, A. E. *Aristotle*. New York: Dover, 1955.

Teilhard de Chardin, Pierre. *Let Me Explain*. New York: Harper & Row, 1970.

———. *Man's Place in Nature*. New York: HarperCollins, 1973.

———. *The Phenomenon of Man*. New York: HarperCollins, 1955.

Tetalman, Jerry, and Byron Belitsos. *One World Democracy: A Progressive Vision for Enforceable Global Law*. San Rafael, CA: Origin Press, 2005.

Tolle, Eckhart. *The Power of Now: A Guide to Spiritual Enlightenment*. Novato, CA: New World Library, 1999.

Van Gennep, Arnold. *Rites of Passage: A Classic Study of Cultural Celebrations*. Chicago: University of Chicago Press, 1960.

Walker, Williston, Richard A. Norris, David W. Lotz, and Robert T. Handy. *A History of the Christian Church*, 4th ed. New York: Simon & Schuster, 1985.

Wheatley, Margaret. *Leadership and the New Science: Discovering Order in a Chaotic World*. San Francisco: Berrett-Koehler Publishers, 1999.

White, Michael L. *From Jesus to Christianity: How Four Generations of Visionaries and Storytellers Created the New Testament and Christian Faith*. San Francisco: HarperSanFrancisco, 2005.

Wilber, Ken. *The Atman Project: A Transpersonal View of Human Development*. Wheaton, IL: Quest Books, 1980.

———. *A Brief History of Everything*. Boston: Shambhala, 2000.

———. *Integral Psychology: Consciousness, Spirit, Psychology, Therapy*. Boston, Shambhala, 2000.

———. *The Marriage of Sense and Soul: Integrating Science and Religion*. New York: Random House, 1998.

———. *Up from Eden: A Transpersonal View of Human Evolution*. Wheaton, IL: Quest Books, 1981.

Wilhelm, Richard. *The I Ching or Book of Changes*. Trans. Cary F. Baynes. Princeton, NJ: Princeton University Press, 1950.

Williamson, Marianne. *Imagine: What America Could Be in the 21st Century*. Emmaus, PA: Rodale Press, 2001.

ANODEA JUDITH, PHD, is a groundbreaking thought leader and bestselling author who has worked as a therapist in private practice for over 20 years. Today she is the director of Sacred Centers (SacredCenters.com), a teaching organization she founded that offers workshops worldwide, including the United States, Canada, Europe, Asia, and South and Central America. Judith holds a doctoral degree in Psychology and Human Health, is a 500-hour registered yoga teacher (E-RYT), and has engaged in lifelong studies in psychology, mythology, sociology, history, systems theory, evolution, and comparative religion. She is considered the foremost Western writer on the subject of the chakra system, bridging the philosophies of East and West, especially in the field of psychology. She also is a faculty member of the Shift Network, as well as other major organizations worldwide.

The author of five bestsellers, Judith is best known for the classic *Wheels of Life: A User's Guide to the Chakra System* (Llewellyn, 1987, revised 1999); it is considered the definitive work on the subject of human chakras, with over 200,000 copies sold in English and additional printings in 15 languages. Her most recent book, coauthored with Lion Goodman, is *Creating on Purpose: The Spiritual Technology of Manifesting Through the Chakras* (Sounds True, 2012). The first edition of *The Global Heart Awakens* won two literary awards in 2007, including a Nautilus Gold, and her DVD, *The Illuminated Chakras,* won the best-animation award at the New York Film Festival in 2004.

A teacher, healer, activist, writer, priestess, musician, artist, yogini, and "co-heart," Anodea Judith is also a dynamic and experienced keynote speaker, workshop presenter, and visionary, who is dedicated to healing our world and evolving human consciousness.

INDEX

C

the call, 42–43, 53
Calvin, John, 162
Campbell, Joseph
    on birth imagery, 65
    on Hero's Quest, 38, 58, 109,
        113–14
    on history's Great Reversal, 98
    on life's journey, 43, 49, 56
    on maturation in myths, 1
    on power impulse in religion, 140
    on shifts of perspective, 53
    on supernatural aid, 50
    on survival instincts, 70
Camus, Albert, 255
caring, practice of, 249–54
Caring Institute, 253–54
Carr, Sheva, 253
Carson, Rachel, 230
Çatal Hüyük, 89
caterpillars, metamorphosis of, 39–40,
    60, 302
Catholic Church
    Crusades, 150–52
    immaculate conception, doctrine of,
        134, 174
    Index of Prohibited Books, 166
    indulgences, 150, 151, 158, 159
    Inquisition, 126–27, 152–53, 160,
        163
    Jesuits, 161, 167
    original sin, doctrine of, 145–46,
        174, 204
    Protestant break from, 159–63
    scientific discoveries and, 156, 163,
        165–66, 171
    women's current status in, 234
    See also Christianity
celebration, practice of, 264–65
chakra, first
    charts showing correspondences,
        26, 28
    as historical era, overview of,
        285–86
    matter and, 227
    roots of human culture and, 68
    second chakra, movement to, 80,
        83–84, 88

chakra, first (continued)
    Static Feminine and, 74, 77
    survival instincts and, 23, 70, 83–84,
        198
chakra, second
    charts showing correspondences,
        26, 28
    emotions and, 24, 96, 227
    as historical era, overview of, 23,
        285–86
    sexuality and, 26, 83–84, 86, 198,
        227
    water and, 26, 80, 84, 88
chakra, third
    aggression and, 123, 269
    charts showing correspondences,
        26, 28
    child development and, 26, 86,
        94–98, 100
    dualistic struggles and, 244
    free will and, 146
    as historical era, decline of, 23–24,
        31, 288, 306
    as historical era, emergence of, 23,
        93–95, 100, 105
    as historical era, overview of, 23,
        285–88
    impulse control and, 120
    individualism and, 112, 172, 252
    matter and consciousness, synthesis
        of, 227
    as navel chakra, 114
    power, as era's organizing principle,
        23, 198, 285, 290
    power as attribute of, 24, 95–96,
        112
    Renaissance and, 156, 157–58
    Roman Empire and, 129, 132, 140,
        143
    Static Masculine's emergence and,
        123, 290
chakra, fourth (heart chakra)
    arrested development in, 23–24, 26,
        147, 156–58, 198
    caring and, 250
    charts showing correspondences,
        26, 28
    child socialization and, 119–22

Christianity (*continued*)
    sexuality, views of, 143–47, 160–62,
        164
    See also Catholic Church
chrysalides, 39–40, 60
circle, as symbol, 74–75, 185
Circus Maximus, 128
city-states, rise of, 23, 94, 117–19
civil rights movement, 178, 190
Civil War, U.S., 190
civilization and nature, synthesis of,
    229–32
Clement of Rome, 148
climate change
    caring and, 251–52, 253
    as collective initiatory ordeal, 45–46,
        52, 240
    denial of, 52, 291, 292–93
    economic vs. environmental costs,
        231
    evolution and, 4, 12, 29
    ice ages, previous, 12, 70, 71, 87, 88
    military vs. environmental spending,
        37
    motorized transportation and, 20,
        179
    mythic scale of, 211
    population growth and, 15
    Static Masculine and, 195
    statistics on, 45
    water resources and, 81
co-hearts, 302, 318n59
Cohen, Andrew, 247
Co-Intelligence Institute, 294
Colisseum, Rome, 129
collective unconscious, 55, 70, 91, 102
Colony Collapse Disorder, 47
Columbus, Christopher, 156
Comedy Central, 193
communication
    fifth chakra and, 27, 156–58, 176,
        199, 220, 227, 270
    technology's enhancement of, 4,
        12–13, 24, 175–76, 187, 193
compassion
    Buddha's message of, 134, 184, 267
    as daily practice, 257–58
    fatigue, 250, 252–53
    fourth chakra and, 121

compassion (*continued*)
    natural disasters and, 60
    neurobiology of, 258–59
    as weakness, 31
Confucius, 195
consciousness
    ancient trade/travel and, 88–89
    Axial Age religions and, 306
    balance of power and love in, 32
    in chakra theory, full spectrum of,
        24, 227
    collective unconscious, 55, 70, 91,
        102
    Descartes's view of, 167, 170, 196
    evolution and, 11, 13
    Freudian theory of, 177–78
    Gnostic view of, 313n77
    Greek philosophy and, 118–19, 124,
        158
    Hero's Quest and, 113–15
    Internet as global organ of, 197,
        199, 205, 296–97, 301
    Jesus's teachings and, 136
    lawmaking and, 122
    matter and, 226–28
    nature and, 73, 78, 104, 111
    planetary harm and, 12
    prepersonal, undifferentiated state
        of, 74, 103
    separation myths and, 101
    seventh chakra and, 195, 197, 227
    Shiva and, 228, 242
    '60s consciousness raising, 183–84,
        188–89, 191, 196, 239
    spiritual practices and, 17, 261, 262
    survival instincts and, 70
Constantine, Emperor, 141–42
consumerism
    caterpillars' metamorphosis and, 39
    disengaging from, 263
    ego and, 178–79
    humans' identity as consumers, 108,
        207
    in new economy, 283–84
    pollution and, 179, 247, 279
    '60s and, 183
Copernicus, Nicolaus, 156, 165
Corinth, 139
Craigslist, 282

economic disparities (*continued*)
    death of old structures and, 51
    elimination of, in new era, 32, 53
    in feudal system, 154, 277
    gender pay gap, 233–34
    as global sin, 206
    Industrial Revolution's reduction of, 172
    Jesus and, 135–36
    modernism's shadow side and, 179, 190
    Occupy movement and, 65–66, 277–78
    See also poverty
Economic Policy Institute, 277
economics, new, 280–85
ecstatic experiences, 185
Edinger, Edward, 105
Edison, Thomas, 176
ego
    birth of, in age of power, 38, 95
    consumerism and, 178–79
    death or dissolution of, 54, 58
    denial and, 20
    Freudian theory of, 177–78
    power displays and, 106, 113–14
    as power-paradigm characteristic, 33
    self-improvement and, 260
    third chakra as ego-based, 23
    See also individualism; self
Egypt, modern, 288–89
Egyptian civilization
    Abu Simbel, 106
    bull symbolism, 91
    irrigation projects, 94, 285
    separation myths of, 101, 102
    slavery, practice of, 110, 111, 128
    third-chakra era's emergence and, 94
Einstein, Albert, 173, 176
Eisenstein, Charles, 279–80
Eisler, Riane, 90
Eisner, Elliott, 156
electricity, harnessing of, 175–76
Eleusinian Mysteries, 57, 143
Elgin, Duane, 14, 226–27
Eliade, Mircea, 91, 133
emotions
    Christian views on, 149
    feeling function, 82

emotions (*continued*)
    nature's effect on, 78
    Renaissance embrace of, 155–56
    repression of, and violence, 82, 109, 250
    second chakra and, 24, 96, 227
    triune brain and, 296
    watery initiations and, 80
    as weakness, 84, 108–09
Enlightenment
    child development and, 164–65, 169–70
    Darwin's theory of evolution, 170–72
    individualism and, 171, 172–73
    Scientific Revolution, 165–68, 205
    spirit–matter debate, 166–68, 174, 175
entelechy, 36, 211
environment
    adult vs. adolescent attitudes toward, 14–15, 180, 275
    air pollution, deaths from, 46
    back-to-the-land movement, 189, 229–30, 289–90
    balance of power and love in campaigning for, 31, 32, 38
    caring and, 250–52
    consumerism's toll on, 179, 247
    deep ecology movement, 33, 77, 189, 275–77
    economics vs., 231, 277–78
    extinction of species, 12, 29, 79, 179, 252
    industrialization's toll on, 20, 172
    I–Thou relationships and, 221
    military vs. environmental spending, 37
    pollution, as modernism's shadow side, 190
    rape of, as global sin, 206
    Republicans' science-denying platform, 52
    '60s environmental movement, 178, 188–89
    See also climate change; nature; sustainability
Eros
    Dynamic Feminine and, 185, 186

gender equality
    balancing masculine and feminine
        principles, 3, 23, 37, 180–81, 199,
        216, 233–36
    as collective challenge, 53
    current spiritual revolution and, 188
    feminism, emergence of, 174–75
    fourth chakra and, 23
    heart-based realm's need for, 74,
        235, 305
    Jesus's support of, 135
    '60s women's movement, 178, 191
    Socrates's support of, 125
    Western vs. global equality, 194, 234
gender roles
    child socialization and, 119
    dominance and war, as masculine,
        99, 106–07, 109, 112–13
    Dynamic Masculine and, 97–98
    in Greco-Roman world, 130
    Luther's views on, 160–61
    modern questioning of, 191–92
    in prehistoric eras, 79, 80, 88,
        90–91, 99
    in Renaissance, 155
    Static Feminine and, 75–76
gender valences. See valences, masculine
    and feminine
generosity, practice of, 255–57
genetically modified organisms (GMO),
    114, 253
gift economies, 280, 281, 284
Gimbutas, Marija, 73, 99
Global Coherence Initiative, 303
global heart. See heart, global
global warming. See climate change
Gnostics, 138, 142, 312n49, 313n77
God, characteristics of
    as authority figure, 17
    Christian God's purity vs. Pagan
        gods' duality, 149
    as divine architect, 166, 170
    as feared vs. loved, 162
    masculine and animal deities,
        emergence of, 89–92
    masculine gods' overthrow of the
        Mother, 98–103
    as masculine to most modern
        worshippers, 69, 191, 234

God, characteristics of (*continued*)
    masculinity and power of Judeo-
        Christian God, 127–28, 134–35,
        214–15
    sky gods, 99–101, 165, 204, 226
    See also Father, archetypal or divine
Goddess worship
    absence of, in modern world, 69,
        234
    authority figures in religion and, 17
    birth of human culture and, 68–69
    in Greco-Roman world, 130
    Mary, worship of, 134, 160
    nature and, 68–69, 72–73, 149, 203,
        215
    prehistoric representations of,
        71–72, 90, 91–92
    revival of, 189, 191, 196
    See also Mother, archetypal or divine
Goethe, Johann Wolfgang von, 175,
    177, 179, 223
Google, 281
Gorbachev, Mikhail, 51–52
Grateful Dead, 183
gratitude, practice of, 254–55
Graves, Clare, 24
Great Mother. *See* Mother, archetypal
    or divine
Great Reversal, 98–103, 149
Greek civilization
    Alexander's spread of Hellenism,
        127–28
    bull symbolism, 91
    consciousness and, 118–19, 124,
        158
    love, concepts of, 34–35
    mystery cults, 57, 136, 139, 143,
        312n43
    mythic vs. rational thinking, 124–26,
        209
    Renaissance rediscovery of Greek
        works, 155
    Roman assimilation of Greek
        culture, 129–30, 133
    separation myths, 83, 101, 102, 124
    '60s and, 184
    slavery, practice of, 112
    Static Masculine's emergence and, 116
    See also polis, Greek

Greek Orthodox Church, 152
Gregory IX, Pope, 152–53
gun control, 247, 272
Gurdjieff, George, 195
Gutenberg, Johannes, 156

H

Hades, 57, 102
Haight-Ashbury, San Francisco, 182
Harappa, 94
Harman, Willis, 263
Hawken, Paul, 282
heart, global
    acceptance and, 264
    beauty and, 83
    caring and, 249–54
    celebration and, 264–65
    chart of heart-paradigm
        characteristics, 33
    co-hearts, 302, 318n59
    communication necessary to, 27
    community and, 242
    daily spiritual practice and, 248–49,
        260–64
    deep ecology and, 275–77
    economics and, 277–85
    emptiness, beginning in, 247–48
    evolution toward awakening of, 1–5,
        31, 40, 304–07
    forgiveness and, 259–60
    gender equality necessary to, 74,
        235, 305
    generosity and, 255–57
    global brain and, 295–97, 301
    gratitude and, 254–55
    heart-coherence techniques, 302–03
    imaginal cells and, 39–40, 265–66,
        302
    integration of elements in, 199,
        223–25, 243, 305
    I–Thou relationships and, 219,
        245–46
    Jesus's heart-based vision, 132,
        133–34, 140, 143, 147, 164, 184,
        268
    leadership models and, 288–95
    peace worldwide and, 269–74

heart, global (continued)
    small acts of kindness and,
        298–99
    water symbolism and, 81
    See also chakra, fourth (heart
        chakra)
heart, human, 259, 300, 302–03
heart chakra. See chakra, fourth (heart
    chakra)
HeartMath Institute, 253, 259, 302–03
heaven and earth, synthesis of, 225–26
Hebrews, 103, 127–28
    See also Judaism
Hegel, G. W. F., 223, 288
Henderson, Hazel, 275, 283
Hera, 130
Heraclitus, 132
Herod, King, 133
Hero's Quest
    dissolution and surrender in, 58
    individualism and, 38, 109–10, 112,
        208
    initiation process and, 38, 113–15
    Jesus as Hero, 143
    mythic thinking and, 210
    return home, as act of love, 38, 304
Herr, Mike, 298
Hesiod, 124
hieros gamos. See Marriage, Sacred
    (hieros gamos)
Hill, Gareth, 74–75, 97, 123, 140,
    185
Hill, Julia Butterfly, 230
Hinduism
    Kama, 83
    Shiva's third eye, 169
    six-pointed star symbolism, 227–28
    Upanishads, 78, 195
    Vishnu and nectar of immortality,
        242–43
    Western interest in, 189, 239
hippie movement, 182–83
Hiroshima, 107–08
history, human
    Bronze Age, 26, 93–95, 99–103
    chakra system's correlation with, 23,
        26, 28, 285–88
    childhood stages' correlation with,
        21, 26, 28, 40

history, human (*continued*)
  Christianity, during Jesus's life,
    133–38
  Christianity, early period of, 139–47,
    148
  Darwin's discovery of evolution,
    170–72
  feminine side of, as missing, 6, 22
  feminism, emergence of, 174–75
  gender valences as four ages of, 22,
    40, 73–74, 180–81, 184, 236
  Great Awakening, current era as, 3
  Great Reversal, 98–103, 149
  Greek culture, flourishing of,
    117–19, 124–28
  healing collective wounds of, 20–21
  Industrial Revolution, 16, 45, 172,
    285, 290
  Italian Renaissance, 154–58, 163,
    164, 165, 184
  kingship, emergence of, 110–11
  Middle Ages, 149–54, 158, 173, 180
  militarization of ancient cultures, 99,
    103–04, 106–09, 115, 285
  Mother archetype and roots of,
    68–73, 203
  Neolithic Era, 80, 87–92
  Paleolithic Era, 26, 71–73, 79, 87
  population growth as driver of, 16
  Protestant Reformation, 159–63,
    204–05
  Roman Empire, rise and spread of,
    128–31
  Scientific Revolution, 165–68, 205
  sixties (1960s), 178, 182–84,
    188–89, 191, 196, 239, 288
  telecommunications, advent of,
    175–76
  third-chakra era, emergence of, 23,
    93–95, 100, 105
  tribal history taught through rites of
    passage, 19
  walling of ancient cities, 103–05,
    115
Holocaust, 126–27, 182
Homer, 124, 209
Houston, Jean, 17
Hubbard, Barbara Marx, 6, 33, 36, 66,
  224

Human Genome Project, 282
human rights, 23, 111–12, 190–95,
  270, 272
human species
  adolescence, as current evolutionary
    stage of, 13–18, 26, 52
  consciousness as hallmark of, 11–12,
    13
  cultural identity, evolution of, 208
  as facing its denouement, 1–3
  origin of *Homo sapiens*, 71
  survival of, tied to Earth, 75, 78,
    231
  See also history, human
humanism, 155–56
Hume, David, 175
Hurricane Katrina, 30, 45, 51, 52, 247
Hurricane Sandy, 45, 52, 247

I

IBM, 281
Iceland financial collapse, 293
imaginal cells, 39–40, 60, 265–66, 302
immanence and transcendence, 215,
  218, 262–63, 306
Inanna, 56, 102, 309n27
individualism
  agency and communion, synthesis
    of, 241–42
  Enlightenment period and, 171,
    172–73
  Greek culture and, 117–19
  Hero's Quest and, 38, 109–10, 112,
    208
  Internet and, 5
  Protestant Reformation and, 159
  Renaissance and, 155
  social movements and, 178, 190–94
  third chakra and, 112, 172, 252
  See also ego; self
individuation, 37–38, 74, 95
Indonesian tsunami (2004), 30
Indus River, 94, 103
industrialization
  growth, as measure of progress in,
    16, 205

industrialization (*continued*)
Industrial Revolution, 16, 45, 172, 285, 290
pollution and, 20, 172, 288
infancy
in chakra system, 26, 28
of human culture, 13–14, 68, 71–77, 94–95, 203, 206
mother-infant bond, 73–74, 77, 85, 97, 305
Static Feminine and, 192
initiation
authority figures and, 17
the call and, 42–43, 53
current cultural dissolution and, 59–60, 301
disasters as collective initiatory ordeals, 29–30, 44–48, 52, 240, 247
discovering divine power in, 215
into Eleusinian Mysteries, 57
global sins and, 206
Gnostics and, 138, 142, 312n49
Hero's quest and, 38
Jesus and, 133, 136–38, 204, 311n40, 312n43
from power paradigm to love paradigm, 3
prehistoric art and, 71–72
sexuality and, 84
spiritual paths in, 54–55
stages, overview of, 49–53
teaching of tribal history and, 19
war as, 109
watery feminine vs. fiery masculine rites, 80, 113
Innocent VIII, Pope, 163
InnoCentive, 282–83
Inquisition, 126–27, 152–53, 160, 163
integration. *See* synthesis
Internet
Dynamic Feminine and, 193
as global organ of consciousness, 197, 199, 205, 296–97, 301
individualism and, 5
military origin of, 269
modern innovations, compared to past, 158, 180
natural disasters and, 60, 258

Internet (*continued*)
open-source collaboration, 281–83
planetary problem solving and, 12–13, 60
rise and spread of, 197
transparency and, 40
upper chakra capacities and, 24
Iraq, 93, 271, 273
Iron Age, 26, 99, 290
Isabella, Queen, 163
Isis, 102
Islam
ascendant spiritual paths and, 55
Crusades and, 151, 152
divinity as defined in, 215
Muhammad, 195
Spanish exile of Muslims, 163
terrorism and, 207
women's current status in, 234
Italian Renaissance, 154–58, 163, 164, 165, 184
I–Thou relationships
anima mundi and, 262
awakening of global heart through, 245–46
chart of three relational systems, 222
empathy and, 257, 260
overview of, 219–21
peace and, 270
spiritual practices and, 261

J

Jacobi, Jolande, 90
Jantsch, Erich, 219, 222
Japanese earthquake/tsunami (2011), 47, 66
Japanese mythology, 101
Jefferson, Thomas, 31
Jericho, 89
Jerusalem, 151
Jesuits, 161, 167
Jesus
alteration of his message after death, 139–40, 142–43, 147, 148, 161
forgiveness of sins through, 204
gender dynamics in birth myth of, 134–35

Jesus (*continued*)
heart-based vision of, 132, 133–34, 140, 143, 147, 164, 184, 268
immaculate conception of, 134, 174
mythic thinking and, 209
as "Nazarene," 133, 311n40
restoring eyesight, 136, 312n43
revolutionary spirituality of, 135–38
separation myths and, 102
seventh chakra and, 195
synthesis and, 223
Josephus, 137
Judaism
Christian attacks on Jews, 151, 152, 160, 163
Ein Sof, 215
Hebrew tribes, struggles of, 103, 127–28
Holocaust, 126–27, 182
infant Moses, abandonment of, 213
Jesus and, 133, 135, 136
laws, emphasis on, 127–28
Paul as Pharisaic Jew, 139
Roman Empire and, 130–31, 133, 136, 137
Julian, Emperor, 142
Jung, Carl
on anima/animus, 216
on balance of power and love, 31
chakra studies of, 239
on child abandonment myths, 213
on childbirth, 67
on enlightenment, 148
on feeling function, 82
on individuation, 37
on life and death, 54
on myth's significance, 208
repressed feelings and, 149
on rootless consciousness, 19
on tension of opposites, 242–43
on visions, 188
Juno, 130
Justin Martyr, 141

K

Kama, 83
Kant, Immanuel, 175

Katha Upanishad, 78
Keats, John, 175
Keen, Sam, 76
Keller, Catherine, 98
Kelly, Marjorie, 280
Kepler, Johannes, 166
Kettering Foundation, 294
King, Martin Luther, Jr., 32, 59, 190, 268
kingship, emergence of, 110–11
Kore, 57, 102
Korten, David, 33, 251, 293
Kurgans, 99, 311n22

L

Lannon, Richard, 296, 300–301
Lao-tzu, 184, 195
Lascaux cave paintings, 71
laws, institution of
child development and rule making, 121–22
Christian doctrine, codification of, 148–49
democracy's emergence and, 117–19, 122
Judeo-Christian commandments, 127–28
in Roman Empire, 129
written laws, advent of, 119, 123, 127–28
Leakey, Richard, 71
Leo X, Pope, 161
Leonardo da Vinci, 154, 156
Lewis, Thomas, 296, 300–301
Libya, 288
light bulb, invention of, 176
Linux, 281
literacy, 152, 157, 164–65, 180, 234
living systems theory, 186
Locke, John, 175
logic. *See* rationalism
Louv, Richard, 78, 277
love
Aphrodite/Venus as goddess of, 130
balance of power and, 3, 31–33, 38, 115, 267
child development and, 207, 217–18

love (*continued*)
Darwin on, 170–71
God as more feared than loved, 162
Greek concepts of, 34–35
heart as spiritual center of, 2
Hero's return as act of, 38, 304
I–Thou relationships and, 219, 245–46
Jesus's message of, 136–38, 140, 143, 147, 161, 268
lessons of, 122
as organizing principle, 3–4, 34–37, 219, 305
personal autonomy and, 178
Petrarch's poetry on, 155
physiological signature of, 302–03
small acts of, 298–99
Teilhard de Chardin on, 198, 295
universal love, 35, 36, 305
violence glorified more than, 59
Loye, David, 170–71
Luther, Martin, 159–62

M

Macedonia, 127
MacLean, Paul D., 296
Macon, Council of, 160
Mahesh Yogi, Maharishi, 195
Maiden, archetypal, 57, 135, 215
Malleus Maleficarum, 163
Malthus, Thomas, 16
Manichaeism, 126, 144
Maori mythology, 101
Marduk, 101, 204
Marriage, Sacred (*hieros gamos*)
gender equality in, 235
integration of polarities in, 216, 225, 243, 306
overview of, 212–16
six-pointed star symbol and, 228
Mars (male gender) symbol, 97
Marshall Plan, 182, 225
Martin, James, 48
Marx, Karl, 223
Mary, mother of Jesus, 102, 134–35, 160, 174
Mary Magdalene, 134–35

matter
Christian rejection of, 144, 149, 165
consciousness and, 226–28
Enlightenment views of, 166–68, 174, 175
Greeks' spirit–matter debate, 125–26
Mother archetype and, 174
Sacred Marriage's integration of spirit and, 216
scientific relativity and, 176, 186
May, Rollo, 115
McTaggart, Lynne, 233
Meade, Michael, 42, 79, 80
medicine, field of
alternative medicine, 60, 186–87, 189
in Greco-Roman world, 124
holistic methods, increase in, 4, 186–87
mental health and, 189, 228
in Middle Ages, 153–54, 180
modernism's shadow side and, 179
three eras in, 233
meditation
crime reduction and, 264
current spiritual revolution and, 186, 187, 261, 262
'60s consciousness raising and, 189, 196, 239
as vehicle for transcendence, 248, 263
Medusa, 130
megalithic monuments, 28, 92, 310n18
men's movement, 191–92
Mesopotamia, 93–94, 104, 106, 110, 285
Mexico City earthquake (1985), 48, 51
Meyers, Hari, 106
Michelangelo, 156
microlending, 284
Middle Ages, 149–54, 158, 173, 180
middle class, emergence of, 118, 154–55
midwifery, 153
militarism. *See* war
Mill, John Stuart, 174
mind–body relationship, 167–68, 189, 228–29, 233, 305
Minos, King, 114

mirror neurons, 258
Mohenjo-Daro, 94
Moors, 160
Moses, 127–28, 213
Mother, archetypal or divine
    agriculture and, 88–89
    authority figures in religion and, 17
    birth of human culture and, 68–73,
        203
    Daughter archetype and, 6
    Divine Child and, 305
    Dynamic Masculine's overthrow of,
        98–103, 122, 135, 149, 181
    Earth Mother, worship of, 68–69,
        72–73, 99–101, 204, 226
    Father's ascendancy over, 68–69,
        148–49, 165, 180, 204–05
    Good Mother vs. Bad Mother,
        85–87
    as Hera/Juno, 130
    Mary, worship of, 134, 160
    matter and, 174
    nature and, 68–69, 72–73, 149, 203,
        215
    power over humanity, as
        unequivocal, 70–71, 95
    prehistoric representations of,
        71–72, 90, 91–92
    Son archetype and, 89–92, 100–102,
        105–06, 180, 212
    vision for the future and, 61
    waning influence of, 105, 111,
        148–49
Move Your Money campaign, 284
MoveOn.org, 293
Moyers, Bill, 140
Muhammad, 195
music, 156, 183, 185, 186, 262
Muslims. See Islam
mythic system, 219–20, 222
mythic thinking
    modernism's shadow side and loss
        of, 180
    need for new guiding myth, 5,
        210–11
    vs. rationalism, 24, 33, 124–26,
        208–11

N

Nag Hammadi, 312n49
Nagasaki, 107–08
Nagler, Michael, 271, 274
namaste, defined, 214
National Issues Forum, 294
natural disasters
    as birth contractions, 65, 66
    as collective initiatory ordeals,
        29–30, 44–48, 52, 240, 247
    Internet and, 60, 258
nature
    agriculture and humans' relation to,
        87–88, 91, 100
    beauty and, 82–83
    civilization and nature, synthesis of,
        229–32
    consciousness and, 73, 78, 104, 111
    crime reductions in green areas, 249,
        276–77
    daily spiritual practice and, 249
    demonization of, 163, 164
    Enlightenment views of, 165,
        166–68, 175, 205
    Mother Nature, power of, 70–71, 95
    Mother Nature, worship of, 68–69,
        72–73, 149, 203, 215
    Romantics' embrace of, 175, 285
    separation from, in modern world,
        78, 180, 205
    survival instincts and, 60–61, 69–71,
        78
    walling out, in ancient cities,
        103–05, 115
    See also environment
nature-deficit disorder, 78
Nazarenes, 133, 311n40
Nazism, 171
Neolithic Era, 80, 87–92
Neumann, Erich, 101
neuroscience, 258–59, 300–303
New Age philosophies, 55, 193
New Orleans, flooding of, 30, 48
New World, discovery of, 156, 180
Newton, Isaac, 103, 168
Nicaea, Council of, 142
Niebuhr, Reinhold, 288
Nietzsche, Friedrich, 173

polis, Greek (*continued*)
  Renaissance cities and, 154
pollution
  air pollution, deaths from, 46
  Carson's *Silent Spring* and, 230
  consumerism and, 179, 247, 279
  industrialization and, 20, 172, 288
  light pollution, 247
  as modernism's shadow side, 190
  as power's shadow side, 37
  as transcending national borders,
    295
population growth
  in Bronze and Iron Ages, 93–95,
    104–05, 285
  global disasters and, 30, 46
  in Greco-Roman world, 117
  in Neolithic, 89
  replacing old leadership models and,
    291
  reproductive rights and, 16, 192,
    194
  sustainability and, 15–17, 52, 79
  unchecked growth, as act of
    immaturity, 275
  water resources and, 81
poverty
  caring for those in, 35
  civil rights movement and, 190
  as collective challenge, 46
  ending, by synthesizing heaven and
    earth, 226
  good vs. evil dialectic and, 126–27
  increasing prosperity gap, 277–78
  Industrial Revolution's reduction of,
    172
  Jesus and, 135–36
  microlending and, 284
  peace of *anahata* and, 269
  population growth and, 15
  See also economic disparities
power
  balance of love and, 3, 31–33, 38,
    115, 267
  banking system and, 283
  chart of power-paradigm
    characteristics, 33
  current age of, 23, 37–38, 198, 276
  dawning of age of, 92, 103–09

power (*continued*)
  dissolution and surrender vs. force of
    will, 57–58
  economic disparities and, 111–12,
    277–78
  global cooperation and, 207–08
  Hero myth's emergence and, 109,
    112–15
  human evolution of godlike powers,
    29
  of Judeo-Christian God, 127–28,
    134–35, 214–15
  kingship, emergence of, 110–11
  lawmaking and, 121–22
  of Mother Nature, 70–71, 95
  of popes, 150–51, 152–53, 158
  replacing top-down models of,
    288–95
  Romanized Christianity co-opted by,
    140, 146–47
  Static Masculine's
    institutionalization of, 116, 123
  as third-chakra attribute, 24, 95–96,
    112
  as third-chakra era's organizing
    principle, 23, 198, 285, 290
  women's current share of, 233–34
prayer, 50, 186, 187, 233, 256, 262
Pre-Socratic philosophers, 124–25
printing press, advent of, 156–57, 164,
  180
Protestant Reformation, 159–63,
  204–05
psychotherapy
  author's practice of, 19–20, 259, 273
  caring and, 252
  Freudian theory, 177–78
  repressed feelings and, 149
  for self-improvement, 192, 261
  '60s consciousness raising and, 188
  Western Civilization as "client,"
    20–21, 68
Ptolemy, 156
Public Agenda, 294
pyramids, Egyptian, 110

Roosevelt, Theodore, 249
root chakra. *See* chakra, first
Rosenberg, Marshall, 270
Roth, Gabrielle, 261
Rousseau, Jean-Jacques, 175
Rumi, 13, 195

S

Sacred Marriage. *See* Marriage, Sacred
  (*hieros gamos*)
sacred partnership, 22, 36, 217–18
Sahtouris, Elisabet, 39, 275
San Francisco earthquake (1906), 48
SARS, 46
Schiller, Friedrich, 177
Schmookler, Andrew Bard, 93, 107–08,
  115
science and technology
  biomimicry, 231–32
  in Bronze and Iron Ages, 92, 94
  Catholic opposition to, 156, 163,
    165–66, 171
  climate change, scientific agreement
    on, 45
  communication enhanced by, 4,
    12–13, 24, 175–76, 187, 193
  Darwin's theory of evolution,
    170–72
  in Greco-Roman world, 110, 118,
    124
  holism/holarchy and, 233, 305
  impulse control and, 120–21
  materialism, peak of, 174
  mythic significance, lack of, 210–11
  nature's mysteries exceeding, 69
  neuroscience, 258–59, 300–303
  open-source collaboration in,
    282–83
  planetary crises solved by, 12–13, 29
  problems both created and solved by,
    20, 114, 179, 206
  relativity in new dimensions of, 176,
    186
  religion and science, synthesis of,
    232–33
  Renaissance advances in, 156

science and technology (*continued*)
  Republicans' science-denying
    platform, 52
  Scientific Revolution, 165–68, 205
  See also Internet; medicine, field of
Seeger, Pete, 183
self
  agency and communion, synthesis
    of, 241–42
  ascendant spiritual paths and, 54
  child socialization and, 119–22
  collective awakening of, 178–79
  Descartes's view of, 167
  evolution and, 13
  individuation, 37–38, 74, 95
  I–Thou relationships and, 219–21
  Renaissance, as first self-conscious
    period, 158
  Sacred Marriage and, 216
  third chakra and development of,
    95–96
  See also ego; individualism
Seneca Fall's women's conference,
  174–75
September 11 terrorist attacks, 30, 48,
  51
sexism
  birth myths, women's absence from,
    126
  Christian views of female inferiority,
    143, 160–61, 162
  convergence of crises and, 4
  Greco-Roman subordination of
    women, 117, 118, 130
  Inquisition's targeting of women,
    152, 153
  in Jesus myth, 134–35
  language, sexist, 271
  modernism's shadow side and, 190
  overcoming, as collective challenge,
    53
  in public institutions, 233–34
  See also gender equality; gender roles
sexuality
  adolescence and, 169
  censorship of, in modern culture, 59
  Christian condemnation of, 143–47,
    160–62, 164

sexuality (*continued*)
    current spiritual revolution and, 186, 188
    feeling function and, 82
    medieval condemnation of, 149
    phallic sculptures, 91–92
    privitization of, 173
    second chakra and, 26, 83–84, 86, 198, 227
    Virgin Mary stripped of, 134
Shakespeare, William, 39, 156
Shakti, 227–28
Sheldrake, Rupert, 195
Shelley, Percy Bysshe, 175
Shift Network, 66, 253
Shiva, 169, 228, 242
Shlain, Leonard, 190–91
Siegel, Daniel J., 259
Siegel, Dylan, 299
sin, doctrine of original, 145–46, 174, 204
sixties (1960s)
    consciousness raising in, 183–84, 188–89, 191, 196, 239
    Dynamic Feminine and, 182–84, 188–89
    heart chakra and, 184, 288
    social movements, blossoming of, 178, 183
Sixtus IV, Pope, 158
sky gods, 99–101, 165, 204, 226
slavery
    abolition of, 174, 178, 190
    construction of ancient monuments and, 106, 110, 130
    economic role of, in ancient world, 111–12, 115
    Greek citizenship of emancipated slaves, 118
    Hebrew tribes, enslavement of, 128
    in Roman Empire, 111–12, 129, 130
Slick, Grace, 183
Socrates, 125, 127, 223
Solnit, Rebecca, 48, 51
Son, archetypal
    Father archetype and, 134–35, 204
    Mother archetype and, 89–92, 100–102, 105–06, 180, 212
Spanish Inquisition, 163

Spencer, Herbert, 170
spiral, as symbol, 185, 262, 306
Spiral Dynamics, 24–25, 28
spirit–matter relationship. *See* matter
spirituality
    ascendant vs. descendant paths, 54–55, 143
    beauty and, 82–83
    current spiritual revolution, 4, 185–88, 196, 261–62
    daily practice, establishment of, 248–49, 260–64
    Eastern and Western traditions, synthesis of, 238–39
    in Enlightenment period, 173
    fundamentalism vs. spiritual diversity, 60
    initiation process and, 44
    of Jesus, as revolutionary, 135–38
    seventh chakra and, 24, 183, 187, 199
St. Bartholomew's Day massacre, 161
Static Feminine
    charts showing correspondences, 28, 237, 238
    child development and, 73–74, 85–87, 89, 192
    Dynamic Masculine's overthrow of, 95, 97, 135, 148
    in historical arc of gender valences, 22, 180–81, 184, 236
    as humanity's primal thesis, 73–77, 79, 89, 184
    need for gender wholeness and, 193
    Son archetype's rise and, 90–92
Static Masculine
    charts showing correspondences, 28, 237, 238
    child development and, 164–65, 192
    Christianity as central myth of, 133
    codification of Christian doctrine and, 148–49
    cross as symbol of, 123, 140
    Dynamic Feminine's undermining of, 182, 185–86, 194–95
    Dynamic Masculine's development into, 116, 122–23
    educational institutions and, 234
    Enlightenment thought and, 168, 175

Static Masculine (*continued*)
  good vs. evil dialectic and, 126–27
  in Greco-Roman world, 116, 127
  in historical arc of gender valences,
    22, 180–81, 184, 236
  need for gender wholeness and, 193
  replacing top-down control of, 290
  scientific relativity's undermining of,
    176
  Son's ascension in, 135
Stewart, John, 241
Stewart, R. J., 56–57
Stonehenge, 92, 310n18
Sumerian civilization
  bull symbolism, 91
  Enlil myth, 101
  Inanna myth, 56, 102, 309n27
  leadership structure, 110
  third-chakra era's emergence and,
    93–94
Sumner, William Graham, 171
survival instincts
  evolution and, 57, 60–61, 69–71, 78
  first chakra and, 23, 70, 83–84, 198
  reptilian brain and, 296
  unknown and, 105
  warfare and, 103
sustainability
  as collective challenge, 53, 61
  human creativity and, 4–5
  joys of, 231–32
  love's reciprocity and, 35
  NGOs and, 282
  population growth and, 15–17, 52,
    79
  progress vs., 224
  of self, 241
  vs. sentimental environmentalism,
    193
  Western vs. global progress, 194
synthesis
  of agency and communion, 241–42
  of civilization and nature, 229–32
  of darkness and light, 239–41
  of East and West, 238–39
  evolution and, 223–25
  in heart chakra, 31, 198–200, 227,
    244, 262, 297
  of heaven and earth, 225–26

synthesis (*continued*)
  of masculine and feminine, 233–36
  of matter and consciousness, 226–28
  of mind and body, 228–29
  in Sacred Marriage, 216, 225, 243,
    306
  of science and religion, 232–33
  of static and dynamic, 236–37
  tension of opposites, 242–44
  thesis, antithesis, and, 223, 224, 244
Syria, 288
systems theory, 186, 219, 291, 293

T

Tacitus, 128
Tagore, Rabindranath, 257
Taliban, 234, 253
Tantric tradition, 227–28, 243
Taoism, 189, 215, 239
Tapscott, Don, 281
Tarnas, Richard, 119
technology. *See* science and technology
Teilhard de Chardin, Pierre
  on faith in the future, 304
  on harnessing God, 267
  on love as unifying force, 198, 295
  on matter, 174
  on noosphere, 297
  on polarities, 223
  on universe, 219
telecommunications, advent of, 175–76
Teresa, Mother, 195, 253–54
terrorism
  as collective initiatory ordeal, 44, 46
  deaths from, 51
  Islam and, 207
  perceptions of weakness and, 31
  Roman crucifixion campaign as, 137
  September 11 attacks, 30, 48, 51
Tertullian, 160
Thagaste, 143
Theodosius, Emperor, 142, 312n48
Thomas Aquinas, 160
throat chakra. *See* chakra, fifth
Tiamat, 101, 204
Tigris-Euphrates valley, 93–94, 277
Torah, 127–28

transcendence and immanence, 215, 218, 262–63, 306
Transcendental Meditation Society, 263
Transition Network, 292
Tribe.net, 187
triune brain, 296–97
tsunamis, 30, 44, 66
Tunisia, 288–89
Turks, 142, 155, 160
Twain, Mark, 259
Twist, Lynne, 11

U

unconscious, discovery of the, 177–78
Underworld
    as archetypal womb, 58, 61, 67
    collective initiatory ordeals and, 6
    death phase of initiation and, 55
    Divine Feminine's relegation to, 149
    Hero's journey to, 38, 58
    Inanna's descent to, 56, 102
    Kore's descent to, 57, 102
    mythic thinking and, 209
    violence, and current Underworld state, 59–61
United Nations, 45, 205
universal love, 35, 36, 305
Upanishads, 78, 195
Urban II, Pope, 151
Ur-Nammu, 106
Uroboros, 74, 87
Uruk, 104
U.S. government, problems with, 291–92

V

valences, masculine and feminine
    charts showing correspondences, 28, 237, 238
    child development and, 192
    Gareth Hill's work on, 74, 97, 185
    historical arc of, 22, 40, 73–74, 180–81, 184, 236
    wholeness, need for, 184–85, 199, 234–35

valences, masculine and feminine (*continued*)
    See also specific dynamic and static valences
Vedas, 83, 195
Venice, 155
Venus, 130
Vietnam War, 60, 182, 183
violence
    caring and, 250, 251
    as collective challenge, 37, 46, 240
    declining rates of, 53, 59, 170, 251, 271–72
    emotional repression and, 82, 109
    green spaces and reduced rates of, 249, 276–77
    gun control and, 247, 272
    in Inquisition, 152–53, 163
    magnification of, in modern culture, 59–61, 270–71, 274
    nonviolence advocacy, 190, 268, 270, 274
    in Roman Empire, 129, 130, 137, 141, 312n48
    as self-perpetuating, 20, 107
    St. Bartholomew's Day massacre, 161
    See also war
Virgin Mary. *See* Mary, mother of Jesus
Vishnu, 242–43
Vivekananda, Swami, 238–39
vocational arousal, 36
volunteerism, 254
voting rights, 118, 174–75, 233, 291–92

W

war
    battlefield deaths, decline in, 272
    Catholics vs. Protestants, 161
    Christian view of, as natural, 149
    as collective initiatory ordeal, 44, 46
    Crusades, 150–52
    Dynamic Feminine's questioning of, 190
    ending, to achieve world piece, 269–74

war (*continued*)
  as global sin, 206
  good vs. evil dialectic and, 126–27
  humans' godlike powers and, 29, 47, 79
  kingship and military structure, 110–11
  magnification of, in modern culture, 59–61
  militarization of ancient cultures, 99, 103–04, 106–09, 115, 285
  personal freedom vs. national security, 122
  Roman Empire and, 129, 130
  as self-perpetuating, 20, 107–08, 115
  spending for military vs. other programs, 37, 116, 194, 273, 274
  suppression of feeling in, 250
  as transcending national borders, 295
  See also specific wars
water, as symbolic element, 80–82, 84, 88–89, 113
Whatley, Haley, 299
Wheatley, Meg, 293
Whitehead, Alfred North, 98
Whole Earth Catalog, 212
Wikipedia, 281
Wilber, Ken
  on democracy, 172
  on differentiating, 263
  on early humans, 87
  on infantile state, 73
  on kingship, 111
  on modernity, 180
  on science and religion converging, 232–33
  Spiral Dynamics, adoption of, 24–25
  synthesis and, 223
Wilde, Oscar, 226
Williams, Anthony D., 281
witch hunts, 152, 163, 165, 168, 179, 272
Wittenberg, 160
women's rights movement
  Daughter archetype and, 6, 134, 135, 175, 212
  Seneca Fall's conference, 174–75

women's rights movement (*continued*)
  in '60s, 178, 191
  See also gender equality; sexism
World Health Organization, 46
World Parents, 100–102, 136–37, 206, 245
World Parliament of Religions, 238
World War I, 126, 271, 288
World War II, 107–08, 126, 182, 225, 269, 288
World Wide Web. *See* Internet
writing
  advent of, 72, 94, 100, 164
  Christian doctrine, codification of, 148–49
  Jesus's teachings, posthumous recording of, 139
  laws, advent of written, 119, 123, 127–28
  as left-brain function, 191
  printing press, advent of, 156–57, 164, 180
  Protestant emphasis on scripture, 159–63
  Socrates's eschewal of, 125

Y

Yahoo!, 281
Yahweh, 127–28
Yellow River, 94
Yemen, 288
yoga
  ascendant spiritual paths and, 55
  author's practice of, 119, 252
  current spiritual revolution and, 185, 186, 187, 196, 261
  Eastern traditions and, 22, 189, 238–39
YouTube, 5, 193, 282

Z

Zen, 55
Zeus, 102
ziggurats, construction of, 106, 110
Zoroastrianism, 126